HISTORY OF THE WORLD

HISTORY OF THE WORLD

FROM THE STONE AGE TO THE TECH REVOLUTION

MICHAEL KERRIGAN

This book first published in 2024 by

Amber Books Ltd
United House
North Road
London N7 9DP
United Kingdom
www.amberbooks.co.uk
Facebook: amberbooks
YouTube: amberbooksltd
Instagram: amberbooksltd
X(Twitter): @amberbooks

Copyright © 2024 Amber Books Ltd

All rights reserved. With the exception of quoting brief passages for the purpose of review no part of this publication may be reproduced without prior written permission from the publisher. The information in this book is true and complete to the best of our knowledge. All recommendations are made without any guarantee on the part of the author or publisher, who also disclaim any liability incurred in connection with the use of this data or specific details.

ISBN: 978-1-83886-450-7

Project Editor: Michael Spilling
Picture Research: Terry Forshaw
Design: Mark Batley, Keren Harragan and Jerry Williams

Printed in Italy
by Vincenzo Bona S.p.A.

CONTENTS

INTRODUCTION 6

EARLY HISTORY
8000 – 1200 BC 8

THE ANCIENT ERA
1200 BC – AD 500 24

THE MEDIEVAL PERIOD
500 – 1453 68

THE RENAISSANCE
1460 – 1600 120

AGE OF REASON
1600 – 1760 164

CONQUEST AND REVOLUTION
1760 – 1850 202

AGE OF EMPIRE
1850 – 1914 270

WORLD ON FIRE
1914 – 1945 312

TIME FOR CHANGE
1945 – 2000 372

THE DIGITAL AGE
21ST CENTURY 422

INDEX 446

PICTURE CREDITS 448

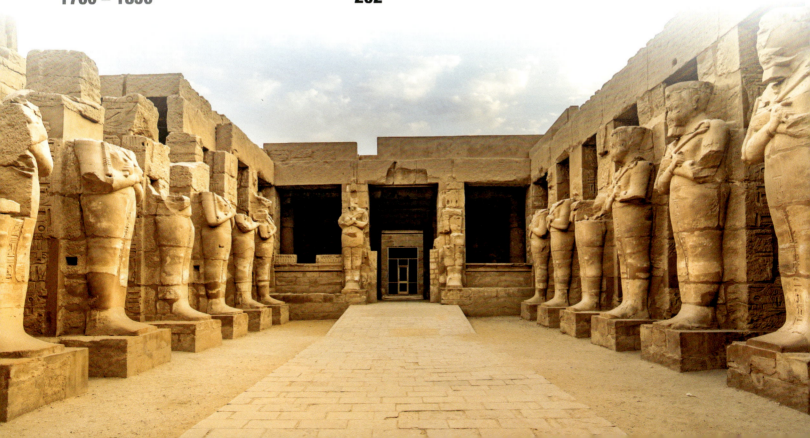

INTRODUCTION

This book sets out to tell the whole human story, from 'Lucy', the first australopithecine, to the *Mona Lisa*; from the Neanderthals to 9/11; from the pyramids to Putin. There's a lot to pack in and so, inevitably, to achieve anything like a clear and coherent narrative, an indecent amount has had to be left out. The shortest shrift has been given to the earliest times. Isn't this a dereliction of duty? Isn't history supposed to be about the past?

True, but our 'past' encompasses everything up to yesterday. We're also constrained by our lack of information. It isn't that the lives of people in ancient Egypt or Peru were less interesting or important than those of twentieth-century Cubans or modern-day Americans, but we know comparatively little about what they were like. Rich as the insights of archaeology have been, they've inevitably left an enormous amount untold. As important, though, is the way in which human progress appears to have moved ever more swiftly down the centuries, going into fast-forward in modern times.

A NUMBERS GAME

It is partly a matter of numbers: 10,000 years ago, there are believed to have been 4 million people in the world; by the beginning of the Common Era (AD 1) there were 160 million. An enormous expansion – but still nothing compared to the 600 million there would be by 1700 or the 990 million there'd be by a century after that. By 1900, the figure was to stand at 1.65 billion. By 1970, that figure had already more than doubled; by 2011, it stood at 7 billion and was rising fast. All told, it is believed that 108 billion people have ever lived. Some 6.5 per cent of them (8 billion) are alive today. We generally come across such figures in the context

RIGHT:
THE ROAD NOT TAKEN
Named for the fact that their first known fossil remains were found in Germany's Neander Valley, the Neanderthals were the closest early relatives of humankind. Still extant some 40,000 years ago, they disappear from the record not long after. DNA evidence suggests their development diverged from modern humanity's half a million years ago.

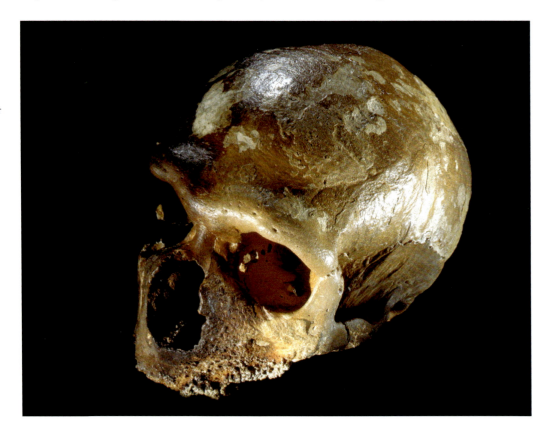

of more or less doom-laden discussion of the coming crisis in food supply or climate change. But they also have their application in explaining why in important ways history appears to have accelerated in recent times. History hasn't really sped up, but as the number of lives has expanded exponentially, so has the sheer amount of human activity, human endeavour.

PREHISTORIC PRELIMINARIES

History is an afterthought. Humankind had existed for many tens of thousands of years before the development of written scripts allowed the record keeping required for any meaningful idea of 'history' to be initiated. Something very like humankind – if not quite *Homo sapiens* – had existed for millions of years before that.

The East African Rift Valley appears to have been a focal point for human evolution. It was here that the fossil remains of 'Lucy', a female member of the hominid species *Australopithecus*, 3.2 million years old, were excavated and assembled in the 1970s. Other hominid species emerged over the following millennia – though some were to be evolutionary blind alleys.

Evolving in parallel from a common ancestor who lived three-quarters of a million years ago, the Neanderthals (*Homo neanderthalensis*) and modern humans (*Homo sapiens*) emerged. Both were sophisticated enough to manufacture tools. Neanderthal remains about 450,000 years old have been found in Spain's Sima de los Huesos ('Pit of Bones'); the oldest *Homo sapiens* fossils date from 300,000–200,000 years ago. At this time, they remained concentrated in east and southern Africa, appearing some 130,000 years ago. Supplanting the Neanderthals who had preceded them, they expanded across the length and breadth of Eurasia.

And beyond. Some 50,000 years ago, Australia's first inhabitants found their way across the Torres Strait, between modern Papua New Guinea and Cape York in Australia. The great glaciations of the Ice Age 'locked up' water, lowering sea levels and reducing the area the oceans covered. It was this that also allowed early humans to find their way across the 'land bridge' of Beringia from eastern Asia via what is now Alaska into North and South America – perhaps as much as 25,000 years ago.

LEFT:
INGENUITY
Mars' atmosphere may be too thin to breathe, but it can support a special helicopter. NASA scientists proved that with Ingenuity, 2019. Space is still the 'New Frontier' John F. Kennedy said it was in 1960, a territory to be contested in the coming years.

EARLY HISTORY
8000 – 1200 BC

In this the Palaeolithic or 'Old Stone Age', people lived in family groups of up to 30, pursuing what is known as a hunter-gatherer lifestyle. The men (mostly) hunted big game – at this time 'megafauna' (mammoth, giant deer, bison, wild cattle …) existed in abundance – while the women (mostly) gathered – nuts, berries, seeds and herbs; and, near seas and rivers, shellfish.

Seasonal variations (plant availability; animal migrations ...) and the need for nutritional range left these communities reliant on an array of different food sources, which in turn dictated a nomadic life, over extended territories. The need to travel light meant they didn't leave much of a material 'footprint' behind them – just odd stone blades and axe- and arrow-heads, and occasional examples of their art on rocks or in caves.

THE NEOLITHIC REVOLUTION

This all changed some 10,000 years ago with the advent of the Neolithic ('New Stone Age'). People began taking greater control of their environments. They started tilling the soil and domesticating animals. It made sense to settle down, building permanent shelters and establishing villages.

For the first time, it became possible for surpluses to be accumulated, giving rise to disparities in wealth and power. Local chiefs emerged; other families worked

OPPOSITE:
BEGINNINGS
On the eastern bank of the Euphrates, in Birecik Urfa, southern Turkey, the ruins of one of the earliest known human settlements have been unearthed. Mezraa-Teleilat is thought to have been established some 10,000 years ago.

RIGHT:
HUMANITY SEES ITSELF
These rock-paintings at Tassili n'Ajjer, on the edge of the Sahara Desert in southeastern Algeria, are believed to have been created around 12,000 years ago. A range of what are clearly human forms may be seen.

EARLY HISTORY

RIGHT:
AFRICAN ORIGINS
The rugged backdrop to several million years of early human evolution, the Great Rift Valley runs all the way up through the East African interior from Mozambique to Ethiopia, before extending up the Red Sea to Lebanon. The oldest hominid fossils have been found here.

for them. Set free from productive labour, a dominant elite emerged, justifying its idleness by its role in defending its subject communities. There was spare capacity too for a class of craftworkers to create luxuries. 'Civilization' gave rise to a cultural richness inconceivable in former times, though for most it meant exploitation, if not oppression.

From about 7000 BC, such civilizations were taking shape in parts of Asia, most famously in the 'Fertile Crescent' arcing across from what is now Israel through Lebanon, Syria and southern Turkey to Iraq. But there were centres too in India, in the valley of the Indus River, and along China's Yellow River. A little later (around 3500 BC), similar centres started springing up in the Americas on the coastal plain of Peru (the Caral-Supe civilization) and in Mexico, where the Olmec people were emerging in what would later be Veracruz.

A NEW TECHNOLOGY

The possibilities of Neolithic life were constrained by the limitations of stone technology. Bone-splinters might be used for needles or bodkins and there were always wood, sinew and hide, but for serious points and blades there was only stone. This was hard to work and heavy, and didn't keep its sharpness.

The rise of metalworking changed all this. It was recognized fairly early that metal made attractive ornaments. From around

LEFT:
A BUXOM VENUS
Thought to have been fashioned some 25,000 years ago, this limestone statuette, the so-called 'Venus of Willendorf', was found in a cave in southern Austria. Her voluptuous curves appear to indicate that our palaeolithic ancestors placed a premium on fertility and childbearing ability.

EARLY HISTORY

ABOVE:
FIRST TECHNOLOGY
These rudely fashioned flakes of flint would only too easily be overlooked outside their archaeological context but they represented a major technological breakthrough in their time. Roughly contemporary with the Venus of Willendorf (opposite), they were excavated in the same cave-system near Aggsbach, Austria.

ABOVE:
A HEAD FOR THINKING
Popular lore has retroactively bestowed a boorish air and lumbering manner on the Neanderthals but skulls like this (found near Tbilisi, Georgia and dated to around 70,000 years ago) suggest that they were every bit our intellectual and imaginative equals.

LEFT:
FIRST LADY?
Scientifically reconstructed here, 'Lucy' was given her name by the paleoanthropologists who in 1974 pieced her together from fragments found at Hadar, Ethiopia. A female of the hominid species Australopithecus, she is believed to have lived approximately 3.2 million years ago.

EARLY HISTORY

3500 BC, though, copper was being toughened with tin to make bronze for tools and weapons in the Middle East. (Copper, gold, silver and a range of other metals were being produced in the Americas from around the same time, but only, it seems, for ornamental use.)

THE FIRST CITIES

By 2500 BC, the Indus Valley Civilization was at its height. Based along the river's floodplain, sophisticated systems were in place to regulate water supply for crops and for the people of what were becoming sizeable cities. Mohenjo-daro and Harappa, in modern Pakistan, had populations of up to 60,000. The challenges of urban life were being faced: people lived in houses of sun-baked or fired mud-brick, and arranged around a grid-like street-plan. They appear to have worked as artisans or traders, relying for food on the production of a peasantry in the countryside.

It isn't clear who was in charge, but most of these 'Bronze Age' cultures had what are now known as 'Palace Economies'. Agricultural produce (and labour on public projects from roads

ABOVE:
BROKEN BEAUTY
Ceramics represented an intermediate stage between Stone Age technology and metalworking, but also allowed more sophisticated food preparation and storage on a larger scale. Pottery also offered a medium for the development of the decorative arts. This sherd originated in the Indus Valley, around 3000 BC.

LEFT:
BIRTH OF BUREAUCRACY
Agrarian development brought booming production, the accumulation of wealth and its concentration in the hands of a new elite. The rulers themselves were represented by armies of scribes and officials: this unicorn seal was made in the Indus Valley around 2000 BC.

to royal tombs) was given by the farming people as tribute to their ruler. Whilst holding on to the majority for him- (or her-) self and their household, the ruler also maintained a caste of warriors, administrators and artisans. And perhaps priests, though ancient societies in which they were to the fore have tended to be characterized as 'Temple Economies'.

A SPIRITUAL DIMENSION

Every human culture that we know of has had its own culture, its own set of values and practices, in everything from art to etiquette. And, of course, its spiritual beliefs. Hunter-gatherer societies seem to have bestowed 'totemic' status on certain animals in hopes of gaining a share of their life and strength. Settled agrarian civilizations were in some ways more secure, but were utterly at the mercy of the seasons. The dwindling of the day into the depths of winter was viewed with anxiety, and so the sun's return was welcomed; people pleaded with the gods for regular rainfall – a golden mean between drought and flood. Certain springs, mountains, trees and hollows took on special significance for those who lived around them. Often they were seen as having their particular deities or spirits.

In the Indus Valley, the foundations of Hinduism appear to have been lain this way in the third millennium BC, though they were modified by the arrival of Aryan invaders from Central Asia from around 1900 BC. The main tenets of this new religion

BELOW:
JAUNTY JARS
The Neolithic achievement is nicely summed up in these anthropomorphic storage containers from the Indus Valley (3000–2500 BC). The accumulation of food brought wealth to an elite and, further, freed up a new class of craftworkers, setting off an explosion of cultural innovation.

EARLY HISTORY

were recorded in a succession of Vedas from the fifteenth century BC. We'd say that these were 'scriptures', except that they were memorized and transmitted orally by recitation and wouldn't be 'scripted' or written down for another thousand years.

THE WRITTEN WORD

The recording of religious lore – or, for that matter, its 'creative' use in literature – was of secondary importance when writing came along. Its first use was functional, in allowing the accounting needed to keep the palace or temple economy running smoothly. Rulers employed enormous staffs of scribes to keep track of who'd paid what and of how much produce they held in their stores. The first known form of writing was the so-called 'cuneiform', used by scribes in Sumeria. Carved sticks were used to make indentations in damp clay tablets.

Centred on the city of Sumer, this was one of the first of a succession of states to emerge in Mesopotamia (literally, 'land between the rivers' – the Tigris and Euphrates) in what is now Iraq, and parts of Syria, Turkey and Iran. As the centuries went by, Sumeria rose and fell and was to some extent supplanted by

RIGHT:
A CHRONICLE OF KINGSHIP
'Civilized' societies were hierarchical in a way that hunter-gatherer groups don't seem to have been. Rulers shored up their status by appeal to tradition and dynastic right. Dating from the first half of the second millennium BC, this Sumerian stone prism is inscribed with a list of kings.

EARLY HISTORY

ABOVE:
FROM ACCOUNTANCY TO INSPIRATION
Made in clay tablets while they were soft and damp, cuneiform script was a means of record-keeping. This inscription (c. 3000 BC) notes quantities of grain. Once the system was established, though, it was endlessly adaptable: the *Epic of Gilgamesh* would be written down this way in c. 2100–1200 BC.

BELOW:
PREDYNASTIC PATTERNING
This handsome vessel was made in Egypt some time in the fourth millennium BC, which places it firmly in the Predynastic Period. What we think of as 'ancient Egypt' – the realm of the pharaohs – still lay several centuries in the future but a sophisticated civilization was already taking shape.

other Mesopotamian civilizations. Akkadia (c. 2300–2100 BC) and Assyria (c. 2100–1400 BC) would be followed by Babylon, which was founded around 1900 BC but be crushed by Assyria a century later. (A second, neo-Assyrian Empire, ascendant from 911–609 BC, would be supplanted by a neo-Babylonian Empire from 609 to 539 BC.

THE COMING OF THE PHARAOHS

Meanwhile, another civilization had been growing up in Egypt, along the Nile, whose annual flood sustained a prosperous 'palace economy'. The earliest signs of civilization here date from around 4300 BC. This is known as the Predynastic Period because it was followed by long lines of rulers, known as 'pharaohs'. From 3200 BC, scribes were keeping records in a form of writing, 'hieroglyphs' – special forms, written on 'paper', prepared from papyrus reeds, in charcoal ink.

In addition to tribute of grain, the pharaoh's subjects provided labour on prestigious projects, like the great pyramids (stylized

EARLY HISTORY

LEFT:
AN EARLY KING
Dating from around 2900 BC, this ceramic sherd is inscribed to Qa'a, a king of the First Dynastic Period. The hieroglyphic record tells us that his reign went on for an impressive 33 years but offers no details of its events.

RIGHT:
A FORCE FOR UNITY
Mentuhotep II, seen here in his funerary frieze, was important in beginning the reunification of Egypt from around 2010 BC, bringing the chaos of the First Intermediate Period to an end. Watching him over on his trip to the afterlife is the sky-goddess Hathor (right, but damaged here).

BELOW:
THE GREAT PYRAMID
Ancient Egypt's achievements were innumerable and astonishing, but there's no dispute over which was the most imposing. The Great Pyramid of Giza remains a wonder almost 5,000 years after its construction as a tomb for the pharaoh Khufu (or Cheops), of the Old Kingdom, at the beginning of the twenty-sixth century BC.

EARLY HISTORY

stone versions of the earthen burial mounds they'd used before) built from 2780 BC. Elaborate funerary practices were at the centre of ceremonial and civic life. Carefully embalmed and mummified, pharaohs were lain to rest in sumptuous tombs surrounded by treasures and equipment for the afterlife.

It isn't clear why, around 2150 BC, this Old Kingdom of Egypt collapsed, but it appears to have done so. After an Intermediate Period, which is only sketchily understood, a second state arose in around 1980 BC. This is now known as the Middle Kingdom because 350 years later a Second Intermediate Period began, before a New Kingdom held sway from 1530 BC. Lavish burial practices were still very much at the centre of ceremonial life, but pharaohs were now lain to rest, not in pyramids, but in grandiose tombs dug out of the side of the Valley of Kings.

HISTORY AND MYTH

Another state had arisen on the island of Crete in the Mediterranean in around 2500 BC. So vast and complex in its layout was the 'Minoan' ruler's palace, with its living

LEFT:
BEAST OF KINGS
The sphinx – a figure with a man's face and a lion's body – emblematized the Egyptian pharaoh in all his regal power and strength. This one represents Amenemhat III, a pharaoh of the Middle Kingdom, who reigned around the end of the nineteenth and the beginning of the eighteenth century BC.

EARLY HISTORY

RIGHT:
AMENEMHAT ASCENDANT
This colourful frieze was made some time around 1970 BC to celebrate the 30-year jubilee of the pharaoh Amenemhat I. We see him attended on one side by Horus, falcon-headed god of sun and sky, and on the other by Anubis, jackal-headed deity of the underworld.

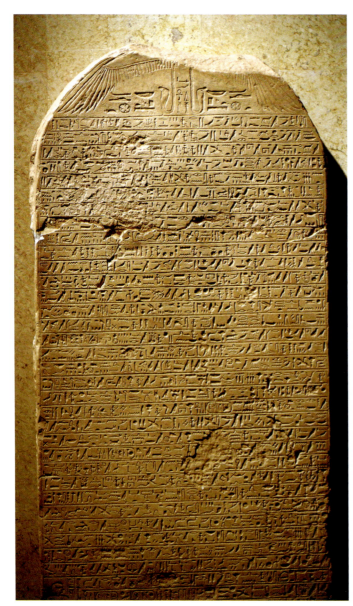

accommodation and storage chambers, that it's believed to have given rise to the later legend of the labyrinth. This was home to the legendary Minotaur – a monster, half-man, half bull. The bull seems to have been a cult-animal in Minoan culture.

Drawing a boundary between history and legend is often problematic, but particularly difficult to do for ancient times. It's tempting to think that the Great Flood of Gun-Yu, which reputedly took place in China in around 2300 BC, is the same as that recorded in the great Babylonian poem *Epic of Gilgamesh*. This seems to have dated from about the same time, though it wasn't to be written down till early in the second millennium BC. The Jews would not start putting together the texts that would make up their Bible for another thousand years, but a world-destroying flood was of course to feature in the Book of Genesis.

IRON ARRIVES

A big step forward had come in about 2200 BC with the introduction of ironworking technology in Anatolia (modern Turkey). Iron was easier to work than bronze. Tougher and more durable, it increased the quality of everything from swords to ploughshares, transforming just about every area of life. Alloyed with carbon (from charcoal, mostly), it made steel, which was even stronger.

LEFT:
KAMOSE THE CONQUEROR
The Second Intermediate Period had seen much of Egypt fall to the Hyksos, Middle Eastern invaders. Kamose's victories helped reclaim the country for Pharaonic rule and establish the New Kingdom. This inscribed stele records his triumphs in detail, though it was made some centuries later (1100 BC).

OPPOSITE:
THE VALLEY OF THE KINGS
The pyramids, iconic though they are, are only half the Egyptian story, ceasing to be built after the fall of the Old Kingdom. For 500 years, pharaohs were lain to rest in this necropolis across the Nile from Thebes, the New Kingdom's capital, in discreet but often still more sumptuous tombs.

EARLY HISTORY

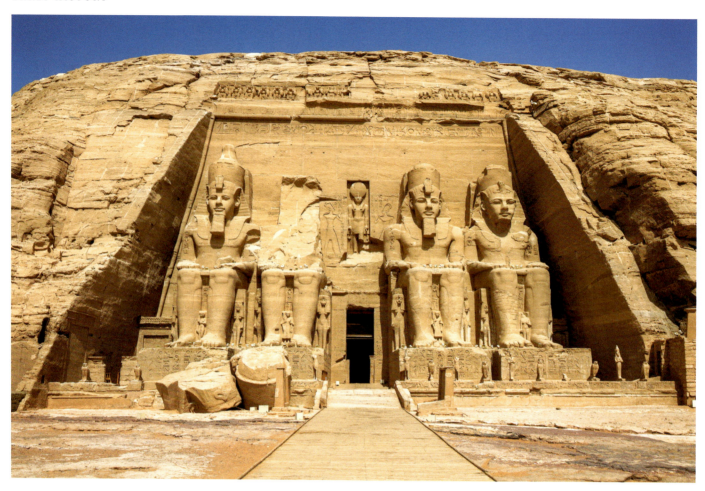

LEFT:
SHANG DYNASTY WINE CONTAINER
Created as a bold display of political power, this large wine container closely resembles two monumental vessels excavated from the tomb of the royal consort Fu Hao (died c. 1250 BC) at Anyang, Henan province.

The Hittites, who built an empire in Anatolia between about 1650 and 1150 BC, were once credited with the discovery of ironworking, but seem only to have been beneficiaries of a technology that was already well-advanced.

The arrival of the 'Iron Age' more widely was actually quite slow. The skill took several centuries to spread across the ancient world. It is known to have reached China during the time of the Shang dynasty (c. 1600–c. 1046 BC) but large-scale ironworking didn't take place till the middle of the first millennium BC. Japan didn't even get bronze until then – brought in by the 'Yayoi' people, immigrants from somewhere on the east Asian mainland. Japan's iron age didn't begin until the first century AD. (In the Americas it didn't happen at all: people there would have to wait for the arrival of the Spanish in the sixteenth century to have access to iron weaponry and tools.)

THE MYCENAEAN MOMENT

Greece, meanwhile, had only comparatively recently left the Neolithic. Island-hopping immigrants had brought Bronze Age technology early in the second millennium BC. Towards

EARLY HISTORY

OPPOSITE TOP:
ABU SIMBEL
Rameses II built a number of temples in Lower Nubia south of Aswan, but none of them are as spectacular as the two rock-cut examples at Abu Simbel. The entrance to the Great Temple is flanked by 20 m (66 ft)-tall statues of Rameses II. Between 1964 and 1968 both temples were cut into blocks and moved to higher ground as Lake Nasser filled behind the Aswan Dam.

RIGHT:
MINOAN MASCOT
An obvious emblem of masculinity and strength, the bull was central to the ceremonial life of the Minoans. This terracotta vessel seems actually to have seen serious use as a rhyton, a ritual jug from which libations (offerings of blood or wine) were poured.

BELOW:
ORTHOSTAT RELIEF: LION-HUNT SCENE
Stone slabs carved in low relief had traditionally decorated the walls of the Neo-Hittite palaces and temples, such as this one dating from the tenth or ninth century BC. Workmanship was often strong, if crude. The figures were carved with little descriptive detail engraved on the surface.

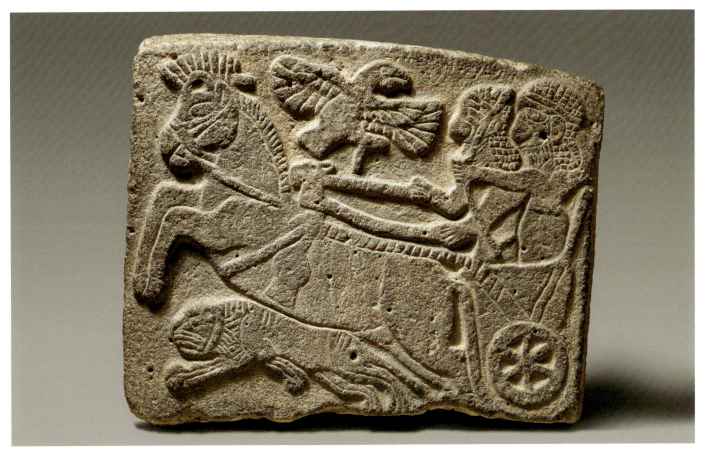

EARLY HISTORY

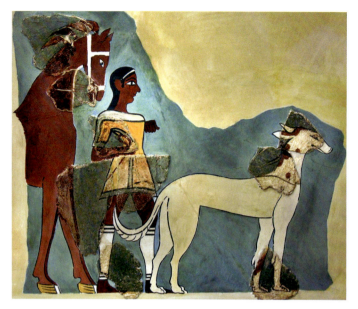

ABOVE:
A CRYPTIC SCENE
A Mycenaean man holds the reins of a majestic horse; before him stands an enormous hound: are they preparing to go hunting or to war? Exhilaratingly splendid as they may have been, the discoveries of Bronze Age archaeology have also often been bemusing.

BELOW:
THE WORK OF GIANTS?
This kind of masonry is called 'Cyclopean' because later generations of Greeks believed that only the ancient race of giants, the Cyclopes, could possibly have raised such stones into place. Even now, in its ruined state, Mycenae's Lion Gate inspires awe.

around 1550, though, the arrival of ironworking allowed the first significant civilization to emerge: its capital lay on the southern Peloponnesian peninsula, at Mycenae. To judge by the ornate armour and weaponry excavated here in modern times, Mycenaean culture would seem to have been strongly militaristic. But its real power was as a merchant state and its biggest army was of scribes: this was another 'palace economy'.

Ironworking was the basis too of northeastern Nigeria's extraordinary Nok culture, which emerged towards the end of the second millennium BC. Despite this, its great legacy has not been its iron artefacts but the terracotta sculptures it produced in the centuries that followed.

By now, we've seen, civilization was old news in Eurasia, Africa and the Americas, but in the Pacific the peopling of the earth remained incomplete. It seems to have been around 1300 BC that colonists from southeast Asia, travelling in family groups in fragile canoes with all their livestock and possessions, reached the islands of Melanesia, Fiji, Tonga and Samoa.

OPPOSITE:
HEAD SCRATCHER
More than two millennia on, we can scarcely even speculate on what the Nok craftworker can have 'meant' by a terracotta head like this. It would be wonderful to know; failing this, though, we are fortunate that we can at least appreciate its extraordinary artistry and skill.

THE ANCIENT ERA
1200 BC – AD 500

Nowhere do history and myth collide more memorably than in the tale of Troy. The city was real enough: it stood on a headland above the Dardanelles on the Turkish coast. It had done so for a long time before its supposed siege. Archaeologists have found signs of settlement from 3600 BC.

AN AFFAIR OF HONOUR

Legend has it that Paris, Prince of Troy, found three goddesses fighting over who was the most beautiful: Aphrodite (goddess of love), Hera (goddess of marriage) and Athene (goddess of wisdom). Asking him to arbitrate, each attempted to bribe him. Aphrodite offering him the world's most beautiful woman, he named her, and won Helen as his prize. It didn't bother Aphrodite that Helen was married, to Menelaus, King of Sparta; nor did it faze Paris, who took her back to Troy.

With Greece's honour at stake, King Agamemnon of Mycenae called together a force from all the country's cities. They sailed across the Aegean and subjected Troy to a ten-year siege. Over the years, sorties were made on to the plain before its gates by the city's defenders, led by

OPPOSITE:
A WORLD OF LEARNING
The Library of Celsius stands in Ephesus, a city founded by the Greeks near Selcuk, on the western coast of what is now Turkey. Celsius had been the Roman governor of the province then called 'Asia'. The library was endowed as a memorial by his son.

RIGHT:
COME TO DUST
True-life Troy as we see it today. The city's 'topless towers' (as the sixteenth-century English playwright Christopher Marlowe called them) would live on in the western memory, as would the 'thousand ships' he said were launched by Helen's face.

THE ANCIENT ERA

THE ANCIENT ERA

LEFT:
COMMANDING HEIGHTS
An austere inspiration for an austere code. Jabal Mousa or Mount Sinai was to become sacred to all three 'Religions of the Book' (Judaism, Christianity, Islam) as the place where in the Bible (Exodus 20) God gave Moses the Ten Commandments.

BELOW:
EPIC EVENTS
A legend in his own right, 'Homer' was a composite of all the bards involved in the evolution of the *Iliad* and *Odyssey* in the oral tradition. But 'his' creations lived on, as in this Roman frieze from the first century AD.

Paris's brother Hector, and repulsed by Greek heroes like Ajax, Achilles and Odysseus. This was to be the stuff of Homer's epic poem, the *Iliad*.

Famously, the city fell when Odysseus devised a plan to stage a withdrawal (as though in finally acknowledged defeat) and leave the Trojans the farewell offering of a giant wooden horse. Jubilant at their deliverance, the Trojans brought the horse into the city – where that night it disgorged a band of warriors, concealed inside. They opened the gates to their fellow Greeks, who had been lurking just along the coast.

WESTERN WAYS

The Fall of Troy traditionally took place in 1185 BC. Whether it actually did is doubtful. It is certain, though, that the classical Greek civilization it came to stand for – and the Roman one which started out in emulation of it – represent one of the most important strands in the history of the succeeding centuries. Arguably *the* most important from the perspective of what we nowadays call the 'West'.

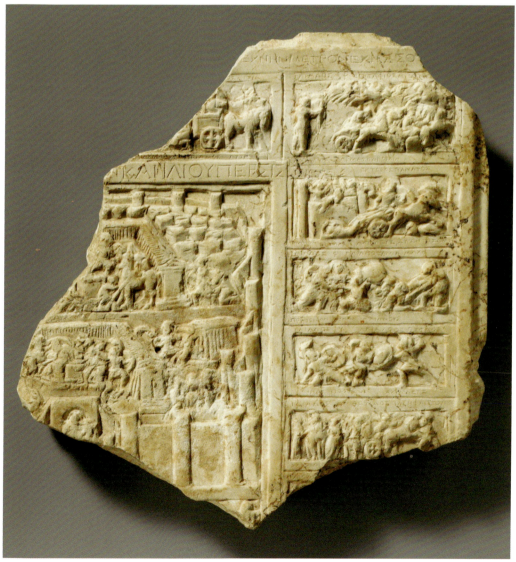

THE ANCIENT ERA

RIGHT:
KING IN THE MIDDLE
King Wu had a brief but vital reign (c. 1047–3) as the founder of China's Zhou dynasty. Its ascendancy was to last for almost 800 years. His descendants built an empire that extended across much of the Middle Kingdom, the area of China that remains central to Chinese historic identity today.

THE ANCIENT ERA

LEFT:
THE AESTHETIC ECONOMY
This rock-crystal vase from the fifth to the second century BC was the work of a Cypriot or Phoenician hand, but might almost as well have been made in the Near East or Egypt. Trade was an important channel of cultural commerce.

BELOW:
MAN OF MARBLE
Embodying the body it was made to contain, this Graeco-Phoenician stone sarcophagus from the fifth century BC may be seen as constituting a sort of sculptural pun. The societies of the Mediterranean were growing rapidly in cultural confidence at this time.

Arguably, but not self-evidently. For, just over a century later, another important influence was taking shape. In 1047 BC, according to the Biblical Book of Samuel, King Saul brought together the two states of Israel and Judah to found the United Kingdom of Israel. Under his heroic protégé David, the Jewish kingdom grew in power. Saul's successor Solomon built his people their first temple.

This story may not be much more historical than Troy's, but it was to be still more far-reaching in its cultural significance. Not only was it central to the identity of the Jews: it underpinned the Christian tradition around which medieval and modern European culture would be constructed. Not, of course, that Europe is the world; or the West and its values the only ones.

For better or worse, though, 'Western' values count in the modern scheme, having made their influence felt across the world at large. From the 'voyages of discovery' of the fifteenth and sixteenth centuries to the colonialism of the nineteenth and on into the 'American Century', a certain set of rules was established as the norm. It went largely unquestioned that this was the way things were and had to be, and other local traditions were marginalized.

THE ANCIENT ERA

CENTRES OF THE EARTH

That said, complacent insularity is a human universal. At this same time, far away in China, in the muddy floodplains of the Huanghe or Yellow River, the kings of the Shang dynasty (c. 1600–c. 1046 BC) were being replaced by those of the Zhou (c. 1046–c. 256 BC). They called their empire *Zhongguo* – literally 'middle'. To the north lay open steppes where wild nomadic herdsmen roamed; to the south were jungles full of savages: their country was the centre of the world. They too took it for granted that their civilization was the only conceivable sort.

Further west, where Asia met Europe and Africa, the Mediterranean (this name too means, literally, 'Middle of the Earth') was assuming a new importance as an arena for imperial expansion and for trade. Setting out from the Lebanese cities of Tyre and Sidon, the Phoenicians were trading with ports in North Africa and Southern Europe. In 800 BC, they established a base at Carthage, near what is now Tunis, which soon became a power in its own right.

BELOW:
PLAYING A GREEK TUNE
A lyre-player cavorts with drunken devotees of Dionysos (or Bacchus) in a fresco from the walls of a tomb in Tarquinia. The Etruscans had imported his cult into Italy along with other Greek luxuries and artistic influences.

Others were establishing colonies too. In Greece, the growing wealth of local rulers had stimulated significant craft-industries and international trade: perfect conditions for the evolution of the *polis* or city-state. Whilst each city typically had a defensive citadel on a hill or elevated outcrop, the focus of everyday life was below, around the *agora*, an open area in which citizens met and talked and made business deals.

Young adventurers from these cities founded trading posts abroad, enriching their home-states still further, and establishing a two-way channel of cultural communication. Byzantium (later Constantinople and then Istanbul), Massalia (Marseilles), Neapolis (Naples) and Odesos (Odessa) were among almost 500 of these colonies.

While individual cities grew independently, their sense of a common Greek identity was growing too, fostered by a shared mythology of gods and heroes. Almost nothing is known of the poet Homer (some even suggest 'he' was more than one anonymous bard), but his *Iliad* and *Odyssey* would be an enduring inspiration to the Greeks.

CITIES OF THE DEAD

Among the Greeks' best customers in the Italian peninsula were the Etruscans. By 750 BC, they had extended their influence

ABOVE:
GREEK POETRY IN EGYPT
The papyrus reeds the Egyptians wrote on were the original 'paper'. This fragment of Homer's *Iliad* was found in excavation at a Roman site at Al Bahnasa, Egypt. Ancient civilizations didn't necessarily fit the silos we sometimes try to force them into now.

beyond their base in Etruria, central Italy, down the western coast and north towards the Po. Their elites were lain to rest in sumptuous tombs. Crowded together in *necropoleis*, 'cities of the dead', these were more permanently constructed than their actual homes and have, ironically, outlasted them.

The same goes for the Paracas culture, then emerging across the world, on Peru's arid coastal plain. Building irrigation systems to bring water from the few, intermittently flowing rivers, and fishing in the ocean, the Paracas managed not only to subsist but thrive. They lived simply, their huts no more than reed-roofed pits, but their departed dignitaries were housed in elaborate underground burial complexes with courtyards and corridors. The dead were dressed in woven and embroidered cloths of sumptuous luxury and staggering workmanship. Wealthy individuals were wrapped in multiple layers (up to a hundred), with jewellery between. While cotton was cultivated by the Paracas, llama and alpaca wool was obtained by trade from communities in the Andes. So too were gold and other

THE ANCIENT ERA

THE ANCIENT ERA

LEFT:
SKY OBSERVATORY, EL MIRADOR
El Mirador (1000 BC–AD 150) has been called by some 'The Cradle of Maya Civilization'. In its time, it was the largest city in the Americas. It is still the largest known Maya site, encompassing an area of 36 sq km (15 sq miles). At its peak, it is estimated that 100,000 people lived here.

RIGHT:
CAT CARAFE
A feline face adorns this Paracas-made bottle (c. 800–550 BC). The spout, shaped like a stylized bird's head, would have whistled while the liquid poured. A second spout just visible behind here would have helped it to flow smoothly.

BELOW:
A MEANDERING MONUMENT
Ohio's 'Serpent Mound' is the most famous legacy of North America's Adena culture, which flourished in the Midwest between c. 500 BC and AD 100. The Adena hunted in the woods, gathered seeds and nuts, and cultivated squashes and sunflower seeds.

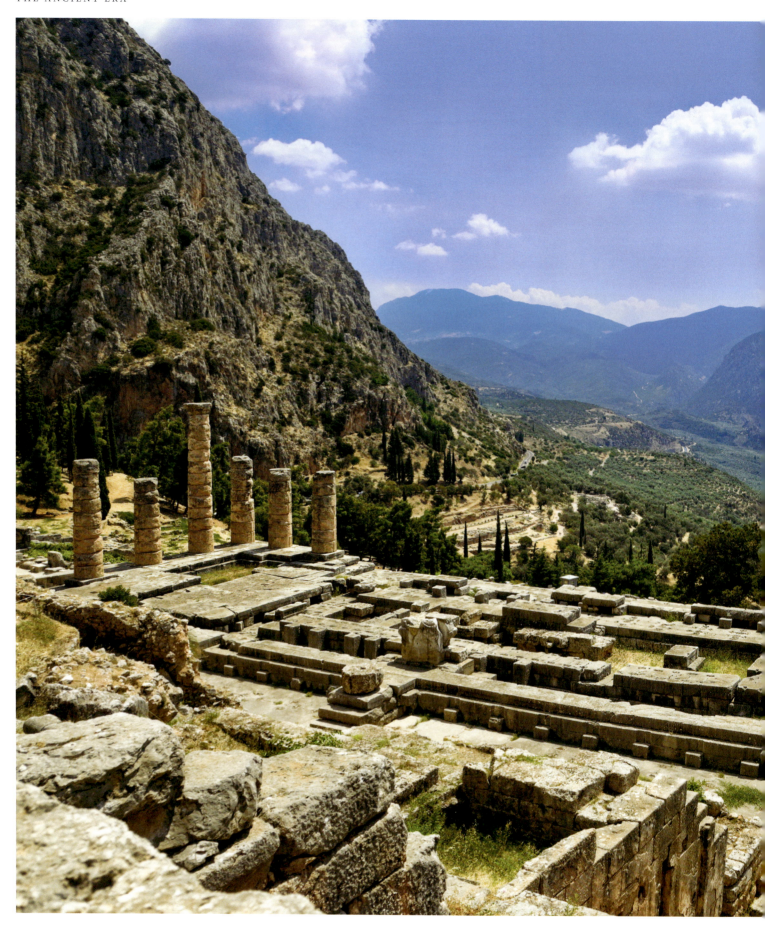

THE ANCIENT ERA

minerals as well as the Amazonian birds' feathers miraculously incorporated into some of the more spectacular fabrics.

BOUNTIFUL BEGINNINGS

Elsewhere in the Americas, on the Pacific coast of Chiapas, Mexico, and the Guatemalan uplands, another culture, that of the Maya, was taking shape. The earthen burial-mounds they threw up were unimpressive by comparison with the pyramids raised by later generations of Maya, but they were arrayed with richly carved standing stones that *were* impressive, and a sign of greater things to come.

At around the same time, the Adena culture was emerging in the North American Midwest. It too left a legacy of earthen mounds. Most were round but some were elaborately shaped, like the 'Serpent Mound' of Peebles, Ohio, its wriggling form some 400 m (1,300 ft) in length.

'BLACK PHARAOHS'

Egypt by now was in its Third Intermediate Period. The New Kingdom had come to an end with the death of Pharaoh Rameses XI in 1077 BC and the Late Period would not begin till the accession of Psamtik I in 664 BC. It was still a significant power, but the exciting development of this time was the ascendancy of the Kingdom of Kush, in Nubia, to the south.

The Egyptians had always disparaged the 'miserable people' of Kush. In 769 BC, however, Kashta became the first of a line of 'Black Pharaohs' reigning over a sort of imitation Egypt here.

LEFT:
DIVINE DELPHI
Apollo's Temple in the Parnassos Mountains was first founded in the eighth century BC. A priestess here, the Sibyl, communicated messages from Apollo, supposedly emanating from an opening in the earth. People came from across the whole Greek world to consult the 'Delphic Oracle'.

ABOVE:
AN ALTER-EGYPT
Kush's cultural debt to its northern neighbour is evident in these pyramids. Over 250 have been found in what is now Sudan. The Nubians worshipped the Egyptian god Amun at Jebel Barkal, a shrine-centre near Karima, on the Nile River.

THE ANCIENT ERA

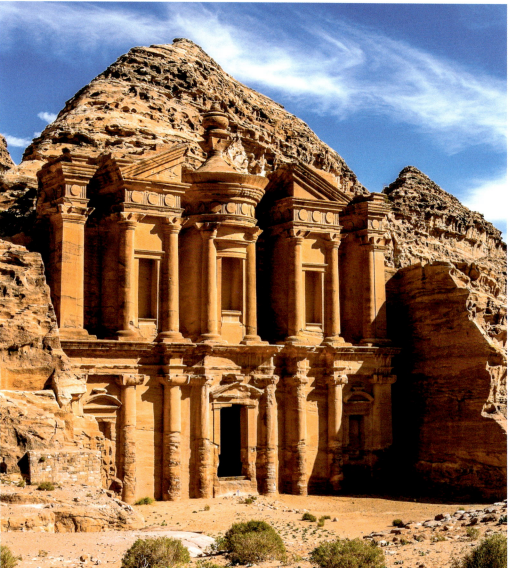

ABOVE:
BABYLONIAN LIONS
Lions pace impressively across the glazed brickwork of Babylon's Ishtar Gate, built by Nebuchadnezzar II in around 569 BC as the climactic point in a processional route into his rebuilt city. Ishtar was the Mesopotamian goddess of love, sex and fertility.

OPPOSITE:
DARIUS AND THE DEITY
The vast Achaemenid Empire encompassed many peoples. The Persian kings took an easy-going multicultural – and multi-credal – view. Cyrus the Great was to treat the Jews to a new Temple; here Darius I (reigned 522–486 BC) makes an offering to the Egyptian god Amun.

LEFT:
A CITY IN THE STONE
Arab nomads, grown wealthy in the incense trade, settled down to start this city in the Jordanian desert in the fifth century BC. Petra (the name is Greek for 'stone') is awe-inspiring in its architecture, classically influenced but carved directly from the virgin rock.

THE ANCIENT ERA

The Nubians were unabashed about their cultural debt to their northern neighbours, adopting Egyptian ways in everything from architecture to religious customs. During the reign of Kashta's son Piye (747–16 BC), they actually conquered Egypt-proper and ruled over it for a century or so.

THE CLASH OF EMPIRES

In Mesopotamia, meanwhile, states had continued to rise and fall. Under Ashurnasirpal II (reigned 883–859 BC), the Neo-Assyrian Empire took Egypt from Taharqo, its last Kushite pharaoh. Successors like Shalmaneser III (reigned 859–824 BC), Sargon II (reigned 722–705 BC) and Ashurbanipal (reigned 669–631 BC) made Assyria the dominant power in the Middle East.

In 605 BC, however, Nebuchadnezzar II became King of Babylon, inaugurating a 'Second Babylonian Empire'. During Nebuchadnezzar's reign (605–561 BC), important territories were conquered and the city of Babylon expanded, rebuilt and beautified – its legendary Hanging Gardens (if they existed) date

RIGHT:
THE SAGE AND THE STATE
Confucius called for the moral self-perfecting of each individual and his induction into the skills that would make him useful to the state. Though not nominally inferior, girls and women were seen as owing their primary obedience to their menfolk and their households.

BELOW:
A MODEST MAUSOLEUM
'Oh man, whosoever thou art,' reads the inscription on Cyrus II's tomb, 'I am Cyrus, and I won for the Persians their empire. Do not, therefore, begrudge me this little earth which covers my body.'

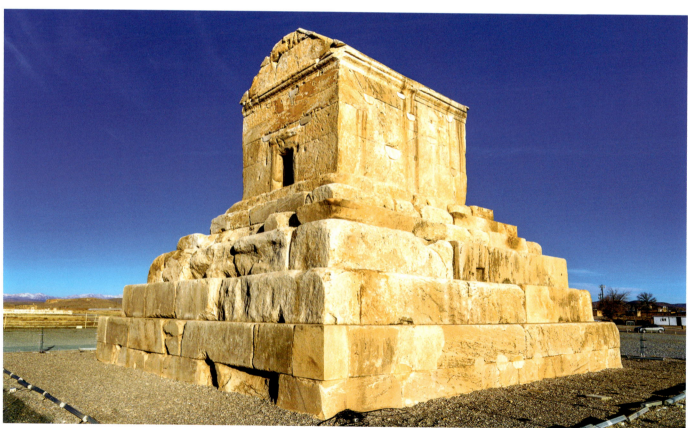

from this time. Nebuchadnezzar features in the Bible, having made an unwelcome appearance in Jewish history, invading Judah in 598 BC and sacking Solomon's Temple in 587 BC.

THE PATH OF PEACE

In 556 BC, by tradition, Gautama Siddhartha was born in India's Himalayan foothills. He's been better known to history as the Buddha. Aristocratic by birth, he had – it's said – been kept in isolation from the ills of the world. Yet, his curiosity growing, he stole out alone into the city, and was shocked by the sights that met his eyes. Signs of suffering and sickness, old age and

BELOW:
PERSIAN POWER
Persian soldiers patrol the walls of Darius I's palace at Susa (now Shush, in western Iran). Greece's victories were impressive but have skewed our perceptions of a Persia which was, through most of this period, the dominant military power in the Middle East.

mortality. Leaving his home to wander as a beggar, he spent six years in poverty and hunger, but this brought him no spiritual return. Realizing he would only find enlightenment within himself, he sat down beneath a tree, resolved not to move until he had attained a state of spiritual ecstasy. Then, for 45 years, he wandered through northern India preaching his message: 'Cease to do evil; learn to do good, and purify your heart.'

RULES TO LIVE BY

Even as Siddhartha was speaking of peace in India, the Chinese general Sun Tzu (traditionally born in 544 BC) was writing his famous treatise on *The Art of War*. As much a philosophical essay as a manual for the field, it pioneered a whole approach to strategic thinking – not just for soldiers but for politicians and businessmen. Sun Tzu's contemporary Kongzi (born c. 551 BC) is known in the West as Confucius. His thinking is influential in China to this day. As much a life-code as a collection of ideas, it places emphasis on individuals' responsibility to their communities – to some extent, their duty to conform.

PERSIAN POWER

In 559 BC, Cyrus the II ('the Great') became King of Persia. One of his successors, Darius I (reigned 522–488 BC), claimed descent not only from Cyrus but from a maybe-mythical hero, Achaemenes, so Persia's ruling house was known as the Achaemenid dynasty. Cyrus, its real founder, conquered the Neo-Babylonian Empire, whose territories at this time included Israel: as a goodwill gesture to the Jews he rebuilt their temple. He also took much of modern Turkey and made inroads into Central Asia. Cyrus's son Cambyses II (reigned 530–522 BC) fulfilled his father's ambition of conquering Egypt. But it was Darius who brought the Achaemenid Empire to its greatest

BELOW:
A ROYAL TOMB
Artaxerxes III, Persia's King of Kings (reigned 358–338 BC), was lain to rest in this sumptuous stone tomb at Persepolis in 338 BC. Eventually beaten by the Greeks, who were eager to discount Achaemenid achievements, Persia was one of the greatest powers of the ancient world.

OPPOSITE:
TREE OF AWAKENING
A frieze at the shrine of Sanchi, Madhya Pradesh, shows the temple King Ashoka (reigned c. 265–238 BC) built around the Buddha's Bodhi Tree at Bodh Gaya, Bihar. Even without the accompanying story, the tree would have been a powerful symbol of spiritual life and growth.

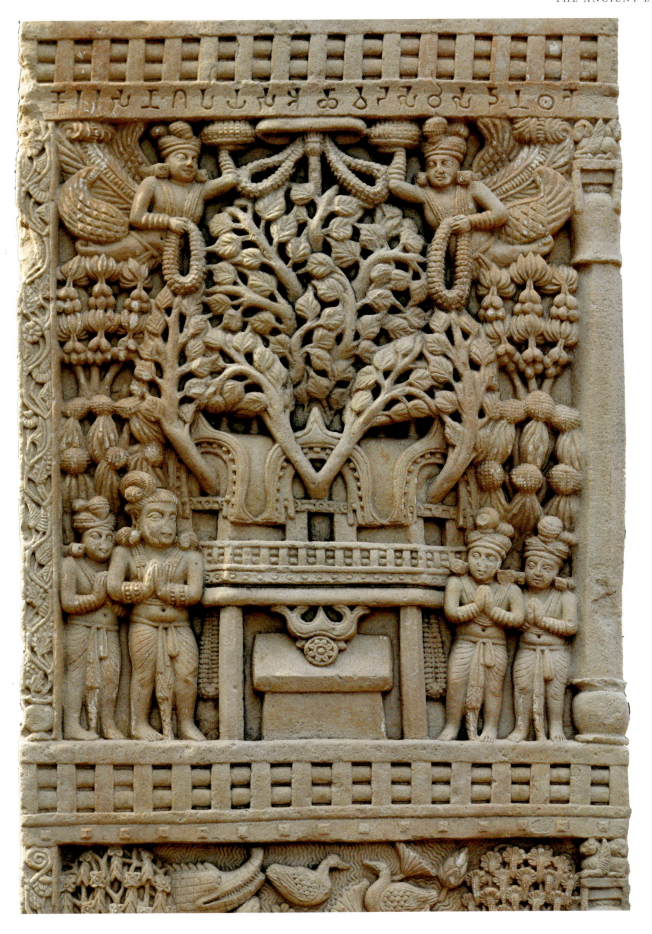

THE ANCIENT ERA

LEFT:
A GLORIOUS GRAVE
The hoplites who died at Marathon were lain to rest in this tumulus or burial-mound, which became a memorial to their victory. In Greek eyes at least, Marathon marked a cultural coming-of-age: a triumph of freedom and enlightenment over oriental tyranny.

BELOW:
CULTURAL CONQUEST
Important in its own right, Greek civilization also provided a paradigm for other aspirational cultures. This krater (a large, two-handled vessel for mixing wine and water) was made by the Etruscans; the Romans too would model their aesthetic on that of Greece.

extent, taking territories in the Indus Valley in the east, pushing north into the Caucasus and establishing a European foothold in the Balkans. This westward expansion brought Persia into conflict with the city-states of Greece – a more formidable enemy than they would have been a few generations earlier.

'GOVERNMENT OF THE PEOPLE, BY THE PEOPLE …'

Athens had been hamstrung by a succession of 'tyrants'. They hadn't all been as oppressive as that word's modern meaning implies, but one-man rule had at best been a brake on progress.

From 594 BC, a campaign by the statesman Solon (c. 630–560 BC) had made it more difficult for tyrants to take power, and weakened the aristocratic elite more generally. It established a hierarchy of officials, answerable to the community. In 508 BC, Cleisthenes inaugurated a system of 'democracy' – rule by the people. Every citizen would have a voice, and vote, in the Assembly.

Athenian democracy was by modern standards staggeringly responsive. Voters didn't just elect a government, but had a say in every decision, every day. On the other hand, women couldn't vote (not that they would be able to in modern democracies until comparatively recently), nor could the mass of slaves

OPPOSITE:
UNAVAILING AUTHORITY
The fourth Achaemenid 'King of Kings', Xerxes I consolidated Persia's hold on Babylon and Egypt and left a legacy of impressive building projects. His subjects called him 'Xerxes the Great' but he is forever remembered for his failure to subdue the city-states of Greece.

THE ANCIENT ERA

and metics (foreign residents), who far outnumbered Athens' approximately 30,000 'citizens'.

There's no doubt, though, that democracy gave Athens a new dynamism and vigour, propelling it to the forefront of the city-states. As its economy boomed and its trade with the rest of Greece and the Aegean took off, it became the richest *polis* of its time. By the beginning of the fifth century BC, only the militaristic state of Sparta could rival it in war. And there only on land: Athens' galley force had grown with the rise of its merchant fleet.

THE UNDERDOG ASCENDANT

Darius was undeterred. In 490 BC, he sent an invasion fleet across the Aegean with an army over 20,000 strong. It landed northeast of Athens, at Marathon, whose wide coastal plain gave his cavalry plenty of room for manoeuvre.

LEFT:
ENLIGHTENMENT AND INTOLERANCE
The Greeks did not always succeed in living up to the values they have historically been celebrated for. Socrates, their founding philosopher, fell foul of powerful political interests in Athens and was forced to commit suicide by drinking hemlock.

BELOW:
ICONIC ATHENS
It was under Pericles' leadership that the Acropolis – the rocky hill that dominates Athens and the site of the city's ancient citadel – was beautified, with a collection of prestigious public buildings. None more charismatic, of course, than the Temple of Athena, the Parthenon.

This was a clash as much of cultures as of militaries. The Persian knights rode horses, a mark of aristocratic status. The 9,000 Athenian hoplites fought on foot, as citizen-soldiers, each man bringing his own armour, shield and long thrusting-spear. They had trained together, acquiring strength in unity and a collective discipline that would save them when the moment came. Facing forward, they presented a solid wall of shields. The Persian cavalry charge shook but didn't break them. Pressing forward in formation, they forced their way to victory. (It

BELOW:
AN ENLIGHTENED EDUCATION
The original 'Academy' was founded by Plato in around 386 BC. Students came here to be schooled in Socratic philosophy and all-round intellectual rigour, learning through directed discussion and disputation. This Roman reimagining, in mosaic, was found at Boscotrecase, near Pompeii.

THE ANCIENT ERA

BELOW:
PERSIA PUT DOWN
Darius looks distraught as his forces fade before the discipline and determination of Alexander's advance at Issus. The presence of this mosaic at Pompeii underlines the importance of the Greek example in establishing a sense of the superiority of the 'West'.

fell to Pheidippides to run back to Athens with news of this extraordinary triumph. The 26-mile (42 km) distance became the basis of the modern marathon.

Another blow for the underdog had been struck in Italy, where the people of Rome had risen up against their Etruscan overlords. Nominally, their city had been founded in 753 BC by Romulus (who as a baby, abandoned with his brother Remus, had famously been suckled by a she-wolf). A line of kings had followed him, but they'd increasingly come under the domination of the Etruscans until, in 509 BC, Rome's leading

citizens had thrown off the authority of conquerors and kings alike to establish a republic. In the 300 years that followed, Rome would extend its imperial sway over the whole Italian peninsula, before pushing on over the Alps into Gaul (now France) and eastward towards Greece – many aspects of whose culture they now embraced.

THE ATHENIAN ACHIEVEMENT

Athens' triumph at Marathon had been achieved alone. The other cities (even Sparta, which had pleaded a religious ceremony) hadn't shown up. This fact did, however, strengthen Athens' position of leadership in Greece.

Ten years later, Darius' son Xerxes led another invasion. He brought a vast army overland around the coast through Thrace. Sparta stepped up this time, Leonidas and his 'Brave Three Hundred' buying valuable time by holding the invaders up at the pass at Thermopylae, though they couldn't keep the Persians out completely. The Athenians withdrew from their city as the enemy advanced, taking refuge in their walled port, Piraeus. Meanwhile, their war-fleet retreated to the nearby Strait of Salamis, whither

THE ANCIENT ERA

it was pursued by the Persian galleys. Instead, the Athenian ships, more manoeuvrable in these narrow confines, turned and savaged and smashed the Persian fleet. Xerxes' force had 'won' but found itself lost without logistical support. It was compelled to make an ignominious retreat.

The stage was now set for Athens' 'Golden Age' under the leadership of Pericles, from 461 to 429 BC. Continuing Cleisthenes' reforms, the justice system was made more democratic, whilst civic pride was boosted by the construction of important public buildings. Against this background, culture thrived more generally. The first tragedies were performed here, as part of religious rituals. The great works of Aeschylus, Sophocles and Euripides (along with the comedies of Aristophanes) become the original classics. Next it was the philosophers' turn. Socrates (c. 470–399) created philosophy

RIGHT:
HANNIBAL (247–183 BC)
One of the greatest generals of antiquity, Hannibal commanded the Carthaginian forces against Rome in the Second Punic War (218–201 BC), famously crossing the Alps with war elephants. He beat the Romans in battle at Trebbia River and Cannae, where his Carthaginian army executed a classic double-envelopment and all but destroyed the Roman forces.

BELOW:
CARTHAGE RUINED
Carthago delenda est – 'Carthage must be destroyed', said the Roman statesman Cato the Elder on the eve of the Third Punic War. Within a matter of weeks he would have got his way. Now the Romans' rebuilt city is itself a ruin.

ABOVE:
A MARTYR FOR MATHS
A Roman mosaic shows Archimedes, the famous Greek mathematician and physicist, being killed by a soldier after the fall of Syracuse (212 BC). The Roman demanded that the scientist come and talk to his commander, but Archimedes – the original unworldly scientist – refused to leave his work.

as a discipline, in which every statement was to be subjected to rigorous questioning. We only know his words because they were recorded by his student Plato (c. 423–348 BC), famous for giving ideas precedence over material forms. *His* student Aristotle (384–322 BC) turned the tables, insisting that knowledge was dependent on perception and experience; we could know only what we had seen verified.

ALEXANDER AND AFTER

Aristotle had a student too. After Plato's death he took a position in the northern kingdom of Macedon, where in 359 BC Philip II had seized power and made himself king. Aristotle became tutor to Philip's son, Alexander (356–323 BC), who, succeeding in 336 BC, set about conquering as much of the world as he could. Defeating Darius III of Persia at Issus (333 BC) and Gaugamela (331 BC), Alexander built the greatest empire the world had yet seen, extending all the way from Greece to northwest India. Taken ill in Babylon, Alexander died, aged only 32. His henchmen squabbled over who would have his empire. When things had shaken down, three separate realms were left. Egypt fell to Ptolemy; Syria and the East to Seleucus; Macedonia and Greece to Antigonus. They all established dynasties and built mini-empires which, through the couple of centuries of what is called the 'Hellenic' era, assumed strangely hybrid cultural characters: part-Greek; part-Egyptian or Asiatic.

EASTERN EMPIRES

Beyond the Indus, the Buddha's had remained a minority religion until, in the third century BC, it was taken up by Ashoka, the

THE ANCIENT ERA

Mauryan emperor, becoming the official religion through most of mainland India. Ashoka also sent out missionaries to spread the word – to Sri Lanka and southeast Asia. Missionaries subsequently set out from these places to preach Buddhism in China, Korea, Japan and Indonesia. It would, ironically, prove more enduring in these far-flung lands than in its Indian birthplace where, after Ashoka's death (c. 238 BC), the Hindu Shungas worked hard to suppress the upstart faith. Another irony would be the co-opting of the Buddha's message – 'First do no harm …' – to militaristic ends, but this certainly wouldn't be the last time this happened (see Constantine's conversion).

While India was being brought together under the authority of the Mauryan emperors, Ying Zheng (259–210 BC) was doing the same for China. He wasn't a great conqueror. The King of Qin (also transliterated 'Ch'in', from which our word 'China' comes), he had ascended his throne at a time when the conflicts

LEFT:
MAURYAN MOTHERHOOD
The Mauryans had many different divinities. This one was associated with motherhood. Her buxom breasts and generous figure are not the only clues. She leans forward as though listening solicitously to her worshippers' pleas, her right palm uppermost, in a giving posture.

OPPOSITE:
IMPERIAL PROGRESS
Having turned a scattering of territories into a single empire, Shihuangdi set out to explore the far-flung corners of his realm. He did so in a series of five inspection tours, visiting cities and sacred shrines, making ritual offerings and setting up monuments wherever he went.

THE ANCIENT ERA

THE ANCIENT ERA

ABOVE:
THE 'SERPENT OF OLD NILE'
Cleopatra VII has been seen as an oriental temptress, sultry and seductive, the ultimate exotic femme fatale. The reality seems to have been that this Macedonian-descended queen surrounded by conspirators at court felt the need to acquire a powerful protector.

LEFT:
A GOD'S EYE VIEW
Straight lines, geometric shapes and a monkey, almost 100 m (325 ft) across, adorn the arid coastal plain in southern Peru. The Nazca carved them, but can't have seen them, since they are only discernible from high above – fashioned, perhaps, for spirits or deities.

of the Warring States Period (475–221 BC) had been coming to an end, with Qin in a strong position and overall authority there for the taking.

His greatness lay in the energy and vision with which he wove his predecessors' conquests into a coherent whole – just as he joined their scattered fortifications into a single structure: the 5,000 km (3,100 mile)-long Great Wall of China. He unified all these former kingdoms into a single gigantic state, taking the title of Shihuangdi or Emperor. This was not an empty, self-congratulatory title: Shihuangdi was reimagining his country and what it stood for.

THE ANCIENT ERA

CERAMIC STRENGTH
Shihuangdi, the first emperor of China (reigned 221–210 BC) hoped to take the afterlife by storm with a 'Terracotta Army' over 7,000 strong. Its life-sized figures included generals, officers, infantry, cavalry and crossbowmen – even acrobats and musicians to entertain them in off-duty moments. All were individualized – no two faces are the same.

THE ANCIENT ERA

A TALE OF TWO CITIES
There were two Teotihuacáns: in one, great pyramids of the Moon (centre) and Sun (right) look down on a solemn, sacred city laid out along a stupendous ceremonial 'Avenue of the Dead'. The other was the sprawling, teeming megalopolis of its age.

THE ANCIENT ERA

LEFT:
FAIYUM FACE
In a (more) modern take on earlier Egyptian rites, patrician citizens of Roman Egypt had their mummified bodies personalized with painted portraits like this one. Some of the finest examples have been found in the oasis-city of Faiyum, south of Cairo.

BELOW:
THE BATTERSEA SHIELD
Discovered by archaeologists on a site south of the Thames in London, this was actually the bronze cover for a wooden shield. Understandably, perhaps, the Romans saw their Celtic enemies as savages, but their arts and crafts show immense sophistication and breathtaking skill.

PUNIC PAIN

Meanwhile, in the Mediterranean, Rome and Carthage were at loggerheads, the former's expanding empire encroaching on the latter's colonies around the region's coasts. In 264 BC, the Romans had attacked the Carthaginian Sicilian base of Akrigas (Agrigento), provoking a protracted naval war. Rome had to build a navy from scratch, copying captured Carthaginian vessels. After 23 years of fighting, Rome prevailed and Carthage was forced to concede Sicily to its enemy's still-expanding empire. A Second Punic War (so-called from the Roman's name for the Phoenician Carthaginians, *Punici*) broke out in 218 BC. The Carthaginian general Hannibal crossed the Straits of Gibraltar into Spain, at the head of a great army equipped with elephants. Pushing on across the Pyrenees through southern Gaul and over the Alps into Italy, he came close to taking Rome but, after 14 years of fighting, was forced to withdraw. In 204 BC, the Romans landed an army in Africa and, in 202 BC, defeated the Carthaginians at Zama. Carthage was finished as a power. It made one more attempt to assert itself in 149 BC. The Third Punic War ended with the Romans victorious, and Carthage razed.

ABOVE:
THE GUNDESTRUP CAULDRON
Made in the Balkans but found in Denmark, this stunningly sculpted silver cauldron bears testimony not only to the extraordinary accomplishment of Celtic craftwork but to the existence of a Europe-wide network of trade and cultural commerce.

AKSUM, ETC

The year 150 BC saw the foundation of the Kingdom of Aksum in Ethiopia. Its influence extended into Arabia's southern tip. It became a major regional power with an important trading empire. At the same time, in the central Mexican highlands, Teotihuacán was founded. With its enormous stone-built pyramids, this ceremonial site was awe-inspiring, but the sprawling city around it (population c. 150,000, many squeezed into multi-storey apartment blocks) was as impressive in its way.

By now, in coastal Peru, the Nazca were building a mysterious culture, most famous for its amazing 'geoglyphs'. Zigzag lines, spiralling whorls, rectangles and trapezoids up to 800 m (2,600 ft) long and 100 m (325 ft) wide were carefully carved out of the desert sand. There are animals up to 300 m (975 ft) in length: a lizard, a spider, a couple of orcas, as well as a stylized human figure.

POWER STRUGGLE

The expansion of its empire had become Rome's *raison d'être*. Its army, now numbering 180,000 (plus local auxiliaries), was its most important institution; its popular heroes were invariably generals. Julius Caesar was one such, celebrated for his victories over the Gauls in what is now France.

The Gauls were just one of many Celtic peoples living across Europe at this time. To the Romans, the Celts were 'barbarians' – uncivilized. Yet the archaeological record shows that they had a highly sophisticated social and artistic culture: but they had a religious taboo against writing, so they left no written record of themselves.

Julius Caesar (100–44 BC), by contrast, blew his own trumpet in his book *The Gallic War*. On the back of its success, he declared himself dictator in 49 BC. A civil war broke out across the empire as his rivals resisted, but Caesar still found time to have an affair with Cleopatra VII, Ptolemaic Egypt's Queen.

THE ANCIENT ERA

RIGHT:
SHIELD OF CONQUEST
The semicylindrical *scutum* shield was carried into battle by every Roman legionary for several centuries. It seems extraordinary now that this is the only one to have survived. It is in a beautiful state, having been lovingly restored, but nevertheless lacks its *umbo* or central boss.

ABOVE:
FROZEN IN FLIGHT
Pompeiians who fled the rain of ash were quickly buried; their decaying bodies left cavities, of which modern investigators made plaster casts. Ghostly forms like this have resulted, caught in the moment of their futile flight, contorted by fear or by the effort to escape.

RIGHT:
AN AUGUST EMPEROR
Rome had rejected rule by monarchy but never really took to democracy. By the first century BC, it was largely being led by groups of strongmen. Caesar's autocratic ambitions had been ended by his assassination but his adopted son Octavian made himself sole leader as Augustus.

Caesar secured his dictatorship at last but was assassinated – stabbed on the steps of the Capitol – in 44 BC. Octavian, his adoptive son, won the second civil war that followed and, in 27 BC proclaimed himself emperor, with the title 'Augustus' ('The August', 'Illustrious').

'YEAR OF THE LORD'

A Jewish preacher, Jesus of Nazareth, very likely *was* born in Roman Palestine – though probably some years before the conventional year of his birth, *Anno Domini*, 'Year of the Lord'. Many scholars agree that he was likely crucified. The view that he was the Son of God, sent to take away the sins of the world and bring us everlasting life, has of course been a great deal more contentious. Even so, a sect of followers sprang up around his teachings. As, over the century or so that followed, it spread around the Roman Empire, involving non-Jews, the authorities cracked down with a series of persecutions.

Meanwhile in Japan, the Yamato Kingdom was coming together. Much remains mysterious about it – including the

THE ANCIENT ERA

THE ANCIENT ERA

ABOVE:
BIRTHPLACE OF CHRISTENDOM
Constantine the Great had the Church of the Nativity built in the fourth century AD. Purportedly, it occupies the site of the stable in which Jesus Christ was born. The star in the centre of the floor marks the exact spot, it's said.

LEFT:
SACRED TO THREE FAITHS
Jerusalem's Temple Mount is so-called as the site of the Jewish Temple; but it was also from here that Muhammad was borne to heaven by angels on his *Lailat al Miraj* or 'Night Flight'. The city is also an important place to Christians. The Western Wall (also known as the 'Wailing Wall', pictured) dates from the Second Temple period, and is believed to have been begun by Herod the Great.

whereabouts of its capital – but its existence was recorded from AD 57 and evidenced by a large number of (characteristically keyhole-shaped) *kofun* burial mounds.

IMPERIAL AFTERNOON

Rome had gone from strength to strength. Though plainly a disaster, the eruption of Mount Vesuvius in AD 79, and the burial of the cities of Pompeii and Herculaneum under a mountain of ash, preserved a vivid record of a highly prosperous and sophisticated civilization.

Roman moralists felt their civilization was getting *too* prosperous and sophisticated, losing sight of the austere virtues that had made it great. While the public were pacified with a regime of 'bread and circuses' (gladiatorial shows), the patrician class were lost to luxury and vice. Clothing and cosmetics were imported from all around an extensive empire. And beyond

– silk was just one of the many exotic commodities brought along what would later be called the 'Silk Road' from China and Central Asia.

By the reign of Hadrian (AD 117–138), the need had been seen to consolidate, establishing fixed frontiers – most famously in Hadrian's Wall, which crossed the breadth of northern Britain, keeping the Celtic Picts (from the Latin *picti*, 'Painted People') of Scotland safely at bay.

By the third century AD, Roman power was waning – though from a very high level. Wealth and power were becoming concentrated in its eastern part. Civil conflict grew. It was before one battle in AD 312 – at the Milvian Bridge over Rome's River Tiber – that the Emperor Constantine saw a vision of the cross in the sky above. A starry motto promised that the sign would bring him victory. He converted to Christianity, making it the official religion of the Roman world.

Elsewhere, other states were on the rise – most notably the Gupta Empire, which ruled over most of India in the fourth and fifth centuries AD. Rome's decline continued, though. In AD 324, Constantine moved the Empire's capital to Byzantium, renaming it 'Constantinople'.

Successive emperors were forced to bring troops back from the periphery to protect Rome, which was increasingly beleaguered by barbarian attacks. Some were Germanic tribes from the Empire's northern borders, others (like the Huns) were nomadic raiders from the Eurasian steppe.

The Iranian rulers of the House of Sasan were also encroaching from the east. From AD 283 to 410, Anglo-Saxon tribes from Germany moved in to take over a Britain abandoned by its Roman protectors. In AD 476, another Germanic people, the Visigoths, sacked Rome, bringing the Western Empire to an end.

OPPOSITE:
THE END OF THE WORLD
Begun in AD 122, Hadrian's Wall remains an awe-inspiring assertion of Roman power, but it was built in a spirit of caution; even hesitation. It marked the emperor's desire to set a limit to what until then had been a story of continuous Roman expansion.

BELOW:
CIVIC AMENITIES
The English city of Bath is named for the complex built there in c. AD 70 by the Romans around natural hot springs that had been held sacred since Celtic times. The Romans were sociable and set a high value on public life: baths were important meeting places.

THE ANCIENT ERA

ABOVE:
THE COLOSSEUM
The ruins of the Colosseum remind us of the awesome scale of the Roman achievement – and, of course, the accompanying cruelty. Amidst this splendour thousands died in gladiatorial shows. Beneath the arena were cages for wild animals, also killed for entertainment.

LEFT:
ARCH OF AMBIGUITY
The Arch of Constantine was built to honour his victory at Milvian Bridge in AD 312. Its inscription tactfully notes 'divine inspiration'. Constantine was to make Christianity Rome's state religion, but he hadn't done that yet and this monument accords with the old pagan conventions.

OPPOSITE:
TRAJAN'S TRIUMPH
Trajan's Column was raised in Rome in AD 113 to commemorate that emperor's victories in the Dacian Wars of AD 101–2 and AD 105–6. Spiralling round it, a frieze presents a continuous narrative of the Roman campaign against the Dacians, who lived between the lower Danube and the Black Sea.

THE ANCIENT ERA

67

THE MEDIEVAL PERIOD
500 – 1453

Bad as it was for its citizens, the Sack of Rome wasn't quite the catastrophe that might be imagined, given the increasing irrelevance of the Italian city. With Constantinople as its capital, the 'Roman' Empire had taken on a different character. Most people spoke Greek; its trading ties with western Asia had fostered a new and richly hybrid culture.

And, largely, a prosperous one. The new Empire – known as 'Byzantine' from Constantinople's former name – recovered much of the territory lost to the barbarian invasions. Great churches were built, with rich mosaics and stunning religious icons, making Constantinople a major spiritual centre. The Pope remained in Rome, but his authority had been damaged. Though officially still subordinate, the Patriarch in Constantinople clearly had a special importance. (In the far west, meanwhile, the Celtic Church was going its own ritual and doctrinal way, as did that of Aksum, Ethiopia, where Christianity became the state religion in AD 330.) Constantinople's

OPPOSITE:
MEMENTO MORI
'Remember that you will die …' The Medieval mind was haunted by the consciousness of death and time and transience – understandably, perhaps, in an age so often afflicted by famine, plague and war.

RIGHT:
BOETHIUS
Imprisonment by Theodoric the Great, the Gothic king of Italy, gave Boethius both the setting and the spur he needed to write his book *The Consolation of Philosophy* (523). It was to remain influential in Christian Europe for a thousand years.

THE MEDIEVAL PERIOD

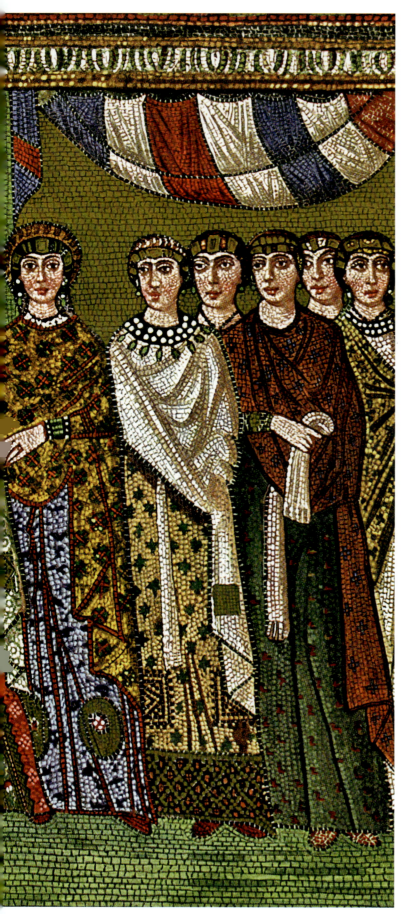

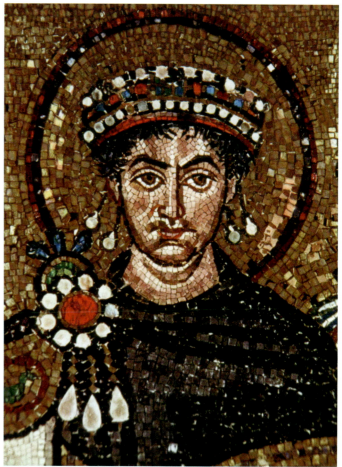

ABOVE:
THE LAWGIVER
The Byzantine Emperor Justinian I undertook an ambitious overhaul of Roman law. His *Corpus Juris Civilis* ('Body of Civil Law') has formed the basis of many modern legal systems.

LEFT:
IMPERIAL SPLENDOUR
Developed by the Romans, the mosaic technique was taken to extraordinary levels of sophistication under the Byzantines. This scene shows Justinian's consort Theodora. Its appearance in San Vitale Basilica, Ravenna, in northern Italy, is a reminder of the progress Justinian made towards recovering the Roman homeland.

capital status was underscored when, in 534, Emperor Justinian I introduced a revised and rationalized code of law.

A PLAGUE OF PROBLEMS

In 541, however, the Empire was hit hard by the 'Justinian Plague'. First breaking out in Egypt, it had spread swiftly to Constantinople and beyond. Plague is caused by *Yersinia pestis*, a bacterium spread by rat-fleas. It is called 'bubonic plague' for the 'buboes' – swellings, in the lymph glands within the groin and armpits – it produces, though there's also a pneumonic version, spread on the breath. On and off, plague would afflict large parts of the world into the early modern era.

Constantinople's relations with the Sasanian Empire, an ancient Iranian dynasty that ruled AD 224–651, had been up

THE MEDIEVAL PERIOD

LEFT:
GOLDEN GRAPEVINE
This beautifully worked gold bracelet with its cunning clasp is testimony to the skill and vision of Byzantine arts and crafts, which have been unjustly overshadowed by the achievements of 'classic' Rome. It dates from the late-sixth or early seventh century.

and down, flaring up into war occasionally without changing the balance of power. But the long-drawn-out, destructive Byzantine–Sasanian War of 602–28 weakened both empires badly.

ISLAM ASCENDANT

In 629, Byzantine Syria was attacked by a new enemy: an army of Arab horsemen led by one Muhammad, whom they hailed as their 'Prophet'. In 610, a middle-aged merchant in the Arabian city of Mecca, Muhammad had started seeing visions. The Angel Gabriel kept appearing to Muhammad, dictating to him the word of *Allah* – God. The name for the new religion, *Islam*, meant 'surrender' to the divine will: it resembled Judaism and Christianity in many respects, notably its monotheism – worship of a single deity.

Muhammad and his followers had inevitably found themselves at odds with the Quraysh, Mecca's elite, and in 622 he had left for nearby Medina. (This emigration or *hijra* became the starting point for the Muslim calendar.) Relations with Medina's three tribes of Jews, though good at first, had worsened as hostilities with Mecca went on, the Muslims fearing that the Jews might make an alliance with their Arab enemies.

In time the Muslims prevailed, though, defeating the Quraysh at the Battle of Badr (624) then taking Mecca, whose *Qaaba* – a pagan shrine already – became the sacred centre of world Islam. By the time the Prophet died in 632, the Arabs had already carried the word by force of arms – and inspiration – through much of the Middle East.

A CONTESTED LEGACY

A meeting of elders elected Muhammad's father-in-law, Abu Bakr, to inherit his authority as *qalifah* or caliph. In so doing, they passed over Muhammad's cousin and son-in-law, Ali ibn Abi Talib, unnerved by Ali's moral rigidity and religious fervour.

OPPOSITE:
MASJID AL-HARAM, SAUDI ARABIA
Muslims worship at the Kaaba, the centre of the Islamic religion, during Ramadan, the holy month. The current structure was built after the original building was damaged during the siege of Mecca by Umayyads in 683. From small, seventh-century beginnings, Islam grew into a major world religion. Its confrontation with Christendom helped shape the medieval history of Europe and the Middle East. Making the Hajj, the pilgrimage to Mecca, was a central duty for every Muslim.

RIGHT:
FOLIATE FINERY
Sasanid aesthetics abhorred a vacuum. Artists decorated every inch of every surface; festooned every wall with stucco, as in this frieze. Stylized vegetal patterns were particularly favoured, suggestive as they were of fertility and abundance.

THE MEDIEVAL PERIOD

In a series of civil wars, first Ali himself and then his sons tried to wrest back the succession they saw as rightly theirs.

Meanwhile, the war of conquest continued, the Muslims taking Syria in 636 after the Battle of Yarmük, in what is now Iraq, and defeating the Sasanians at al-Qadisiyyah the next year. In 638 they entered Jerusalem, to a warm welcome from the city's Jews and Christians, relieved to be freed from oppressive Byzantine rule. The city was as important for the Muslims as for Jews and Christians. (From its Temple Mount, the Prophet had been borne up to heaven by angels in his *Lailat al Miraj* or 'Night Flight'.) Next, in 641, came Cairo and Alexandria, in Egypt.

In 644, Abu Bakr's successor, Caliph Umar, was assassinated. He was followed by Uthman ibn Affan, though not all Muslims were happy with his rule. (His main claim to fame is having brought all Muhammad's visionary pronouncements together in a single sacred volume, the Quran.)

Even so, the Islamic Empire grew as Iran was secured and Afghanistan occupied, an advance-guard crossing the Hindu Kush into what is now Pakistan. In the west, Tripoli was taken and ships sent to seize the strategically vital island of Cyprus. Alien as it was to the experience of most desert-dwelling Arabs,

BELOW:
CENTURIES OF FAITH
St Catherine's is believed to be the oldest continuously inhabited Christian monastery. Greek Orthodox monks have worked and prayed here since the sixth century. Above them looms the mass of Mount Sinai on whose heights, says the Bible, God gave Moses his Ten Commandments.

ABOVE:
'NATURAL' CHURCHES
The Göreme Valley in Cappadocia, Turkey, looks as if it belongs in another world. Uneven erosion of the soft volcanic tufa rock has produced strange 'spires' of stone. Many were hollowed out for churches in what was an early centre of Christian belief.

seafaring did have a place in their country's traditions: ships had long plied up and down the Red Sea and along the seaboard of the Indian Ocean.

BANTU BEGINNINGS

A quieter conquest had been taking place in Africa, where the Bantu nations had – for four or five centuries now – been on the move. If humankind as a whole originally came 'out of Africa', then much of Africa came out of one little corner of the continent. Albeit far more recently.

To this day, by far the majority of West Africa's peoples speak languages belonging to the Niger-Congo group, for many years known to scholars as 'Bantu'. That title is avoided now, being associated with languages found in central and southern Africa. The label is logical enough, though, given that the more southerly Bantu languages were distributed through the continent by a large-scale migration from West Africa almost a thousand years ago.

The migrants didn't just take their language with them. They took all sorts of skills, assumptions, ideas, beliefs and rituals. Their gradual expansion had taken place without regard to either

THE MEDIEVAL PERIOD

BELOW:
RUTHLESS RULER
Li Shimin (reigned 626–49) toppled his father and murdered his two brothers so he could seize power as China's Emperor Taizong. A great, if cruel, ruler, he quelled the nomadic tribes to the north, opening up the great trade routes to western Asia and beyond.

the Western Christian or the Islamic chronology, but is believed to have been completed by about 650.

TO THE EAST

The rise of Islam had undoubtedly been *the* event of the middle of the first millennium AD, but that didn't mean that wider world history had stopped short. China had since 618 been ruled by the Tang dynasty, which enjoyed its golden age in the reign of the Emperor Taizong (626–49). In India, the Pushyabhuti dynasty, having risen in power since the 500s, had built an important empire under Harshavardhana, from around 590, but this began to disintegrate after his death in about 647.

It was around 650 that Teotihuacán in Mexico was destroyed – whether by unknown invaders or its own people remains obscure. The Mayan civilization continued to thrive, but in the early centuries AD its focus had shifted to great cities like Tikal (in what is now northern Guatemala) and Copán (Honduras). By 650 both were starting to be surpassed by an emergent power-centre around Chichén Itzá in Mexico's Yucatán.

In 657, Jayavarman I founded the dynasty which one day, in a century or so, would rule Cambodia's powerful and prosperous Khmer Empire.

In Britain, in 664 at the Synod of Whitby, leading prelates of the Celtic Church agreed to accept the authority of Rome and in 685, the Picts beat the Angles at the Battle of Nechtansmere (its location is unknown), arguably ensuring Scotland's survival as a separate nation.

In southeastern Korea, the Kings of Silla were on the rise. At first, through the Three Kingdoms period, their ascendancy was contested by the rulers of Paekche, in the southwest of the peninsula, and Koguryo in the north, but by the 670s – with the support of Tang China – they controlled most of Korea.

By then, the character of Indonesia was changing. Increasingly important as a centre for Buddhist culture, the emerging trading state of Srivijaya, Sumatra, was establishing extensive contacts in both China and India.

SUNNI VS SHI'A

In the Middle East, meanwhile, Islam had fallen into faction-fighting after Uthman had been murdered by partisans of Ali ibn Abi Talib. Ali's own assassination in 661 brought about the split between the mainstream Sunni and radical Shi'a (the tradition

OPPOSITE TOP:
STONES OF SPLENDOUR
Stone tombs testify to the grandeur of Koguryo, whose name, contracted to 'Koryo', gives us the word 'Korea'. Even so, it was only one of three states vying for supremacy in the first millennium, with Silla in the south and Baekje in the southwest.

OPPOSITE BOTTOM:
'THE CAVES OF THE THOUSAND BUDDHAS'
The murals in northern China's Mogao Caves represent several centuries of Buddhist art. This one dates from around 705. A religious centre grew up here, connected to East and West by the 'Silk Road', along which commerce and cultural influences flowed both ways.

THE MEDIEVAL PERIOD

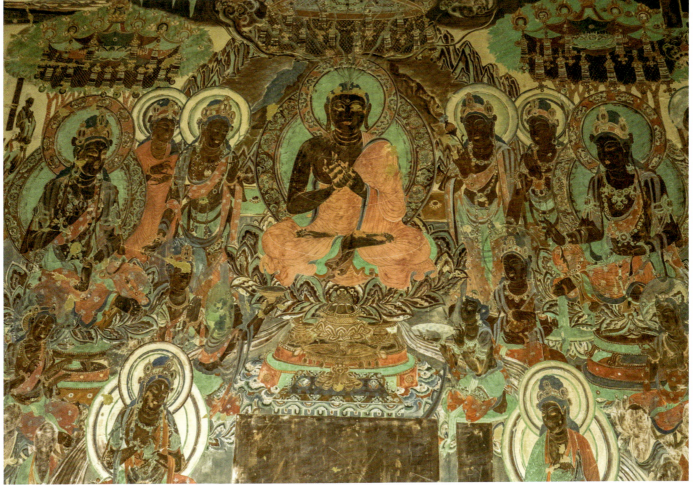

ABOVE:
HOLY GROUND
St Columba is reputed to have prayed and studied in a hut atop this hill on the island of Iona, having introduced Christianity to Scotland. Looking down, we see the seventh-century St Martin's Cross and, farther off, the ruined thirteenth-century Chapel of St Mary.

OPPOSITE:
BARBARIC BRAVURA
One of those 'barbarian' peoples who had inherited the territories of an imploding Roman Empire, the Germanic Anglo-Saxons were not short on civilization, as this extravagantly worked helmet found in a ship-burial at Sutton Hoo, Suffolk, England, makes clear.

which identified with Ali), which has divided Islam throughout the centuries since.

Over time, doctrinal differences developed between Islam's main sects. Those who followed Abu Bakr and the succession of 'Rightly Guided Caliphs' who came after him called themselves Sunni Muslims, because they followed the *sunnah* or 'customs' established by the Prophet. Shi'ites argued that this succession had been corrupted to begin with, and that Islamic tradition should have flowed directly through the person and profession of Ali, and those of the line of teachers or *imams* who came after him.

The massacre of the Shi'ites at Karbala, Iraq, in 680 gave the sect its first martyrs. Though obviously a defeat, it gave the Shi'a movement new impetus.

THE MEDIEVAL PERIOD

UMAYYAD ORDER

For now, though, the Sunni had the upper hand. Mu'awiyah I's Umayyad dynasty, centred in Syria, imposed much-needed unity and order on the Arab world. And building magnificent mosques: the Dome of the Rock, on the site of Muhammad's Night Flight in Jerusalem, and the Umayyad Mosque in their capital, Damascus.

Despite a setback at Constantinople, where in 678 Byzantine forces had deployed 'Greek fire' (a naphtha-based incendiary) to dislodge an Arab fleet that had subjected the city to a seven-

LEFT:
COPYING COINAGE
At its height, the Umayyad Caliphate controlled more than 11 million sq km (almost 4.5 million sq miles) of territory. So swift were the Arabs' early conquests, though, that they had to start their state from scratch. This early coin is based on a Byzantine model.

BELOW:
MOORISH MAGNIFICENCE
Built in 785, the Grand Mosque of Córdoba, Spain, stands as a lasting monument to the glories of al-Andalus – despite its later conversion into the city's cathedral. These horseshoe arches were a feature of the 'Moorish' style.

LEFT:
WINGED HORSE
On this ninth century roundel, the extended tongue and long tail of this winged creature suggest that it may be a griffin, a part-lion, part-eagle emblem of power and protection common to the Byzantine and Islamic worlds. The ultimate inspiration for this fragment may have been Sasanian, as it also resembles a winged horse with ribboned feet.

year blockade, Islam was still carving out new territories. In the early years of the eighth century, Arab armies pushed west from Libya across the entire length of the Maghreb. In 711, the first raiding party of Arabs and Islamicized Berbers – 'Moors', as they were called in Europe – crossed the Straits of Gibraltar into Spain.

Since the fifth century, Spain had been under the control of those Germanic Visigoths who had taken it during the final decline of Rome's Western Empire. They had grown more 'civilized' since, adopting Roman ways – including Christianity. By 718, however, they had been comprehensively defeated by Tariq ibn-Ziyad and his Moorish warriors, and almost all Iberia lay in Muslim hands.

THE FIGHTBACK BEGINS

Only in the far north, in Asturias, did the Muslims fail to impose themselves: in these mountains, a little pocket of Christendom remained. In 720, King Pelagius inflicted a humiliating defeat on an Islamic army at Covadonga, the start of that long, attritional process known in Spain as the *Reconquista*. In 732, a Frankish army led by Charles Martel turned back the Moors at Poitiers/Tours in southern France,

THE MEDIEVAL PERIOD

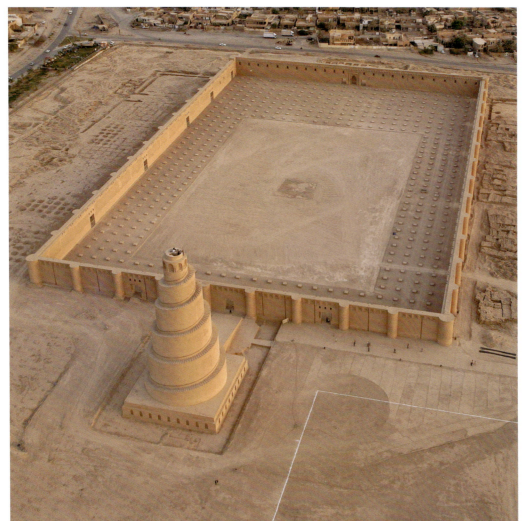

ABOVE:
CHRISTIAN VICTORY
The bloodied heads littering the ground at right suggest that Charles Martel's Christian knights are getting the better of it in this representation of the 732 Battle of Tours. (From an illumination from the *Great Chronicles of France*, 1270.)

LEFT:
HEIRS TO HISTORY
The Abbasids were conscious of their historical status. Built in the ninth century, the Malwiya minaret, at the mosque of Samarra, north of Baghdad, imitates the kind of ziggurat (spiral pyramid), that had been built in Mesopotamian times.

OPPOSITE:
GOD IN HEAVEN
Christ enthroned confers his authority on the scripture we are about to read. An illuminated manuscript like the ninth-century *Book of Kells* was not just a text but a treasure in itself; the sumptuousness of the decoration attested to the truth the work purported to contain.

ABOVE:
LEWIS CHESSMEN
Made from whales' teeth, the 12th century chess pieces discovered on the Isle of Lewis, Scotland, tell us a great deal about Medieval society, demonstrating the international connections of the Norse peoples of the period.

a victory that would subsequently be held to have 'saved' Christian Europe.

The Moors were still very much in charge in the province they called al-Andalus but it might be said that notice had been served. Besides, the Umayyads had more pressing problems closer to home in the Middle East. By 750, they'd been overthrown by the Baghdad-based Abbasid Caliphs. While this wasn't strictly speaking a Shi'ite revolution (Shi'ism recognized no rule higher than that of the imams themselves), the Abbasids could hardly have prevailed without the backing of the Shi'ite scholars. Divisions between Sunni and Shia Islam have persisted to this day, a source of distrust and at times of open warfare.

THE BIRTH OF FRANCE

A Germanic people with territories concentrated in what is now eastern France, the Franks had become the foremost power in western Europe. They had of course won great prestige at Poitiers. The crowning of Carolus Magnus – Charles the Great or 'Charlemagne' – in 768 ushered in a golden age. Charlemagne extended his realms over the Alps into the northernmost parts of Italy. Whilst he didn't occupy any areas farther south, Pope Leo III was sufficiently keen to have his favour that he resurrected the title of 'Roman Emperor' for him.

Charlemagne's son Louis I inherited his empire when he died in 814, but his own death was followed by civil war between his sons. This was resolved in 843 in the Treaty of Verdun. Rather than reuniting Charlemagne's realms, this definitively divided its German and its French domains, setting a course for those two countries into modern times.

THE MEDIEVAL PERIOD

ABOVE:
FIREPOWER
Byzantium's defenders send Arab attackers packing with 'Greek fire'. Its use in 678 had ended a seven-year siege. The widespread use of firearms still lay some centuries off, but this was at least a foretaste of horrific things to come.

LEFT:
ROME RESURRECTED
Pope Leo crowns Charlemagne 'Holy Roman Emperor' (800). Conferring on the Frankish king all the prestige still associated with ancient Rome, the title also implicitly made him and his successors responsible for the protection of the Church.

THE MEDIEVAL PERIOD

The main driver of development – not just religious, but cultural and even economic – through much of the medieval period had been the monastery, a community of monks. According to the 'Rule' lain down by St Benedict at Montecassino, Italy, in the sixth century, monks had to divide their time between spiritual and manual labours. The latter could include everything from agriculture to art ('illuminated' or richly decorated manuscripts). Europe's monasteries became centres of excellence in all these things.

LEFT:
RAMPAGING RAIDERS
Warriors brandish battle-axes and swords on what has come to be known as Lindisfarne Priory's 'Viking Stone', a ninth-century grave-marker. The foundation here had indeed notoriously been attacked by Vikings in 793.

BELOW:
PEACEFUL SETTLERS?
At L'Anse aux Meadows, at the northernmost tip of Newfoundland, Canada, traces of a Viking village may be seen. Established towards the end of the tenth century, the site was soon abandoned. It may only have been a depot for ship repair.

THE MEDIEVAL PERIOD

RIGHT:
FIRST KING OF THE ENGLISH
Aethelstan (894–939) gives a book to St Cuthbert at that saint's shrine. The King of Wessex, in southern and southwestern England, Aethelstan led Anglo-Saxon resistance to the Danish kingdom being established to the north and east – following on from his father Edward the Elder and his famous grandfather, Alfred the Great. Uniting the old Anglo-Saxon kingdoms of Wessex, East Anglia, Mercia and Northumbria, many consider him to be the first king of the English from 924 to 939.

THE VIKINGS

In 793, wild raiders had attacked the quiet monastery on the island of Lindisfarne, off the coast of northeast England. The advent of the 'Vikings' sent a shockwave through Christian Europe. Young warriors struggling to establish themselves in a Scandinavia short of productive land, they found an easy route to wealth through piracy overseas.

In the century or so that followed, Vikings from Norway attacked coastal communities from Ireland to France and even Umayyad Spain (raiders sailed up the Guadalquivir to Seville in 844). Eventually they would start to settle – in northern France (where their descendants became the 'Normans'); in

BELOW LEFT:
TRANSLUCENT BEAUTY
This globular green-glass beaker, discreetly decorated with 'trails' of dribbled molten glass, was made in Anglo-Saxon England at some time between the fifth and seventh centuries.

BELOW RIGHT:
ANGLO-SAXON ADORNMENT
Intricately patterned in copper alloy, silver, gold and glass paste, this seventh-century disc brooch was made in Anglo-Saxon England – very likely Kent. Close as it was to the continent, Kent was a centre for jewellery manufacture and the hub of an international trade.

THE MEDIEVAL PERIOD

THE MEDIEVAL PERIOD

LEFT:
PRESTIGIOUS PRAMBANAN
Near Yogyakarta, southern Java, stands a ninth-century temple complex – the Hindu Sajaya kings' competitive response to Buddhist Borobudur. Abandoned only a few decades later, it sank slowly into dereliction but has been being gradually reconstructed since the early twentieth century.

ABOVE:
RICH RELIEFS
Built as a stupa – a stylized symbolic mountain – Borobudur's rising terraced walls are adorned with over 2,600 ornate bas-reliefs. Whilst some are purely decorative, many show stories from Buddhist mythic tradition or simply scenes of Javanese daily life.

Iceland (which in 870 they effectively discovered); in Greenland (from 958). In 1001, they'd establish a settlement at L'Anse aux Meadows, on North America's Newfoundland coast, which they called 'Vinland', because of its grape vines.

Danish raiders directed their attention to eastern England; their raids became an invasion and eventually an occupation. They set up a rival state to that of southern England's Anglo-Saxon kings. Vikings from Sweden sailed across the Baltic, finding their way down the Russian river system all the way to the Black Sea, raiding and trading, till they reached Constantinople, where several of their number hired themselves out to the Byzantine emperor as an imperial guard.

Known as Varangians, the Vikings in what are now Russia, Belarus and western Ukraine set themselves up as protectors of the local Slavs against raiders from Central Asia. In 879, Prince Oleg became the first ruler of the Rurik dynasty in what was to become the kingdom of Kievan Rus.

EMPIRES OF THE EAST

More peaceable migrants, it seems, the communities that had for many generations now been making their island-hopping progress across the Pacific completed the colonization of Polynesia by some time in the tenth century. The Pacific Islands didn't really lend themselves to the construction of extensive empires, and – while there would be any number of local rivalries and even wars – an easy-going anarchy existed overall.

Since the middle of the eighth century, the kings of the Shailendra dynasty had fostered an Indianized culture in the island of Java. Between 778 and 850 they built Borobudur,

THE MEDIEVAL PERIOD

BOROBUDUR
Stupas stand upon stupas here, the whole straining upwards towards enlightenment, the spiritual plane, the ultimate aspiration of the Buddhist believer. The world's biggest Buddhist temple is believed to have been built in the ninth century, but was abandoned after a few hundred years: the Indian influence in Java seems to have ended with the decline of local Hindu civilizations. After that, it was overgrown and all but obliterated by successive volcanic eruptions until its rediscovery by British archaeological enthusiasts in the early nineteenth century.

THE MEDIEVAL PERIOD

a spectacular Buddhist temple. Meanwhile, in Cambodia, Jayavarman I's Khmer Empire had come of age with the accession of Jayavarman II in 802. He brought a lengthy period of conflict to an end, uniting much of southeast Asia under Khmer rule.

Divided during the Yayoi period, Japan had slowly been unified in the Kofun period as the Yamato kingdom expanded its influence across the archipelago. In 538, Buddhism arrived – from now on it would co-exist with local Shinto traditions. A capital was established at Asuka, in central Honshu, and this is now referred to as the Asuka period. From the seventh century, leaders of the Fujiwara tribe took power in Japan – though they'd wield it discreetly, through the medium of the emperor. Though revered as *Tenno*, 'Ruler of Heaven', he was a puppet of the Fujiwara: this system would remain in place until the 1860s.

Tang China was badly shaken by the Huang Chao Rebellion (874–84), an attempted coup that very nearly succeeded. The Emperor Xijong was put to flight, and though the revolt petered out after Huang Chao was assassinated by his own nephew, the Tang dynasty was severely weakened.

BIG BANG

Further revolts followed. During one, a siege of Yuzhang (Nanchang) was the scene of the first known use of gunpowder as a means of making 'fire arrows'. The divisions that followed the overthrow of the Tang by another military governor, Zhu Wen, in 907, allowed ample opportunity for the new weapon to

BELOW:
PRINTING IN PORCELAIN
Four centuries before Gutenberg in around 1040, China's Bi Sheng carved characters into clay tiles and fired them to make what is believed to have been the world's first moveable type for printing.

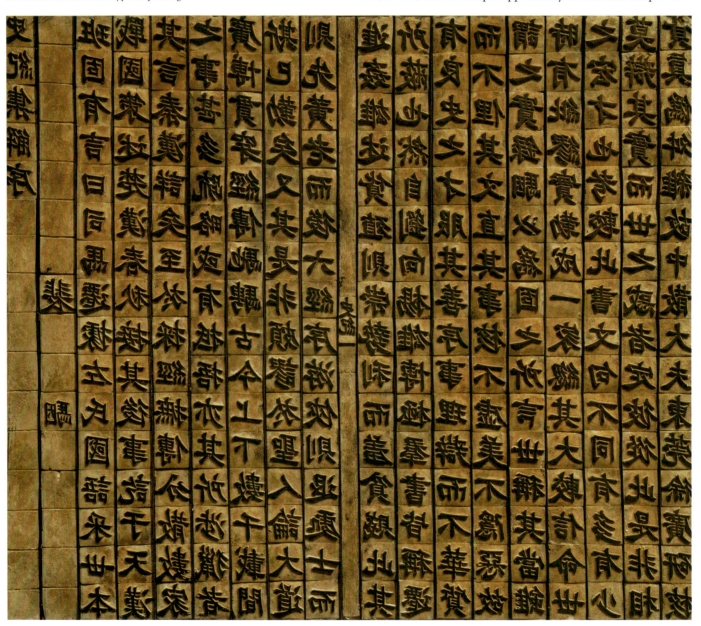

THE MEDIEVAL PERIOD

ABOVE:
THE FIRST FIREARMS
Buddha's temptations on the way to enlightenment mostly came down to earthly power. Gunpowder weapons could be key to this – see the fire-lance and grenade at upper right. This tenth-century mural from China's Mogao Caves is the first known representation.

be developed further. By 969 (by which time some stability had been restored under the Song dynasty), it was being used as a propellant for simple rockets.

The relative peace and prosperity of this period had positive implications culturally. It is seen as something of a golden age for Chinese landscape art.

In the Americas, the Mayan Empire appeared to be ending not with a bang but a whimper. It now entered a long-drawn-out decline. On the coastal plain of Peru, though, the Chimú state had picked up the baton from the Paracas – both in stunning craftwork and in power.

Building slowly, from a homeland in the Moche Valley, some 500 km (311 miles) north of Lima, it would amass an impressive empire by the twelfth century. From a point just north of modern-day Lima, this extended 1,000 km (621 miles) up the coast to a point just south of the present-day Ecuadorian border. Constructing a network of canals and ditches, the Chimú brought 20,000 ha (50,000 acres) under irrigation, a figure modern Peru wouldn't match till 1960. Chan-Chan, their coastal capital, covered 20 sq km (7.7 sq miles) and was home to over 30,000 people, the biggest city in the Americas at this time.

In southern Africa, meanwhile, Great Zimbabwe was being built. A major city, it seems certain that it was the centre of some important state. If it was, however, we know almost nothing about it.

THE MEDIEVAL PERIOD

THE MEDIEVAL PERIOD

A MYSTERIOUS METROPOLIS
The ruins at Great Zimbabwe seem to have belonged to some great city – which should surely have been the centre of some great state. Something like 18,000 people might have lived here – yet the reality is that the history of the place remains unknown.

THE MEDIEVAL PERIOD

ABOVE:
EMBROIDERED EXPLOITS
Shortly after landing on England's southern coast, the invading Normans defeated the defending Anglo-Saxons on a hillside near Hastings. The events of the Norman Conquest were recorded by Norman ladies back in France, in the so-called Bayeux Tapestry.

RIGHT:
ABBASID INVENTION
Castle Water Clock. The engineer Ismael al-Jazari designed this ingenious castle clock in 1206. A water-driven mechanism didn't just move the arch of hours (the roundels) and the wheel of the zodiac but at regular intervals make the drummer and the buglers play.

KOREA COMPLETE

Back in the East, in Korea, the Koguryo kingdom had risen at the expense of Silla. In 918, General Wang Geon overthrew King Gung Ye to seize power in Koguryo, which he renamed Koryo. His successors would rule Korea as a unified state for the next few centuries, making it an important Buddhist centre.

In the Middle East, the Abbasid Empire was coming apart at the seams. In 909, a new dynasty had taken power in Egypt. Strong Shi'ites, they claimed descent from Muhammad's daughter Fatima and her husband Ali. The fourth 'Fatimid' Caliph, Ma'ad al-Muizz Li-Deenillah, built a splendid new capital in Cairo, which became the base of a powerful caliphate.

The reign of Basil II (976–1025) brought the Byzantine Empire to its height. So confident did it feel that, in 1054, in

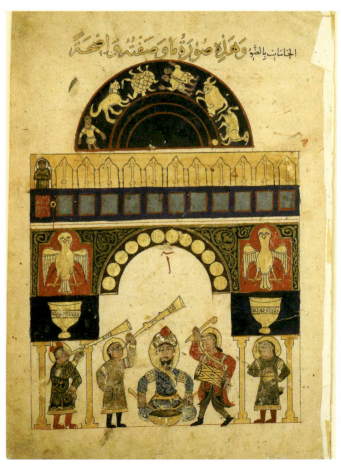

THE MEDIEVAL PERIOD

the reign of Constantine IX, the 'Great Schism' took place, its church-leaders formally rejecting the authority of Rome. From now on the Orthodox Church would run itself. One of its strongholds was to be the kingdom of Kievan Rus, which reached its height in the reigns of Vladimir the Great (ruled 980–1015) and his son Yaroslav the Wise (ruled 1019–54).

In 1066, a force of Normans under William I, 'the Conqueror', invaded England. The south and Midlands fell swiftly, and William was able to make a systematic survey of his new territory, collecting the findings in his 'Domesday Book'. But his anger at a succession of rebellions prompted the so-called 'Harrying of the North' (1069–70), a well-nigh genocidal campaign to put down resistance there.

THE CRUSADING SPIRIT

From the sixth century, a succession of Turkic peoples – nomadic herding communities – had moved west- and southward out of the eastern steppe, rather as the Huns had done before. The Uyghurs and Kazakhs had both established empires but had soon been displaced by the Seljuk Turks. In 1071, at Manzikert, they defeated the Byzantines, capturing their emperor, Romanos IV Diogenes. This decisive victory opened the way to the west for them – including the Byzantine territory of Palestine.

Here it was of course that the Christian 'Holy Places' were – though as we've seen, Jerusalem was sacred to the Jews and Muslims too. In 1095, Pope Urban II called the kingdoms of Christendom to send their forces to recover the Holy Land. This 'crusade' was successful, capturing Jerusalem in 1099, with atrocities against not just Muslims but Jews ('Killers of Christ').

A parallel, parodic 'People's Crusade', whipped up in France by the wandering preacher Peter of Amiens or 'Peter the Hermit', raised 100,000 volunteers who marched into western Germany and carried out a series of pogroms against that country's Jews. The partial recapture of the Holy Land by the Turks provoked a Second Crusade (1145–9), which was partially successful.

These Crusades had underlined the military importance of the mounted knight for the Western army. A whole 'chivalric' ethos arose around his gallantry and a cult of 'courtly love' around his idealized passion for his lady. Poetic romances about the knights of England's mythical King Arthur were read Europe-wide.

BELOW:
A CRUEL COUP
The Byzantine Emperor Leo V ('the Armenian') was assassinated by supporters of Michael II in 820. Here his body is carried through Constantinople's Hippodrome (racetrack) while members of the Viking Varangian Guard stand idly by.

THE MEDIEVAL PERIOD

LEFT:
A LION IN LEAD
Jean, Vicomte de Tripoli was a Frankish nobleman set to reign over the crusaders' County of Tripoli, in northern Lebanon, towards the end of the twelfth century. He would have pushed this 'bulla' into warm wax to make a seal for important documents.

OPPOSITE:
KEEPING THE CITY HOLY
The Knights Templar – an order of military monks established in Jerusalem to support crusaders – made this map of the city (somewhat stylized here). At the bottom we see an upbeat scene, red-crossed crusaders chasing frightened Muslim knights. It didn't always end this way, of course.

These gracious lives were of course made possible by the workings of a 'feudal' system, which saw the aristocrat owing 'fealty' and military service to his king, the peasant loyalty (and labour) to his lord.

OF TEMPLES AND TROUBLE

Suryavarman II died in 1150, having brought the Khmer Empire to its greatest height with the completion of the great temple complex Angkor Wat. Its construction corresponds (very roughly) with that of the great Gothic cathedrals in Europe, like those of Chartres, Reims and Notre Dame in France, Salisbury and Lincoln in England, Burgos in Spain and Cologne in Germany. These were collective efforts, craftsmen working together to produce thoroughly integrated artistic masterworks, from their soaring spires to their sumptuous carving and stained glass. Less edifying events were happening in Europe too. In 1171, England's Norman king Henry II set about the conquest and colonization of Ireland, storing up centuries of trouble for both countries.

In Japan, the Genpei War broke out in 1180. This set the Taira and Minamoto clans against each other in hopes of gaining control of the emperor. Minamoto no Yoritomo won, and appointed himself *shogun* ('commander') in 1192.

CRUSADING CATASTROPHES

The war for the Holy Land went on. In 1187, the charismatic Kurdish leader Salah ad-Din or 'Saladin' recaptured Jerusalem. Richard I ('the Lionheart') of England and other Christian kings mounted a Third Crusade in 1189, but this was unsuccessful. The victorious Saladin was able to set himself up as sultan, establishing his own Ayyubid dynasty. Antisemitism remained a theme: in 1189, the Jewish community of York were besieged in a tower by an angry mob; all 150 committed suicide.

The Fourth Crusade (1202–04) was a stain on Christian history. Short of funds, the Crusaders diverted to Constantinople and sacked the city, massacring thousands. A more creditable Christian development came in 1208, when St Francis of Assisi established his order of Franciscan Friars. Eschewing property and comfort, they would take to the roads of Europe and beg for their sustenance while spreading Christ's word. (In 1212, his friend St Clare founded a sister order, the

'Poor Clares'.) Grim farce followed when, in 1212, young people in France and Germany joined the 'Children's Crusade'. Long before they could reach the Holy Land they had starved or been sold into slavery in North Africa. The Fifth Crusade (1217–22) proved no more successful than its predecessors. In 1228, the Holy Roman Emperor, Frederick II, negotiated Jerusalem's return diplomatically.

THE NOMADIC MOMENT

Hardened by steppe-life, skilled in horsemanship and pushed into expansionism by environmental and demographic pressures, warlike nomads did much to shape the course of medieval history. Even as the Turks had been expanding westward, the Jurchen – later known as the Manchu – were pushing south from Manchuria. In 1104, they had started mounting raids into Korea.

1165 saw the birth of Temujin, or Genghis Khan. From 1206 he would lead his Mongols all the way across western Asia into Europe. Though they became expert in siege tactics, their principal weapon was terror. They killed 30 to 60 million people in the process of building the largest land empire ever known.

Nomadic pastoralists had made their mark on Africa as well. Through the middle of the first millennium, this had been the lifestyle of the Hausa. Their territories had extended northward

BELOW:
SACRED MYSTERIES IN STONE
An entrance to Chartres Cathedral, France. Saints stand arrayed around as the Virgin Mary is crowned by Christ to reign as Queen of Heaven after her 'assumption' – body and soul.

OPPOSITE:
TO WAR
The bas-reliefs at Angkor Wat go on for kilometres, crowded with extravagantly realized moments from myth and literature, as well as extraordinary battle-scenes. Here warriors brandish their weapons as they advance; their commander is carried into battle in a howdah on an elephant.

THE MEDIEVAL PERIOD

A SPIRITUAL SPOT
Atmospheric in the morning light, Ta Prohm temple is part of Cambodia's Angkor Wat complex – among the most impressive religious monuments in the world. Nineteenth-century France would justify its colonial takeover of Cambodia by the need to protect such sites.

THE MEDIEVAL PERIOD

ABOVE:
A SHIELD ON A SWORD
This sword pommel bears the arms of Pierre de Dreux, Duke of Brittany, who was taken prisoner in Egypt at the Battle of al-Mansurah, 1250, during the Seventh Crusade. He was subsequently ransomed and released, but died on his voyage home.

RIGHT:
CIVIL STRIFE
The Minamoto meet the Taira at the Taiken Gate to Kyoto's Imperial Palace during the Heiji Rebellion (1160). Unfinished business from this conflict would bring about the Genpei War (1180–5). Kunisada, who painted this scene, was an artist of the Ukiyo-e period.

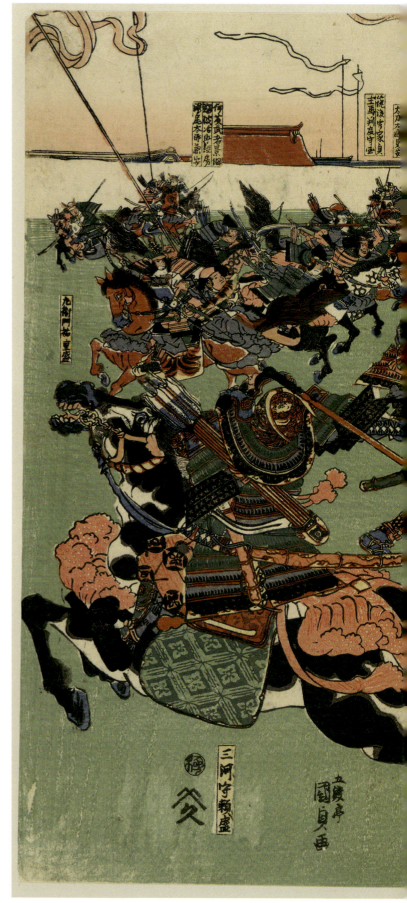

across present-day Nigeria and Niger, and east to Central Africa's Lake Chad.

From the seventh century, however, Arab expansion into the Maghreb had begun to have a 'billiard-ball' effect south of the Sahara. Tuareg nomads had made inroads into the northern fringes of the Hausa homeland, whilst rival herders from Borno had encroached from the east.

Powerful peoples to the west had boxed the Hausa in on that side. So they'd settled down, creating successful city-states along the Niger Valley. These had come into their own in the eleventh and twelfth centuries when the Hausa Kingdoms had been among the richest in Africa.

RULERS' RIGHTS

In 1215, England's King John was bullied by his barons into signing Magna Carta, agreeing to be bound by his country's laws. It was important in guaranteeing some of his subjects' most basic liberties – a first step on the road to constitutional monarchy.

In eastern Europe, Kievan Rus had faded through the eleventh and twelfth centuries, power shifting north, to the merchant

city of Novgorod and the republic of potent magnates in power there. In the thirteenth century, the Novgorod Republic found itself beleaguered in its turn, but stood firm against a succession of enemies. In 1240, Prince Alexander Nevsky saw off a Swedish invasion. Two years later, the Teutonic Knights, an order of military monks from Prussia, northeastern Germany, were defeated on a frozen lake in the so-called 'Battle of the Ice'. Under Nevsky's son Daniel, Muscovy – the least valued of his father's territories – grew in importance to eclipse the others.

By 1248, the Holy Land had fallen into Muslim hands again. King Louis IX of France mounted a Sixth Crusade, with disastrous results. But it also ended badly for Sultan al-Salih Ayyub, who fell in battle. He had been defended ferociously by his Mamluks – soldiers bought as slaves in boyhood, brought up to total loyalty and trained in warlike skill. Their allegiance had been to their late master, though. A few months later they murdered his son and heir Turanshah and took over Egypt in their own name.

RIGHT:
MASSACRES OF THE INNOCENTS
King Herod's soldiers slaughter new babies over their parents' protests. The 'Massacre of the Innocents' (Matthew 2, 16) formed a gorily exciting climax to the York Mystery Plays. Ironically, it had been here that the entire Jewish community had committed suicide to save themselves from a pogrom of 1190.

THE MEDIEVAL PERIOD

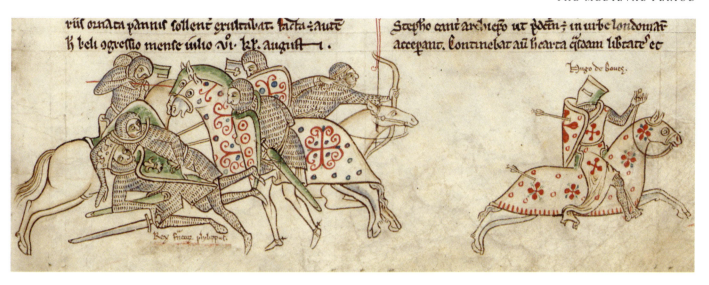

ABOVE:
DECISIVE VICTORIES
Philip II's victory at Bouvines in 1214 was a disaster for the Holy Roman Emperor Otho IV but also for his ally, King John. So badly weakened was the English king that he had to find an accommodation with his barons. The following year he signed Magna Carta.

BELOW:
EAST MEETS WEST?
Marco Polo's caravan makes its way along the Silk Road in this illustration from the *Catalan Atlas* (c. 1375). How far his travels really took him remains unclear, but there is no questioning the contribution he made to the opening up of the European mind.

THE MEDIEVAL PERIOD

THE MEDIEVAL PERIOD

MAGNA CARTA
Few of his subjects were even aware that, in 1215, King John had signed *Magna Carta Libertatum* ('The Great Charter of Freedoms'); even fewer were to benefit directly. But his bullying barons had still struck a blow for freedom in the longer term, establishing the principle that an English monarch was not above the law.

THE MEDIEVAL PERIOD

LEFT:
MAN OF THE PEOPLES
A Chinese artist's posthumous portrait acknowledges the Mongol background of the Yuan emperor, showing Kublai Khan in the white robes of a shaman of the steppe. Genghis's grandson had felt strong loyalties both to his wilder antecedents and to his Chinese realms.

FROM THE MAMLUKS TO MARCO POLO

The Mamluks successfully resisted an attack by the advancing Mongols. Had the invaders lost some of their toughness, some of their edge, since the death of Genghis Khan in 1227? Under his grandson, Kublai Khan, the Mongols took a whole new approach to conquest. In 1279, he made himself emperor of China, as head of the Yuan dynasty. He was still a military leader, undertaking campaigns in Korea and Myanmar – and attempting, unsuccessfully, to invade Java and Japan. But he also took an eager interest in the culture of his adoptive homeland.

And, if his account is to be believed, in showing these off to his guest from Venice, Marco Polo, who arrived here with his father and uncle in 1275. Kublai Khan didn't just welcome him: he made Marco his emissary; he stayed for 17 years before returning home to Venice and writing his memoirs. Recently, scholars have suggested that these were one of history's great hoaxes: Marco may have gone no farther east than the Black Sea.

BELOW:
BATTLE OF MOHI (1241)
At the bridge over the Sajó at Mohi in Hungary the Mongols swept aside a royal army before rampaging through the country killing half the population. Europe had no answer to the threat they posed, though guerrilla actions discouraged them from settling. Internal divisions eventually caused them to withdraw.

OPPOSITE:
THEOLOGICAL TREATISE
St Thomas Aquinas was undoubtedly a great thinker. His *Summa Theologica* ('Summary of Theology', 1274) represented a high point of medieval thought. Yet this is itself a reminder of how remote this 'Age of Faith' was from any intellectual approach we could imagine now.

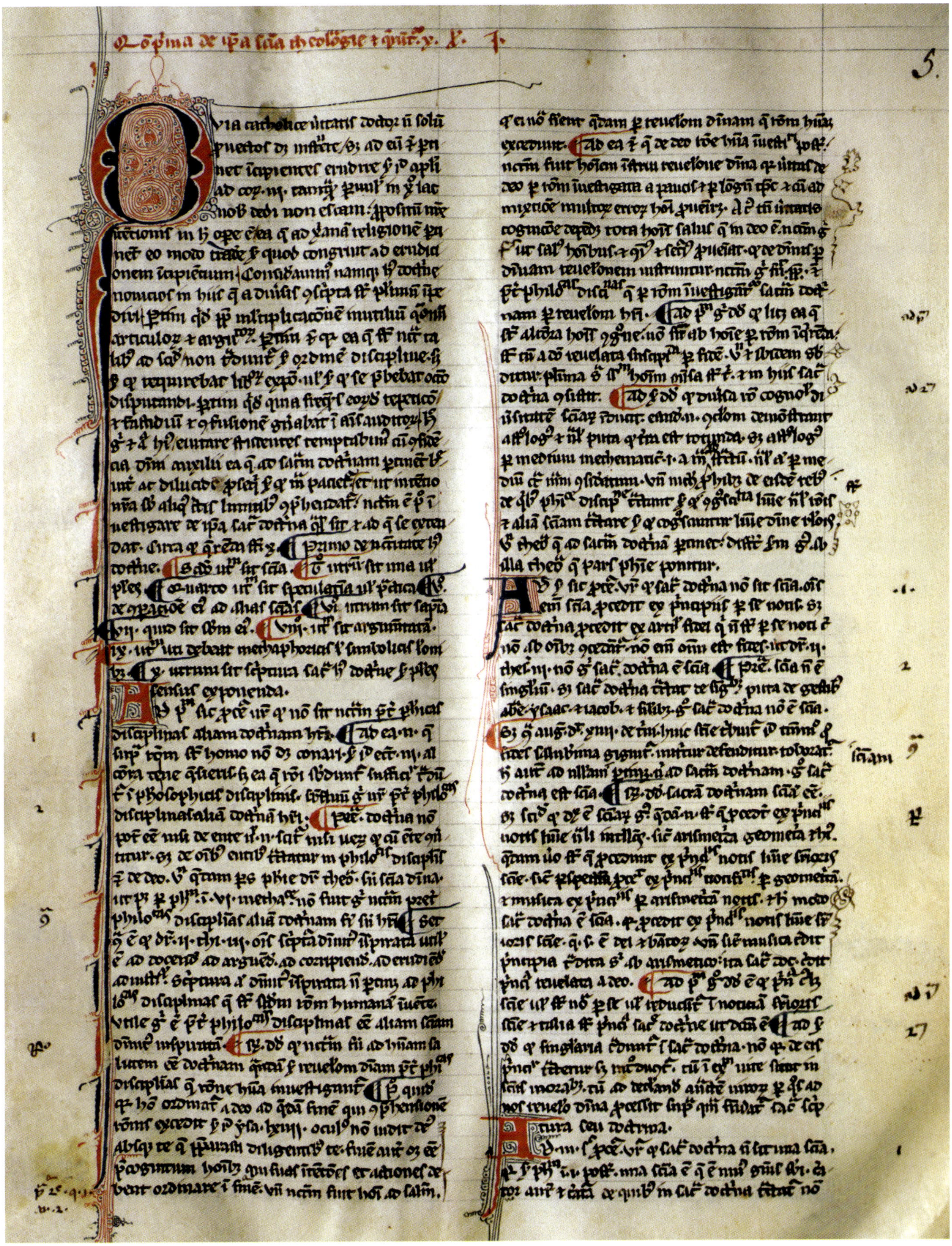

THE MEDIEVAL PERIOD

LEFT:
RUMI THE MYSTIC
Jalal al-Din Rumi, the thirteenth-century Persian poet, was an adherent of the Sufi school of Islamic mysticism. Among the most moving articulations ever of romantic passion, his lyrics at the same time explore the divine love he sees infusing the universe.

Another major empire had been taking shape in West Africa, where King Mansa Musa was making Mali an important power. The city-state had grown wealthy as a terminus of the trans-Sahara trade (in everything from gold to kola nuts, from salt to slaves). In 1320, Mansa Musa captured Timbuktu from the Tuareg and made it his capital.

BELOW:
FINANCIAL SERVICES
Banking had its breakthrough during the Crusades, when knights needed considerable sums to be available far from home. Thereafter, the industry took off in Italy: this fourteenth-century fresco shows us (above) the clerks in the counting-house and (below) a queue of customers.

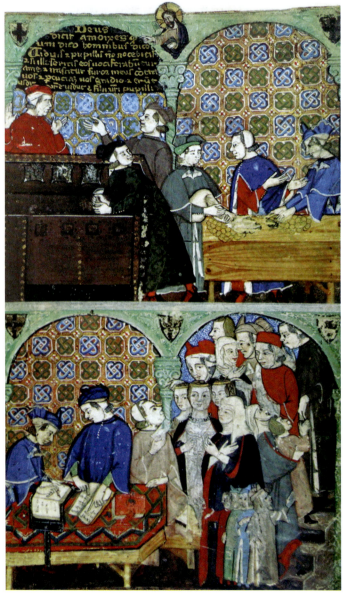

Much of what he reports is to be found in contemporary Persian accounts and there are startling omissions in what purported to have been an eyewitness account.

HAMMERING OUT AUTHORITY

Within Britain, England's ascendancy had been strengthened by Edward I, king from 1272 to 1307. Known as the 'Hammer of the Scots' for the defeats he inflicted on that people, he dealt as harshly with the Prince of Wales, Llywelyn ap Gruffudd. The Welsh held out bravely against the English but were eventually put down. Edward left a chain of castles around North Wales as his legacy.

By the beginning of the fourteenth century, the Aztecs were extending their rule through the Valley of Mexico. Soon their empire would extend across the Isthmus and cover an area of 220,000 sq km (85,000 sq miles). At much the same time, the Inca were building an empire in the high plateau (*altiplano*) of the Andes in Peru. Two American superpowers were emerging.

THE MEDIEVAL PERIOD

RIGHT:
DECORATED IN DEATH
Bodies mummify naturally in the arid Peruvian coastal plain, so the dead were dressed up to attend the shamanistic ceremonies of the living. The slanted eyes and the conspicuous jewels in the nose and ears are typical of the death masks of the Chimú.

BELOW:
THE PEASANTS' REVOLT
'When Adam delved and Eve span,/ who was then the gentleman?' asked the radical priest John Ball in 1381. Here he exhorts a crowd of English peasants to rise up against their exploitation. His comrade Wat Tyler can be seen in red in the front row.

THE MEDIEVAL PERIOD

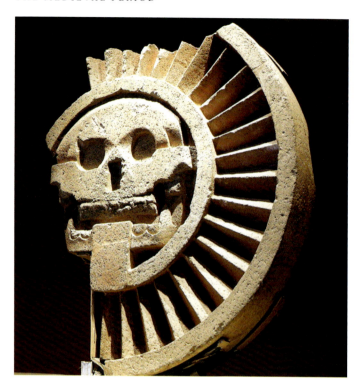

It was also at around this time that the ancestors of the Maori – Polynesians – reached New Zealand, or *Aotearoa* ('Land of the Long White Cloud'), as they called it.

THE FOUR HORSEMEN

In Europe, crop failures and cattle diseases caused the Great Famine of 1315–17. Mass-starvation and sickness resulted, whilst there were widespread reports of cannibalism. Southern England may have lost as much as 15 per cent of its population; northern France more like 10 per cent. In 1337, Philip VI of France invaded Gascony – a territory in southwest France which

LEFT:
DISC OF DEATH
Mictlantecuhtli, the Aztec god of death, gapes grotesquely, tongue lolling forth. The burst of basalt radiance around him in this (damaged) disc suggests that he may specifically represent the death of the sun, whose return each day the Aztecs secured by offering human sacrifice.

BELOW:
REALM OF GOLD
Mansa Musa holds up a gold coin here – as well he might. Not only was his realm of Mali rich in goldfields, it controlled the cross-Sahara caravan routes on which so much of the region's trade depended. An illumination from the *Catalan Atlas* (c. 1375).

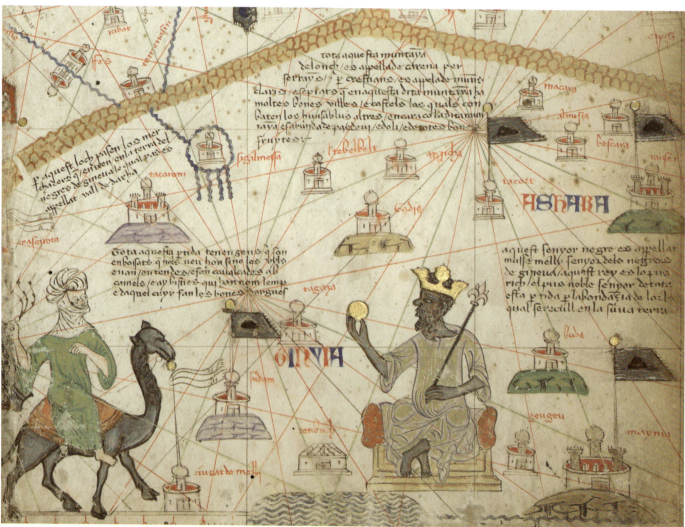

ABOVE:
ARTISTIC JUDGEMENT
The frescos Giotto painted around the walls of Padua's Scrovegni Chapel (1305), marked a milestone in the history of European art. The sequence centres on the life of the Virgin Mary and the part she plays in helping mortal humans attain salvation.

Edward III of England claimed by dynastic right. Hostilities continued on and off till 1453, hence its being known as the 'Hundred Years' War'. England's longbowmen came through for their country in a couple of famous battles: Crécy (1346), and Agincourt (1415). In the end, though, it would be France that won the war. Not, however, before the English archers' influence had given an early indication that the reign of the Knight at Arms – and with it the whole chivalric ethos – was approaching its end.

The fighting was interrupted – well, just about everything was – after a bout of bubonic plague broke out in China in 1346. It reached the West within a few months, its progress ironically facilitated by the ease of travel the stability of the Mongol Empire allowed – but didn't really reach its peak there until the following year. Overall, the 'Black Death' would rage till 1353, by which time 100 million people may have died worldwide. It's thought to have killed about 33 per cent of the population of the Middle East; 30 per cent of that of western Europe.

The Black Death, we've seen, had been born in China, which had been afflicted by famine too, and revolts which had swept the Yuan dynasty away. In 1368, Zhu Yuanzhang took the reigning name of Hongwu, becoming the first Ming emperor of China. The Ming dynasty would remain in power for almost 300 years. Between 1405 and 1433, it sent out a series of 'treasure fleets' on voyages of exploration around the South China Sea and Indian Ocean. These reached India, Arabia and East Africa.

OTTOMAN ADVENT

The career of Timur Lenk or Tamerlane ('Timur the Lame') was like a re-run of Genghis Khan's. He'd been born out on the steppe

THE MEDIEVAL PERIOD

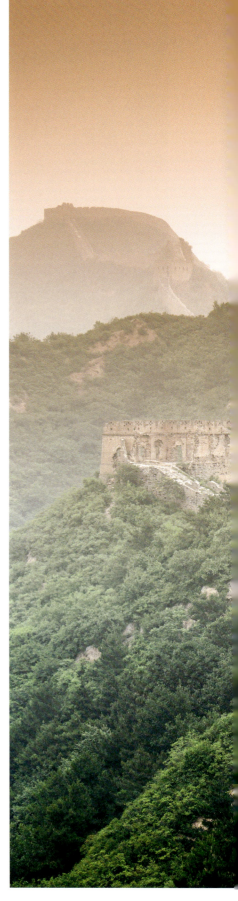

LEFT:
UPSTART EMPEROR
Zhu Yuanzhang led the uprising that overthrew the Yuan dynasty in 1368. The first Ming emperor took the name of Taizu, or Hongwu ('Mighty Military'). He also had a less flattering nickname: the 'Pig-Emperor'. He was quietly derided for his unprepossessing appearance and humble birth.

RIGHT:
MING MONUMENT
The Great Wall of China was first constructed during the reign of the First Emperor Shihuangdi. The wall we see now – as here at Jinshanling, northeast of Beijing – mostly dates from the Ming period (1369–1644).

BELOW:
'DANCE OF DEATH'
Michael Wolgemut's woodcut for the *Book of Chronicles* (1493) captured the mood of medieval Europe perfectly. The fear of plague was never far away. Famine loomed and humanity felt helpless. The imagery of death recurred in literature and art.

THE MEDIEVAL PERIOD

THE MEDIEVAL PERIOD

THE MEDIEVAL PERIOD

OPPOSITE:
TIMUR'S TERROR
The forces of Egypt's Mamluk Sultan Nasir-ad-din Faraj fight a losing battle against Timur Lenk's in a fresco from Tehran's Golestan Palace. Timur's attacks must have brought the Middle East a hideous sense of déjà vu. His was the latest in a long succession of invasions by steppe nomads.

in 1336. A cunning and fearless young warlord, he'd gathered a like-minded group around him and amassed an army which pushed westward, conquering as it went. In 1381, he invaded Iran, then crossed into the Caucasus, killing and pillaging as he went. In 1400, he invaded India. His cruelty was a point of pride – and, of course, a message to his enemies. In a half-circuit of Isfahan's walls after Timur's sacking, a chronicler claimed to have counted 28 pyramids, each comprising 1,500 skulls.

Nomads had done much to shape the history of the medieval period. Now they brought the epoch to an end. The Ottoman Turks had taken their name from their thirteenth-century warlord Osman, though they adopted Islam in the course of their journey west. By 1300, they had established a foothold in Anatolia and begun a bitter struggle with the Byzantines. Finally, after decades of trying, the Ottomans under Sultan Mehmet II captured Constantinople in 1453 after a 53-day siege, providing a huge symbolic victory over Christendom. They made it their imperial centre, Istanbul.

ABOVE:
SULTAN MEHMET II
Venetian painter Gentile Bellini was sent to Constantinople in 1479 specially to paint this portrait of Sultan Mehmet II. His trip had a diplomatic dimension: a devout Muslim but also a highly educated admirer of western Renaissance art, the Ottoman ruler had requested that a painter be sent for this purpose.

BELOW:
DIVINE JUDGEMENT?
The Fall of Constantinople is commemorated by a fresco from the Moldovita Monastery in Romania (1532), an Orthodox foundation for whose monks the event was recalled with trauma even 80 years later.

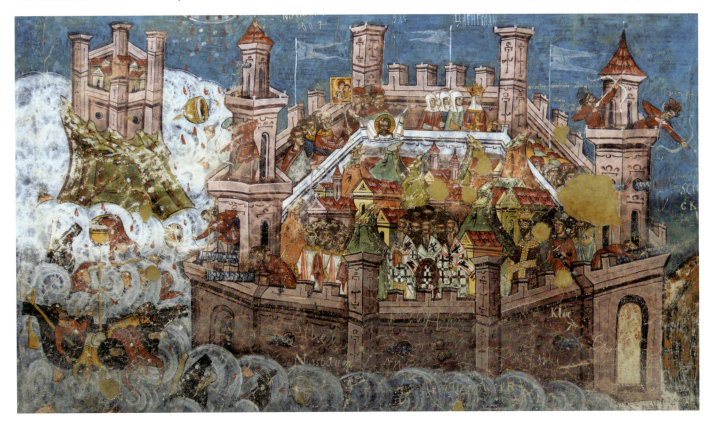

THE RENAISSANCE
1460 – 1600

Europeans already knew that their continent was not the whole world: Africa lay just beyond the Mediterranean, after all. Spices and other luxuries had been brought along the 'Silk Road' from the East for generations: Marco Polo (1254–1324) had brought back tidings from China two centuries before.

But few Europeans had followed him: the Crusades had left the Middle East a hostile environment, and though trade continued, it had been conducted largely by middlemen. The soaring costs of luxuries imported overland had helped motivate the search for a sea route, which received a boost when Portugal's Prince Henry the Navigator established a naval academy around 1450. Portuguese seafarers made the running, Bartolomeu Dias (1450–1500) finding his way down the coast of Africa to the Cape of Good Hope in 1487, while Vasco da Gama (c. 1460–1524) pushed on to India a decade later. By that time, of course, Columbus had reached the Americas.

OPPOSITE:
FROM REFUGEE TO RULER
A descendant of Timur Lenk, Babur (1483–1530) came to India in flight from Uzbek attack in Central Asia. He founded the famous Mughal dynasty (so called on account of its rulers' Mongol origins), which eventually ruled the whole subcontinent apart from the southern tip and Sri Lanka.

RIGHT:
HIS HORRIFIC HIGHNESS
Vlad III of Wallachia (1431–76), a kingdom in the Carpathians, was better known as 'Vlad the Impaler' from his practice of mounting his defeated enemies on spikes. Between his gory nature and his paternal name 'Dracul', he inspired Bram Stoker's novel *Dracula* (1897).

He would be convinced until he died that he had found the westerly route to the Far East – hence his description of the Americas' indigenous people as *Indios* ('Indians'). Before too long, though, Europeans came to realize that he had stumbled on a 'New World'. The Old one was never going to be the same again.

CLEANLINESS AND GODLINESS

Even as geographical horizons were broadening, the world was painfully contracting in other ways. Columbus, though Genoan by birth, had sailed in the service of Spain's 'Catholic Monarchs'. Ferdinand of Aragon and Isabella of Castile were called this because their marriage had united Spain's main kingdoms, though they were also strongly – some would say fanatically – Catholic in the religious sense. Columbus's discoveries hadn't been the only great event of 1492. That same year the capture of Granada from the Moors completed the *Reconquista*.

For good measure, Ferdinand and Isabella expelled the Jews from a Spain they wanted to see religiously (and, arguably, racially) purified. *Limpieza* – 'cleanness' – was to be the criterion by which a person's Spanishness would be judged in the centuries to come. The Holy Office (or 'Inquisition') was established to root out secret Jewish and Muslim affinities, as well as any signs of heresy (departures from orthodoxy in belief).

BELOW:
DIABOLICAL DISCOVERER
Sebastiano del Piombo's (1485–1547) *Portrait of a Man* (1519) is widely believed to show Christopher Columbus. He had got colonialism off to a brutal start in the Americas and was tried by the Catholic Monarchs for cruel acts against the '*Indios*'.

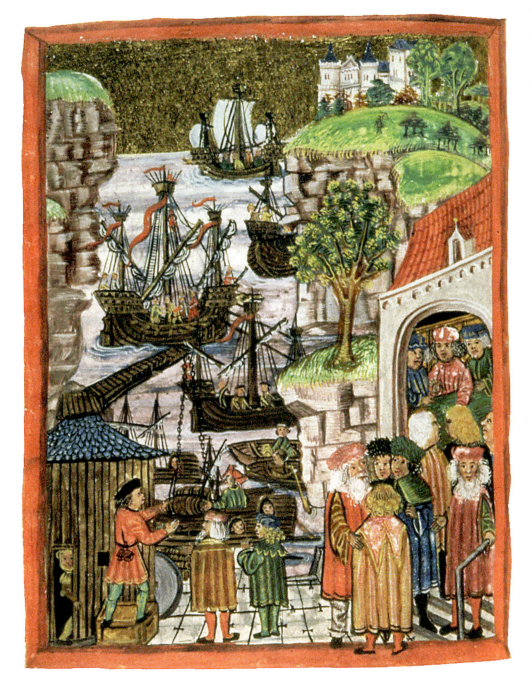

LEFT:
HANSEATIC LEAGUE
A cover from a document on Hamburg ship law, 1497. Hamburg was a part of the Hanseatic League, an association of more than 200 trading ports and settlements that stretched throughout the North and Baltic Seas, from modern-day Netherlands to Estonia. The organization was founded by north German towns and local merchant guilds, and dominated commercial activity in northern Europe for much of the fourteenth and fifteenth centuries.

FAIR EXCHANGE?

In other ways it was a time for sharing. Under what has come to be called the 'Columbian Exchange', items like maize, potatoes and chillies were brought back to the 'Old World', while wheat, rice and sugar cane, as well as livestock – including horses – were introduced to the Americas.

Less fortunately, the inhabitants of the New World were completely unprotected against diseases to which their visitors had long since acquired immunity. These cut a swathe through indigenous communities in the first few generations of European settlement, killing anything up to 90 per cent of the population. Others were massacred by colonists, 'clearing' lands for development, or enslaved and worked to death on lands they'd seen as theirs.

Spain and Portugal agreed to share the world's unclaimed territories according to a formula proposed by Pope Alexander VI (1431–1503), formalized in the Treaty of Tordesillas, 1494. A line was imagined running down the mid-Atlantic halfway between the (Portuguese) Cape Verde islands and (Spanish) 'Indies' – the Caribbean islands. Lands to the east of this would belong to Portugal; lands to the west to Spain.

The voyages of discovery went on, Vasco Núñez de Balboa (1475–1519) in 1513 becoming the first European to see the Pacific Ocean. The years 1519–21 saw Ferdinand Magellan's

OPPOSITE:
MAPPING THE WORLD
The Portuguese seaman António Pereira supposedly made this map showing the route of Orellana's expedition. The other sections of what was once a world map are missing. Quirky as it is, Pereira's map (1545) is accurate in essentials. A sophisticated geographical understanding was taking shape.

(1480–1521) voyage to the East Indies – which turned into the first circumnavigation of the globe. In 1540, Pedro de Valdivia (1497–1553) established a Spanish colony at Santiago de Chile.

That same year, Francisco Vázquez de Coronado (1510–54) led an expedition into what is now the American southwest, while in 1541 Hernando de Soto (1500–42) and his party, pushing westwards across Georgia, discovered the Mississippi River and crossed it to explore parts of Arkansas and Texas. Meanwhile, marooned in the Upper Amazon region after crossing the Andes from what is now Ecuador, Francisco de Orellana (1511–46) and his men were floating downriver to the Atlantic.

But heroic exploration tended to be followed fairly quickly by cruel exploitation, often after brutally bloody conquest. Even as Magellan had been making his historic voyage, the Spanish conquistador Hernán Cortés (1485–1547) had been subjugating Mexico's Aztec Empire. Backed by only 600 men but equipped with firearms, steel armour and horses – which the Americas' indigenous peoples had never seen before – he

ABOVE:
FRESH VISTAS
When he led an expedition across the Isthmus of Panama in 1513, Vasco Núñez de Balboa became the first European to see the Pacific Ocean from the New World side. He was later executed for allegedly plotting against the colonial administration in the Indies.

BELOW:
AZTEC ATTACK
Cortés's right-hand man in Mexico, Pedro de Alvarado leads the defence of the conquistadors holed up in Tenochtitlán against Aztec warriors rising up against Spanish atrocities (1520).

ABOVE:
NEW HORIZONS
All manner of marvels accompany Ferdinand Magellan's discovery of the strait which bears his name in a woodcut of 1522. Europeans found their imaginative – as well as their geographical – world extended.

had also been assisted by the Aztec legend that predicted that the departed god Quetzalcóatl would make a second coming over the eastern sea.

TAKING TENOCHTITLÁN

The Aztec capital, Tenochtitlán (modern Mexico City), rising up out of a lake bed and reached by a causeway, was, recalled Cortés' comrade Bernal Díaz del Castillo, an 'astounding' sight. 'Indeed, some of our soldiers asked whether it was not all a dream.' The Aztec ruler Moctezuma II (reigned 1502–20) was 'feared near and far', according to contemporary accounts. His name translates as 'he who grows angry like a lord' and he had 'conquered forty-four nations'. He walked on jaguar pelts so he wouldn't have to make contact with the ground. He had brought his people to the height of their power and magnificence.

That magnificence was steeped in blood: like other Mesoamerican civilizations, the Aztecs appeased their angry gods with human sacrifice – often, it appears, on a colossal scale. The need to acquire captives for this was one of the main reasons why they went to war.

Cortés and his men became convinced (quite possibly rightly) that should they be captured they would be sacrificed, which lent an edge of desperation to their courage. Despite their technological advantages, they did well to resist the attacks of armies, many thousands strong, which came out to meet them as they made their way inland.

Cortés forged alliances with the Aztecs' enemies, who sensed an unprecedented opportunity to avenge old wrongs. He took a Nahua woman – La Malinche – as his mistress. (She became a hate-figure in the Mexican mythology of later generations as her country's great betrayer but appears to have been a slave with no real control over what she did.) The Spanish also had an ally in smallpox, which spread rapidly among a population with no immunity protection, a pattern that would become grimly familiar in the Americas over the generations that followed. Even so, more than 100,000 Aztecs were killed in the fighting of the final battle for Tenochtitlán (August 1521); perhaps a quarter of a million in the campaign overall.

THE RENAISSANCE

'UNKNOWN TO MEN'

'Where have men ever seen the things they have seen here?' marvelled Pedro de Cieza de León (1520–54), a sixteenth-century Spanish visitor to Peru. If it seems pedantic to point out that the country's indigenous people were 'men' (and women) and that they had certainly seen it, it's also an interesting insight into the colonialist psyche as it was now developing.

Cieza de León arrived in the high Andes just a few years after the invasion of Francisco Pizarro's conquistadors (1531–2) and

BELOW:
THE VIEW FROM VENICE
A plan of 'Temistitan' (Tenochtitlán) by the Venetian cartographer Benedetto Bordone (1460–1531). His *Isolario* ('Book of Islands', 1528) depicted North America and the northern part of South America as a single island; Pereira's 1545 map (p. 124) shows how far knowledge advanced over a single generation.

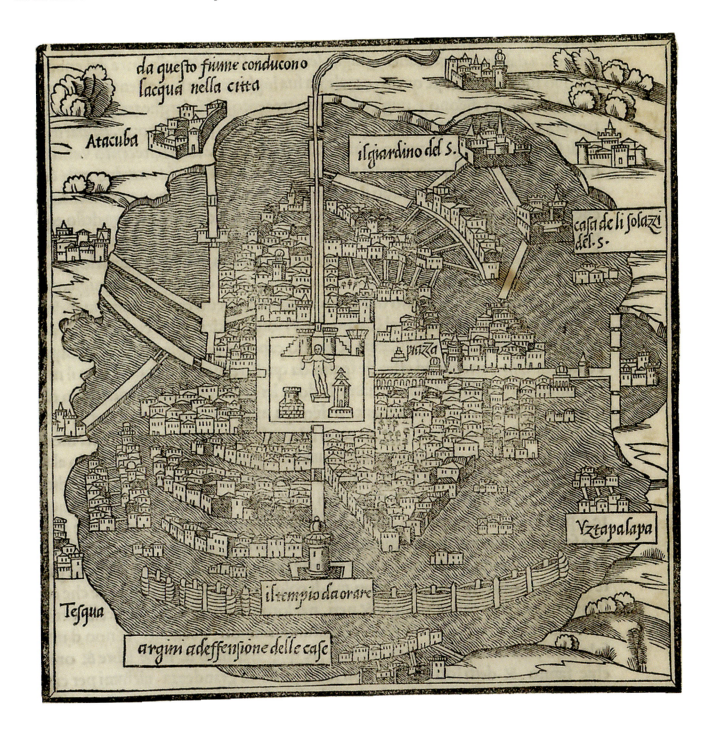

ABOVE:
SILVER CITY
The *Cerro Rico* ('Rich Hill') rises high above Potosí. For centuries its silver underwrote Spain's imperial economy. Mule trains took it down to the coast for shipment to Panama; then it was carried across the Isthmus before being sent in 'treasure fleets' to Spain.

could scarcely believe the splendours that he saw. Despite the depredations of his countrymen, the sacking of the cities and the stripping of the shrines, evidence of the awesome Incan achievement was all around. 'And to think', he wondered, 'that God should have permitted something so great to remain hidden from the world for so long in history, unknown to men…!'

DENUNCIATION AND DEBATE

But growing numbers worried that God was permitting too many atrocities. Published in 1542, Fray Bartolomé de Las Casas's (1474 or 84–1566) *A Short Account of the Destruction of the Indies* denounced the cruelty of Spanish colonization in the Americas. Sometimes, it's suspected, in exaggerated terms. Either way, that same year, the Spanish Crown introduced its 'Laws of the Indies', including the abolition of *encomienda* – the right of colonists to exact tribute and labour from indigenous inhabitants of the lands they settled.

Spain took its responsibilities as colonial power seriously. An important debate in Valladolid in 1550–1 discussed the respective rights of settlers and indigenous communities. But the temptation to exploit the New World and its people was proving irresistible. Since 1545, the richest mine in the Americas had been on-stream at Potosí, Bolivia. Silver was being sent back to Spain by the shipload.

Nor were the New World's *Indios* the only people being exploited. Slavery had existed in ancient times and been the norm in the Byzantine and Muslim worlds. As long ago as 1444, a Portuguese ship had become the first European vessel chartered to sail down the coast of Africa and bring back slaves. The Atlantic Slave Trade would build only slowly, but as Old World diseases took their toll in the Americas – and the Spanish Crown stepped in to protect the indigenous peoples from being enslaved, Africans would be shipped out there to fill the gap.

BUSINESS AND BEAUTY

In 1494, the year in which the Treaty of Tordesillas had balanced out the colonial entitlements of Spain and Portugal, the Venetian friar Luca Pacioli (c. 1447–1517) had published his textbook *Summary of Arithmetic, Geometry, Proportions and Proportionality*. Among many other things, this had first set out the principles of double-entry bookkeeping.

The last two terms of the title, 'Proportions and Proportionality', make clear the method's original appeal: there was a certain mystic beauty in the way the figures balanced. But it was also of course an eminently practical aid to doing business which would come in very handy in what was to be a golden age of trade. It already was, to some extent. In the great city-states of Italy, especially. Trade between them was flourishing, as was commercial (and cultural) contact with the wider world – Florence in particular had grown wealthy through its wool trade. The confidence of the cities was the stronger for their freedom: Florence was a republic in its own right.

FLORENTINE FLAIR

Not that it was what we'd call a democracy: powerful magnates ruled the roost. But they owed no allegiance to kings or emperors: they were self-made men – independent, and extremely proud of it. The local Medici family boosted both its own and its city's prestige by commissioning handsome

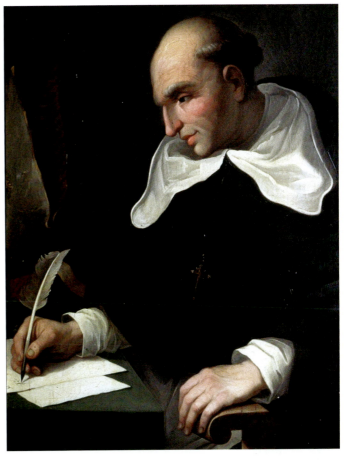

RIGHT:
'PROTECTOR OF THE INDIANS'
Officially at least, the Spanish took their responsibilities as colonizers seriously. Columbus had been investigated for cruelty to the *Indios*. Fray Bartolomé de Las Casas was able to have himself appointed 'Protector of the Indians' in 1516 and spent half a century advocating for this cause.

BELOW:
MEDICI VILLA LA PETRAIA IN FLORENCE
The Medici family dominated banking and politics in the Republic of Florence under the leadership of Cosimo de' Medici (1389–1464), through intermarriage with other powerful families and often achieving their ends through bribery and violence. Cosimo was also an important patron of the arts, commissioning Donatello's *David*, the first freestanding nude male sculpture since antiquity.

THE RENAISSANCE

buildings and beautiful works of art. As Lord of Florence, Lorenzo de' Medici ('the Magnificent'; 1449–92) commissioned the architect Filippo Brunelleschi (1377–1446) to design a new *duomo* (cathedral), famous for its gravity-defying dome and exuberantly patterned walls.

Poets and scholars also found patronage in Florence. (In other Italian cities too: wealthy nobles vied to surround themselves with the most sophisticated and creative courts they could.) Men of art and learning could hold their heads up high: the feeling naturally boosted their self-esteem, but also enhanced their sense of what humankind might be capable of in general.

BELOW:
LUCA PACIOLI
Jacopo de' Barbari (1440–1516) is believed to have painted this portrait, perhaps with the help of Leonardo da Vinci (1452–1519). German artist Albrecht Dürer (1471–1528) may be the man behind. Pacioli's theories of accountancy drew on the same aesthetic sense of symmetry that inspired Renaissance architecture and Leonardo's *Vitruvian Man* (c. 1490).

HUMANIST VALUES

'Humanism', as articulated by scholars like Marsilio Ficino (1433–99), saw the human form as the height of physical perfection and the human intellect as the ultimate earthly reflection of the divine. Looking beyond the established orthodoxies in medieval thought – which had seen humanity's duty as simply to obey divine and ecclesiastical authority – it found inspiration in the achievements of classical Greece and Rome. Albeit now in ruins, the monuments of these civilizations still stood in their midst: they marvelled at their grace and symmetry. The name 'Renaissance' (in French 'rebirth') was given to this great artistic, cultural, philosophical and scientific gear shift only subsequently, but it doesn't seem exaggerated in its implications.

At the time, though, it must have felt more like evolution than revolution: the Church remained enormously important as a patron and religious art was still important. Fra Angelico's (1395–1455) frescoes (wall paintings done directly on to damp plaster)

THE RENAISSANCE

LEFT:
GREAT MEN MEET
Babur's grandson Akbar the Great (1542–1605) took enormous pride in his Mughal lineage. He had the great man's memoirs, *The Book of Babur*, translated into Persian for wider readership. This illustration shows the Mughal founder meeting his cousin, Sultan 'Ali Mirza, outside Samarkand.

ABOVE:
WICKED OR REALISTIC?
'It is far safer to be feared than loved,' wrote Niccolò Machiavelli in his infamous guide to government, *The Prince* (1532). Posterity made a pantomime-villain from a thinker who was arguably only offering a dispassionate account of politics in practice.

RIGHT:
MICHELANGELO'S MASTERPIECE
A treasury of Renaissance art, the Sistine Chapel has frescoes by Botticelli, Ghirlandaio and Perugino; tapestries by Raphael line the lower walls. Here we look eastwards along the ceiling, past a series of scenes from Genesis, to Michelangelo's spectacular *The Last Judgment* (1536–41).

clearly continued the work of the medieval church painters but had a wonderful new warmth and human interest.

Increasingly, artists were scientifically informed. Paolo Uccello (1397–1475) and Piero della Francesca (c. 1416–92) enjoyed considerable reputations as mathematicians. Their paintings use geometry and perspective to give an arresting sense of depth. By the late-fifteenth century, the wind of Renaissance was blowing strongly. The idealization of the human form; a new and more scientific eye for nature; classical inspiration (and a 'neoplatonist' attempt to marry Christian concepts of grace, godliness and virtue with ancient Greek philosophical ideas, like those of Plato). All these new trends are displayed to ravishing perfection in the famous works of Sandro Botticelli (1445–1510).

It wasn't all about high art. It was to Lorenzo the Magnificent's grandson, another Lorenzo, that Niccolò Machiavelli (1469–1527)

THE RENAISSANCE

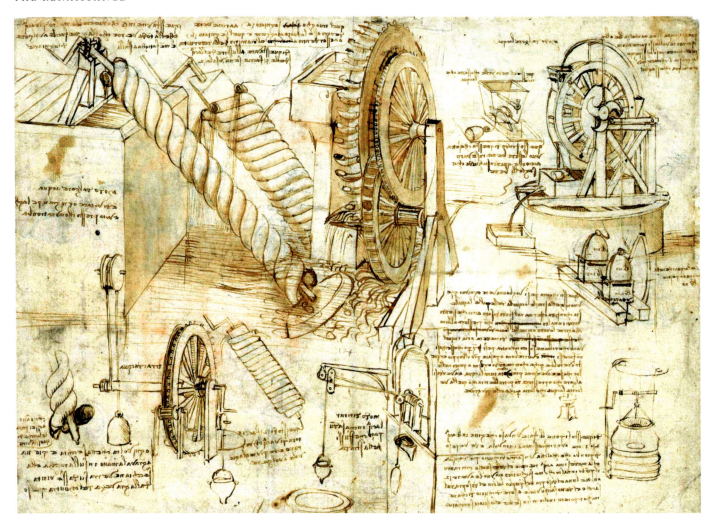

ABOVE:
ENDLESS INVENTIVENESS
Leonardo's curiosity knew no bounds; his ingenuity no limit. He spent hours doing inspired doodles, sketching everything from anatomical studies to flying machines. Here (left) we see a machine for raising water and another (right) for pumping water from a well.

dedicated his book *The Prince* (1532), a no-holds-barred primer on *realpolitik*. The Papacy at this time was an immensely important institution. And not just spiritually but temporally: the Church had huge political influence and vast wealth. Accordingly, Rome exerted a strong cultural pull. Ambitious artists flocked here to find commissions.

One who made the grade was Michelangelo Buonarroti (1475–1564), primarily a sculptor, but a painter at Pope Julius II's (1443–1513) request. It was for His Holiness's new Sistine Chapel that Michelangelo spent four years (1508–12) painting the ceiling – among the undoubted glories of Western art. It was in Rome as well that Raphael created his greatest works, extraordinary in their humanity and grace.

Venice was a great seaport: looking outwards to the Adriatic and the world beyond, it was more cosmopolitan than the other Italian cities. From here Marco Polo had set out on his (supposed) travels to China in the fourteenth century. Contacts with Asia had continued – albeit indirectly and intermittently – ever since. Only now are Western scholars coming to appreciate the cultural implications of this commercial connection; the influence of Eastern silks and ceramics, say, on the decorative arts in Europe.

The consequences for the 'fine arts' are harder to assess: artistic conventions in both East and West were strong. It's intriguing, though, to think that Ming China was undergoing something of a Renaissance itself, artists like Tang Yin (1470–1523) and Qiu Ying (c. 1494–c. 1559 or 61) creating works of irresistible freshness and enterprise. It's in a Venetian painting of 1513, by Giovanni Bellini (c. 1430–1516), that we find the first known representation of Chinese porcelain – a beautiful blue-and-white bowl – in Western art, but there's no obvious indication of any more serious artistic engagement, either in Bellini's work or that of his successor, Giorgione (c. 1477/8– c. 1510), one of the greatest and most enigmatic figures in Renaissance art.

OTTOMAN EXPANSION

The East wasn't just a source of luxuries. The Ottoman Turks hadn't given up their westward expansion with Constantinople's capture – as climactic as that event had clearly been. In 1521, under their new Sultan, Suleiman I, 'the Magnificent' (c. 1494/5–1566), they'd taken the Serbian city of Belgrade. The following year, the island of Rhodes had fallen.

Like the Arabs before them, the Turks had quickly mastered the art of naval warfare. Their commander, Hayreddin Barbarossa (?–1546), a corsair (a sort of licensed pirate) from Lesbos, led the new Ottoman fleet in a series of raids on ports around the Adriatic coast belonging to Austria, at the head of the Holy Roman Empire, before moving westwards and (in 1543) allying with the French to sack Nice and occupy Toulon, both of which also belonged to Austria at that time.

Further raids followed before, in 1545, Suleiman signed an armistice with the Emperor Ferdinand (1503–64). Renewed hostilities were brought to an end by the imperial forces' successful defence of Malta from an Ottoman siege in 1566.

RIGHT:
MING CENSER
The ceramic stillness erupts into writhing life, ferocious-looking dragons weaving their contorted way through the thick green leaves of the stylized peony that forms the centrepiece of the decoration around this stunning censer (1512).

BELOW:
THE WORD SET FREE
The importance of the Gutenberg Bible (1450s) can scarcely be exaggerated. It opened the door to mass education; to modernity. Books had been bespoke till now, each one produced by hand; reading the preserve of the very few.

THE RENAISSANCE

Suleiman the Magnificent died that same year, leaving behind a fitting memorial in Istanbul's majestic Suleimaniye Mosque.

NEW HEIGHTS

The 'High Renaissance' in Italy conventionally begins with Leonardo da Vinci – not just a celebrated artist but an all-round 'Renaissance Man'. It was in keeping with humanist ideals that the individual should cultivate every possible accomplishment. The man who created the *Mona Lisa* and *The Virgin of the Rocks* was also a musician, an engineer, an anatomist, a geologist, a writer and much else besides.

The Renaissance values of regularity and balance and the skills of perspective had by now become almost instinctual for artists: the sheer technical assurance available was staggering. Hence the virtuosity with which the Florentine painter Andrea del Sarto ('Andrea *Senza Errori*' – 'without errors') could breathe life into his human forms. There was still scope for improvement, though: it took the Venetian Teziano Vecelli, or Titian (1488/90–1576), to recognize the possibilities for exploring colour, in all its depth and warmth. A redheaded beauty is still spoken of as 'Titian-haired'; his use of colour opened up a whole new dimension in art.

OPPOSITE:
THE AMBASSADORS
Painted by Hans Holbein the Younger (1497/8–1543) in 1533, the painting shows an array of expensive scientific objects related to telling the time and understanding the cosmos, including globes and dials.

RIGHT:
BUYING REDEMPTION
A woodcut showing indulgence selling in a church from title page of *On Aplas von Rom kan man wol selig werden* ('One can be saved without the Indulgence of Rome').

NORTHERN POWERHOUSE

Further north, in the Netherlands and Germany, city-states were prospering through trade and industry very much as the Italian cities had done before. In art, at least, the 'Northern Renaissance' lagged a little way behind, but the intellectual revolution it brought with it was every bit as far-reaching.

In the Low Countries, centres like Antwerp, Brussels and Bruges were booming on the back of the international trade in woollen textiles – and, increasingly, in finance. What has been described as the 'first modern economy' was under construction here. As in Italy, local patriotism was strong: wealthy magnates were anxious to boost their communities' prestige.

The industrious city-states of Germany were thriving too, their leading citizens acquiring unprecedented wealth, and with it a certain self-confidence and independent-mindedness. Education was more widely dispersed up here than it was in southern Europe, thanks in part to the new medium of print. Johannes Gutenberg had pioneered the use of movable type here in Germany; his 'Gutenberg Bible' had been published in about 1455.

FROM RENAISSANCE TO REFORMATION

For now, though, the 'Northern Renaissance' was overshadowed by the southern. Especially with a new St Peter's being built in Rome. Pope Nicholas V (1397–1455) in the fourteenth century and Julius II earlier in the fifteenth had both wished to replace Rome's increasingly decrepit St Peter's Basilica – world Catholicism's chief church, built by the

ABOVE:
PROPHET OF REFORMATION
Martin Luther's denunciations rang out with the force of an Old Testament prophet's. Lucas Cranach the Elder (1472–1553) captures his uncompromising courage – indeed, his uncompromisingness in general.

ABOVE:
SULEIMAN THE MAGNANIMOUS
Aggressive in his foreign policy, Suleiman the Magnificent was more tolerant at home in the Ottoman Empire. He encouraged literary culture, intellectual enquiry and the arts.

OPPOSITE:
NEW MONEY
A dynasty of bankers, the Fugger family rose up from nowhere in fifteenth-century Augsburg. The founder of the line had been a weaver. In 1511, Jakob Fugger was given noble rank by the Holy Roman Emperor and three years later he was anointed Imperial Count of Kirchberg and Weissenhorn.

Emperor Constantine – but failed to find the funding. It was Pope Alexander VI who actually managed to get things done – by organizing what amounted to a trade in indulgences.

In the Catholic scheme, only the saintliest went straight to heaven when they died, while only the most unrepentantly wicked went to hell. Most souls could hope to be saved, but first they'd have to endure the punishments of purgatory, until they'd literally been purged of the stain of sin. It had always been possible to be sped through the process to some extent: special devotions, prayers and pilgrimages could secure this before death, or be offered by the living on a loved one's behalf. Unscrupulous officials had always abused their positions by offering indulgence in return for bribes, but that the Pope himself should be selling them was a radical new departure.

A deeply shameful one in the eyes of Martin Luther (1483–1546), a German monk. But the last straw atop a pile of abuses. In 1517, he pinned a list of 95 Theses on to the door of Wittenberg's Castle Church. Luther is generally regarded as the first 'Protestant', not only in the obvious sense that he mounted a protest, but in an older sense of the word 'protest', meaning to make a commitment to a cause. 'Here I stand, I can do no other,' he was to say.

Luther's belief that the structures of the Church placed barriers between individual men and women and their God struck a chord with believers in northern Europe. An educated middle class here felt capable of deciding things for themselves, and expected to be allowed to. Lutheranism encouraged this with its insistence on private Bible-reading. Till now Catholicism had expected congregations to wait to be told what to think about their religion by their priests. The 'Gutenberg Revolution' would make it easier for people to study the scriptures for themselves, as would the vernacular translations Luther called for. (In the Catholic Church, the medium of all serious religious reading and discussion was still Latin.)

HENRY AND JEAN

England's 'Reformation' was more opportunistic in its inspiration. Henry VIII (1491–1547) denounced Luther's 'heresies' at first but underwent a change of heart in the 1530s

THE RENAISSANCE

THE RENAISSANCE

thanks to the Pope's refusal to annul an irksome marriage. His zeal was heightened by the fact that he was able to dissolve the Catholic monasteries in his kingdom and confiscate their wealth. The Church of England he established was Catholic in everything except obedience to Rome; in time, however, that would change.

If Luther's objections had been to the institutions of the Church and the conduct of its clergy, his faith in its basic

BELOW:
THE FIELD OF THE CLOTH OF GOLD
What we would now call a 'summit conference' was held in Balinghen, south of Calais, in 1520, between Henry VIII of England and Francis I of France (1494–1547). They were technically on English soil, the 'Pale of Calais' still belonging to England's Crown.

beliefs remained unchanged. In Geneva, however, the French preacher John Calvin (1509–64), rethinking Christian theology altogether, had come up with a creed that was more severe and Bible-based. The faithful, the 'elect', would be saved, he said, but sinners cast into hell forever. He even argued that God knew in advance which group was which, and that some were thus 'predestined' to be damned. The sort of strict 'puritanism' for which Calvin stood was officially frowned on in England, but found its way into the mainstream through the Church of England's *Book of Common Prayer* (1549), whose authors had been influenced by Calvin's teachings.

The political stakes were high – not just because ideas are important but because the potential for social upheaval seemed so real. Protestants were persecuted in Catholic kingdoms, Catholics in the growing number of Protestant ones, but many braved torture and death rather than surrender their beliefs.

THE RENAISSANCE

ABOVE:
ANNE BOLEYN
Second wife of English king Henry VIII and queen from 1533–36, Anne was executed on spurious charges of adultery and treason after failing to provide Henry with a male heir.

RIGHT:
MURKY MOTIVES
Genuine churchmen may have retrofitted it with a real doctrinal reformation, but Henry's motivation for breaking with Rome seems to have been more cynical. First the annulment issue; then the chance to make a fortune expropriating the funds of monasteries like this one, Fountains Abbey, Yorkshire.

SHOW VS SUBSTANCE?

The sale of indulgences aside, Alexander's new St Peter's project emblematized the differences in approach. It was certainly impressive, bringing together a star-studded cast of Italian Renaissance architects, including Donato Bramante (1444–1514), Michelangelo and – a generation later – Gian Lorenzo Bernini (1598–1680). His astonishing *baldacchino* canopies the papal altar and St Peter's bones, below. In its size and showiness, though, and in the 'idolatrous' importance it attached to the supposed relics of a saint, it was a glittering monument to everything Protestantism loathed.

Protestantism presented a whole new challenge to the visual arts, given its emphasis on sobriety and its Bible-based rejection of anything suggestive of the 'graven image' (so statues, icons …). At the same time, its emphasis on the individual conscience

THE RENAISSANCE

144

THE RENAISSANCE

OPPOSITE:
THINKING THE UNTHINKABLE
Copernicus's idea that the Earth and planets might revolve around the Sun seemed so crazily counterintuitive that it was at best mocked, and at worst repressed as 'heresy'. But so strong was the Renaissance spirit of enquiry that, by slow – if admittedly, painful – degrees, it was first taken seriously and then eventually accepted.

RIGHT:
TO ARMS!
Dressed in armour and carrying a lance here, as befitted his chivalric fantasies, Ignatius of Loyola was a sort of Divine Don Quixote. For better or for worse, though, his 'Jesuits' would play an important role in equipping Catholicism to fight back against the rising tide of Reformation.

foregrounded the feelings of real men and women. It's hard to imagine an earlier artist achieving the sort of psychological depth the German artist Hans Holbein the Younger did in the portraits he made at Henry VIII's court.

AN AESTHETIC OF EMOTION

More thoughtful Catholics, meanwhile, were acknowledging the justice of the complaints; envying the energy and passion of Protestantism. As leading churchmen met at the Council of Trent (held in three parts from 1545 to 1563) to discuss reforms, a new corps of Catholic writers and artists – and of course priests – was mobilizing for that intellectual and spiritual movement called the 'Counter-Reformation'.

In Spain, Ignatius of Loyola (1491–1556) was writing his *The Spiritual Exercises*, promoting a more personal and emotional engagement with Catholicism. The 'Society of Jesus' he co-founded with friends like Francis Xavier (1506–52) was explicitly modelled on the chivalric orders of medieval times. It was recognized by Pope Paul III (1468–1549) in 1540. Written in the 1560s, St Teresa of Ávila's (1515–82) memoirs provided a passionately intimate account of her journey into faith.

It was this sort of emotion that Catholic artists and architects started trying to evoke: paintings and sculptures that would move the viewer into faith (like El Greco's [1541–1614] paintings, or Bernini's statue of *The Ecstasy of St Teresa* (1652); 'baroque' architecture so extravagant it would 'wow' people into belief.

PLANETS AND PREJUDICE

In 1543, to show that radical religious reformers could be as reactionary as anyone, Martin Luther wrote a polemical booklet,

THE RENAISSANCE

THE RENAISSANCE

A FAITH OF FEELING?
The Council of Trent gave the Catholic Church the chance to take stock after the shock of the Reformation, and come up with a 'Counter-Reformation' of its own. Though typically top-down in its approach, it could still be seen to be trying to emulate the element of individual engagement and emotional commitment Martin Luther had hit on in his Protestant vision.

THE RENAISSANCE

ABOVE:
A MINISTRY IN MACAU
In 1557, the Ming dynasty leased the island of Macau to the Portuguese for a trading post. As this sixteenth-century woodcut shows, they built churches, along with storage sheds and dwellings. A thriving Catholic community developed.

Of the Jews and their Lies. They were, he informed his reader, 'vermin' who sucked the marrow from the bones of poor, hard-working Christians. He called for their synagogues ('dens of devils') to be burned down and for them to be confined to their own neighbourhoods.

In other respects, though, the Western mind was broadening as its explorations continued – in some cases beyond earthly limits into the universe at large. That same year, another German, Nicolaus Copernicus (1473–1543) published *De revolutionibus orbium coelestium* ('On the Revolutions of the Heavenly Bodies'), suggesting that the planets orbit the Sun.

Others were venturing inward. Also published in 1543 was the Belgian Andreas Vesalius's (1514–64) *De humani corporis fabrica* ('On the Structure of the Human Body'), widely regarded as the founding work of modern anatomical science.

EAST MEETS WEST

Meanwhile, the Jesuit Francis Xavier had begun his mission to Goa, a Portuguese possession in western India. It was by chance that, in 1543, a group of Portuguese seafarers in difficulties accidentally became the first Europeans to set foot on Japanese soil, but St Francis Xavier's mission there was very much intended. And, initially, successful, local people converting to Christianity in their tens of thousands before the imperial authorities cracked down. (In 1597, six Western missionaries and seventeen Japanese converts, including children, were to be publicly crucified in Nagasaki.)

The Chinese took another view, giving the Jesuits at least a cautious welcome. Francis Xavier had been about to embark on his mission to China when he died on an island off Guangdong, on its southern coast, in 1552. Within a few decades, though, his spiritual brothers Michele Ruggieri (1543–1607) and Matteo Ricci (1552–1610), established their own mission in Beijing.

The Chinese elite took to the newcomers, eager for fresh thinking from the West. There were few takers for Catholicism, though, and progress was hampered even further by bad-tempered competition between Jesuit priests and Franciscan friars. Neither would be able to stay long-term: the Manchu invaders who swept away the Ming regime in 1644 would be far less accepting of 'foreign' faiths.

The Japanese authorities were entitled to consider the presence of Westerners destabilizing. Washed up with the Portuguese sailors in 1543 had been Japan's first firearms. After generations of conflict, the Ashikaga (or Muromachi) shogunate had won the bitter Ōnin War of 1467–77, but fighting had continued on and off through the ensuing Sengoku period.

Westerners were certainly helping change the course of events elsewhere in Asia. In 1541, for instance, King Tabinshwehti of Toungou (1512–50), having conquered the neighbouring kingdom of Mon, had made himself ruler of a united Burma (Myanmar). In 1548, however, the expansionism of his new Burmese Empire was brought up short when Portuguese mercenaries repulsed his attack on Ayutthaya, Siam (now Thailand). Tabinshwehti was assassinated in the aftermath.

BELOW:
HOLY WATER
St Francis Xavier saved the day when, Asia-bound, the *Santa Cruz* ran out of water and its crew and his fellow passengers faced death. They dangled him overboard and, where his sacred soles touched the salty waves, the water miraculously turned fresh.

Seemingly secure, though sandwiched geographically between East and West, was the Safavid Empire, founded in Iran by Shah Ismai'l I (1487–1524) in 1501. With territories extending from the Caucasus to Central Asia and what is now Pakistan, it was a wealthy trading state, with an unsurpassed record in the arts and architecture.

TERRIBLE IVAN
Russia was in turmoil now, Ivan IV (1530–84), 'the Terrible', having in 1547 made himself the first 'czar' (from 'Caesar'). Brought up in an already dysfunctionalcourt, he'd nominally been Grand Duke of Muscovy since the age of three, but had been properly in charge since ordering his first assassination at thirteen. It wasn't to be the last. He didn't just have his opponents (real and imaginary) murdered but terrorized the general population with his black-cowled *oprichniki*. This

THE RENAISSANCE

6,000-strong secret police force picked up people pretty much randomly, subjecting them to torture, their lord apparently playing an enthusiastic part. In 1581, he would even murder his own son, Ivan, in a rage.

He was, however, an effective military ruler, in 1552 conquering the former Mongol Khanate of Kazan. The following year, he reopened trade between Russia and the West. He extended his kingdom again in 1556, taking the Khanate of Astrakhan, opening up the way to the Volga, the Caspian Sea, the Caucasus – and ultimately Siberia. In 1558, he attacked the Germanic Livonian Knights, who restricted Russian access to the Baltic, but this turned into a protracted war, involving Sweden, northern Europe's leading power. An appalling reputation aside, Ivan's great legacy is Moscow's St Basil's Cathedral, built on his orders 1555–61.

The year 1569 saw the foundation of the Polish-Lithuanian Commonwealth. A constitutional monarchy (sometimes indeed referred to as a 'republic') before its time, it was to be a major power at the heart of Europe till 1795.

BELOW:
THE ROYAL TOUCH
Ivan the Terrible takes a hands-on approach to torture in this seventeenth-century engraving. It can't of course be verified, but doesn't seem the slightest bit unlikely. Russia's first tsar was seriously unbalanced and psychopathically violent as even his own family could attest.

ROYAL REFORMERS

The Reformation had divided Germany, where an assortment of princes, dukes and other dignitaries had enjoyed considerable autonomy under the Holy Roman Emperor. Religious tensions had put this arrangement under strain, as some states leaned towards Lutheranism, affronting the staunchly Catholic Charles V (1500–58). In 1555, however, he was forced to bow to realities, agreeing to the Peace of Augsburg and the principle *cuius regio, eius religio* ('whoever's be the realm, his be the religion'). Local rulers could decide which faiths would be established within their realms.

Meanwhile, in England, the Reformation had been playing out in pendulum swings. From 1553, under Henry VIII's daughter, Mary I (1516–58), Catholicism was reimposed as state religion. She was married to the devoutly Catholic King Philip II of Spain (1527–98). (So important was his faith to him, he built a majestic monastery-palace for himself outside Madrid at El Escorial where he could hear Mass from the comfort of his bed. It also had a pantheon in which all Spain's monarchs were to be lain to rest.)

Queen Mary's determined persecution of Protestants earned her the nickname 'Bloody Mary'. She had her half-sister, Elizabeth, imprisoned on suspicion of involvement in Sir Thomas Wyatt's Protestant rebellion. It was, however, Elizabeth

THE RENAISSANCE

LEFT:
AN EMPEROR AT EASE
Jakob Seisenegger (1505–67), who painted this portrait, was court artist to the Holy Roman Emperor Ferdinand I (ruled 1558–64). Here we see Ferdinand's older brother, Charles V (ruled 1519–56), in 1532, by which time Charles had been Emperor for sixteen years. Emperor of Spain and later the Holy Roman Emperor, he was seen as the true defender of the Catholic faith and greatest among Catholic kings of the era.

THE RENAISSANCE

ST BARTHOLOMEW'S DAY MASSACRE
François Dubois (1529–84), who painted this scene, was a Huguenot himself, forced to flee France for Switzerland after the killings. Even so, we have no reason to see this representation as in any significant way exaggerated, though it concentrates a scattered action in a single place. The dead body of Huguenot leader, Admiral Gaspard de Coligny (1519–72), slumps out of a window to the right. At rear-left, a black-clad Catherine de Medici comes out to inspect the bodies of those who have been slaughtered on her orders.

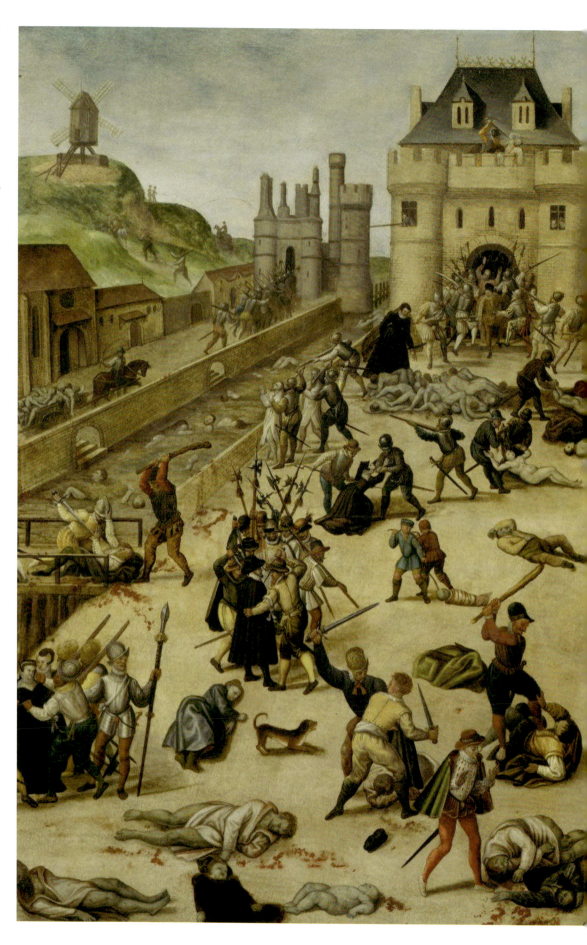

I (1533–1603) who, by dynastic right, succeeded Mary when she died in 1558. Elizabeth restored the Reformation – and the persecution of Catholics. Including her cousin, Mary, Queen of Scots (1542–87), after she was ousted by a group of Protestant nobles who took her son James from her and had him brought up in their faith. Elizabeth gave Mary grudging sanctuary – but held her in prison for eighteen years before finally accusing her of conspiring against her and having her beheaded. Even so, Mary's Protestant son, James VI of Scotland (1566–1625) since his infancy, succeeded Elizabeth as James I of England, bringing about a 'Union of the Crowns' from 1603.

CHRISTIAN CARNAGE

It wasn't just in Britain that the Reformation had brought violent tumult. France's King Charles IX (1550–74) had been alarmed at the rise of his country's Protestant Huguenots, who had held their

BELOW:
PIETY FACTORY
Apart from its Pantheon of Kings, Philip II's El Escorial had three libraries, a school, a monastery and a convent, as well as the basilica where Masses were said in a continuous relay round the clock, seven days a week.

OPPOSITE:
GREAT QUEEN
'Though I be a woman yet I have as good a courage answerable to my place as my father had.' Elizabeth I brushed sexist condescension aside with regal disdain. Here we see her in her coronation splendour.

first national synod or council in 1559. 'Wars of Religion' raged from 1562, throwing France into confusion as the authorities tried to suppress the Huguenots and they resisted. Up to 4 million may have been killed in the fighting and attendant famines. On St Bartholomew's Day (24 August), 1572, on the orders of Charles's mother, Catherine de Medici (1519–89), hundreds of Huguenots were massacred in Paris. In 1598, the accession of Henri IV (1553–1610), who, though Catholic himself, was prepared to grant Protestants the right to worship, brought the conflict to an end.

Affluent, educated and progressive, the Dutch had come early to the Reformation. It was darkly ironic that the Netherlands should have come to Spain's Catholic and reactionary ruling Habsburg monarchs as a legacy of their Burgundian ancestors. The Protestant Dutch weren't comfortable with their Catholic overlordship. Philip II of Spain sent the Duke of Alba to Brussels to put down unrest – which he did, very brutally – but fighting

THE RENAISSANCE

OPPOSITE:
A QUEEN IN COURT
Mary Queen of Scots (top right) is ushered in to face her trial for purportedly plotting against the throne of Elizabeth I. 'Look to your consciences,' she told the jurors, 'and remember that the theatre of the world is wider than the realm of England.'

BELOW:
CLASH OF EMPIRES
The Battle of Lepanto in 1571 was the galley's last hurrah. Don John of Austria (1547–78) deployed over 200, along with six giant galleasses – floating fortresses – armed in all with more than 1,300 guns. Facing them, in Müezzinzade Ali Pasha's Turkish fleet, were 205 galleys, rowed by 19,000 slaves.

THE RENAISSANCE

continued for decades in what was to become known as the Eighty Years' War.

If history teaches us nothing else, it's how good humans are at creating catastrophes for themselves and others, but suffering can come from other sources too. In 1556, China's Shaanxi province had been the epicentre of the world's deadliest ever earthquake. Imperial records show that 830,000 died. 'Mountains and rivers changed places and roads were destroyed. In some places, the ground suddenly rose up and formed new hills, or it sank in abruptly and became new valleys … Huts, official houses, temples and city walls collapsed.'

Less dramatic but more influential on world history, the 'Little Ice Age' seems to have set in some time about now. Average European temperatures dropped around 2–3 °C (3.6–5.4 °F) which, though not spectacular in itself, was serious enough to make life hard for rural communities and the urban poor. 'Ice fairs' on frozen rivers may have been fun, but poor crops and livestock diseases forced food prices up, even when there weren't actually famines. Central England endured its coldest ever month in January 1795, with an average temperature of -3.1 °C (26.4 -3.1°F). Conditions weren't really to ease until the nineteenth century.

FIRE AND STORM

Some scholars have suggested that the stress caused communities to look for scapegoats. Witch-hunts took place in much of Europe. Mary Queen of Scots' son James VI (from 1603, he'd be King of England too, as James I) helped whip up the frenzy in Scotland. In 1590, at North Berwick, east of Edinburgh, over 60 suspects were arraigned for witchcraft. A dozen or more were executed; others may well have died under torture. Over the next century or so, hundreds of people (predominantly women) were to be executed for witchcraft in Scotland. James VI/I had furthered the paranoia, convinced that witches had sent the storm that had almost wrecked his ship as it brought him home from a state visit to Denmark.

That he actually had more to fear from England's persecuted Catholics became clear on 5 November 1605, when Guido

THE RENAISSANCE

OPPOSITE:
FIRESHIP AHOY!
A work from 1796 by the French-born English painter Philippe-Jacques de Loutherbourg (1740–1812) underlines the extent to which the *Defeat of the Spanish Armada* was to enshrine itself in Britain's national mythology.

RIGHT:
SHAKESPEARE IN PRINT
The 'First Folio' of 1623. The dedicatory verses by Ben Jonson (his fellow playwright) worry, as posterity would, at the apparent contradiction between Shakespeare's extraordinary genius and his unassuming appearance and prosaic life. It was new for plays to be collected and published in this way, making popular entertainment into 'literature'.

BELOW:
ST MARK'S SQUARE, VENICE
The Republic of Venice (697–1797) dominated trade in the eastern Mediterranean for much of the medieval era, but suffered a long decline from the fifteenth century onwards with the expansion of the Ottoman Empire.

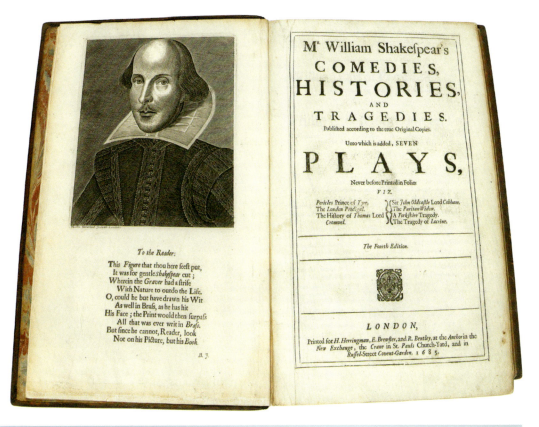

THE RENAISSANCE

THE RENAISSANCE

CULTURE IN A COLD CLIMATE
Heading home with little to show for their efforts (the figure on the left has a dead fox slung over his shoulder), *The Hunters in the Snow* (1565) are pictured by Pieter Bruegel the Elder (c. 1525–59). A dismal scene, on the face of it, but a glorious and ever-popular painting. The Northern Renaissance can seem a little dour next to Italy's sun-soaked version, but it was in its own way as exciting and as enduringly important.

THE RENAISSANCE

Fawkes and his co-conspirators tried to blow up London's Houses of Parliament with him inside.

If their intended inferno proved a damp squib, that couldn't have been said of the Battle of Lepanto (1570), at which the massed galleys (more than 200) of the Catholic 'Holy League', led by imperial Austria, defeated those of the Ottoman Empire off the coast of Greece. 'The sea and the fire seemed as one,' one veteran recalled. How important this victory was strategically can be debated, but its symbolic significance for the West was huge. As was that for England of its triumphant routing of the Spanish Armada, dispatched by Philip of Spain in 1588. As this great fleet made its way up the English Channel to pick up an invasion force waiting in the Netherlands, it was intercepted by the English – who attacked it with fireships – and broken up and scattered. Missing their Dutch rendezvous, the Spanish ships had to go home the long way round the Scottish and Irish coasts: battered by storms, many were wrecked.

A NEW SHOGUNATE

A rainstorm was in 1600 to cast cold water on both armies at the Battle of Sekigahara in Japan, extinguishing the glowing fuses of their matchlock muskets. Toyetomi Hideyoshi (1536/7–98), who had finally unified the country, had been killed in battle by Tokugawa Ieyasu's (1543–1616) forces in 1598. At Sekigahara, Ieyasu defeated the remaining Hideyoshi loyalists, bringing the country under the control of his Tokugawa shogunate. He established his capital at Tokyo, which was then called Edo: the next 250 years of Japanese history is known as the 'Edo period', a time of internal peace and isolationism.

BELOW:
SHOGUNATE SHOWDOWN
Complex coalitions of clans came to blows at Sekigahara. This seventeenth-century screen provides a panoramic view. Ieyasu's victorious 'Eastern Army' advances from the right; Hideyoshi's 'Western Army' pushes back from the left.

AGE OF REASON
1600 – 1760

As in the sixteenth century, exploration and enquiry went along with exploitation. In 1607, England established a settlement at Jamestown, Virginia. Twelve years later, the first cargo of slaves was brought here from West Africa. The following year, another ship, the *Mayflower*, arrived in Massachusetts, carrying the Pilgrim Fathers – Protestant Puritans fleeing harassment in England.

England's American territories were on the one hand a land of opportunity and of freedom; on the other a colony, which would prosper at the expense of Indigenous peoples and imported slaves. In 1641, the General Court of Massachusetts Bay Colony would number the 'right' to own slaves among a 'Body of Liberties' it held sacrosanct. Three years later, local Native Americans would rise up and kill 400 colonists. The pattern would continue. And affect Asia as well as North America. In 1639, Ivan Moskvitin became the first Russian to reach the Pacific Ocean, discovering the Sea of Okhotsk.

OPPOSITE:
ASTRONOMER BY CANDLELIGHT
Dutch painter Gerrit Dou sums up an era in this 1655 work: the spirit of enquiry was abroad. Enlightenment was framed with darkness, hence the *chiaroscuro* (the bold opposition of light and shade) so central to the artistic aesthetic of the time.

RIGHT:
COGITO ERGO SUM ...
'I think, therefore I am …' Descartes' claim became his catchphrase but he might as fairly have said, 'I am, therefore future generations will think that much more clearly.' His *Meditations on First Philosophy*, published 1641, remains a vital textbook to this day.

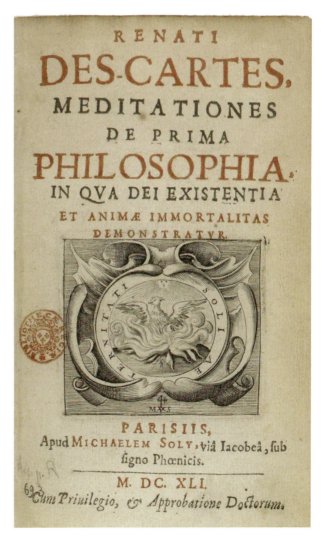

AGE OF REASON

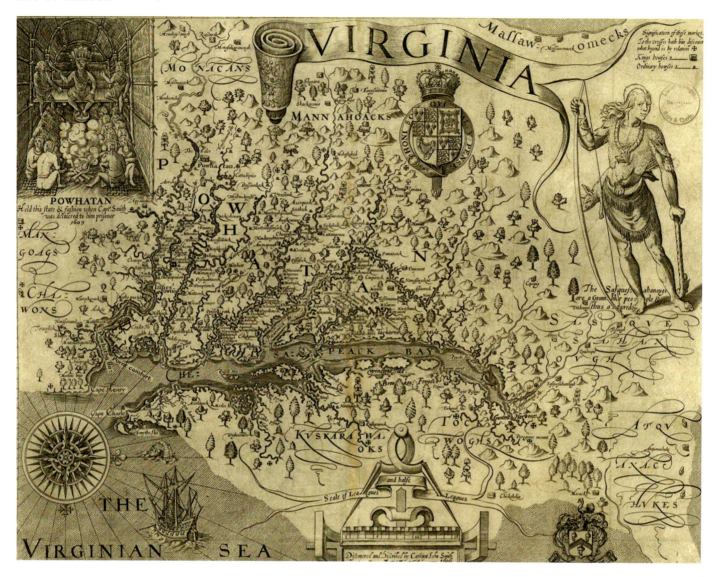

PROGRESS AND PROFIT

In 1610, Italian astronomer Galileo Galilei (1564–1642) used his improved telescope to identify Jupiter's four moons; two years later he would incur the wrath of the Catholic Church for suggesting, after tracking sunspots on its surface, that the sun rotated on its axis – in keeping, he argued, with the theories of Copernicus. Johannes Kepler took scientific understanding even further in 1619. He solved the mystery of the motion of the planets by showing that their orbits were elliptical.

The year 1606 had seen the first recorded landing of any European on Australian soil when the Dutch East India Company's ship the *Duyfken* put in at the mouth of Queensland's Pennefather River. In 1627, another Dutch vessel found the continent's southern coast, while in 1642 Abel Tasman (of the Dutch East India Company) 'discovered' Tasmania and New Zealand.

Two years later, the French philosopher René Descartes (1596–1650) published his *Meditations*. This was to be one of the founding texts of the 'European Enlightenment'. But the profit motive was never to be forgotten long: in 1640, England's East India Company had established a base at Madras (Chennai). In 1641, the Dutch took Malacca from the Portuguese, underlining their dominance throughout the East Indies. Horizons were being broadened, but the new territories being opened up were seen as properties to be taken possession of and fought over. In 1645, the export of slaves from Mozambique to Brazil began.

Not that the world's misfortunes could all be lain at Europe's door. In 1644, struggling with unrest in Shaanxi province, the

ABOVE:
A CARTOGRAPHICAL CLAIM
The English Virginia Company's Captain John Smith mapped the coast around Chesapeake Bay in 1608. He had this more permanent engraving done three years later. No better illustration could be found of the way in which exploration and exploitation went hand in hand.

OPPOSITE:
POCAHONTAS
The daughter of Powhatan, a local chief in Tidewater, Virginia, 'Princess' Pocahontas wed tobacco-planter Thomas Rolfe in 1614. He took her to England where she became a celebrity and the fund-raising 'face' of colonial development. Simon van de Passe made this portrait (1616).

LEFT:
THE UNIVERSE REORDERED
It was with this telescope that Galileo scanned the skies. '*E pur si muove*' ('And yet it moves'), he is reputed to have said to the Catholic Inquisitors who demanded his agreement that the earth stood still while the planets and the stars revolved around it in 'geocentric' orbit, as astronomers had believed since ancient times.

Ming emperor hired Manchu warriors as mercenaries. Their leader, Dorgon, decided to make himself China's emperor, though it would take some 60 years for his Qing dynasty to take over China as a whole. (Despite its barbarous beginnings, the Qing presided over a glittering period in Chinese art. The imperial workshops produced important treasures in arts and crafts.)

Nor could all the world's atrocities be said to be 'colonialist' in origin. In 1646, Amangkurat I (1619–77) marked his accession to the throne of the Sultanate of Java with mass-executions of potential opponents, religious scholars and others. He had some 6,000 killed in his first year.

THE THIRTY YEARS' HORROR

The Peace of Augsburg in 1555 had bought everyone time but, as Protestantism gathered momentum in Central Europe, the Emperor Matthias had continued to be concerned. He had tried to tighten restrictions on the new religion's spread in Bohemia (later the Czech Republic). At the 'Defenestration of Prague' in 1618, however, Protestant nobles had literally thrown Matthias's emissaries out of a third-floor window. They'd survived, but the slight to the emperor had been intolerable. The resulting hostilities had quickly escalated. As Protestant states flocked to Bohemia's aid, France, Sweden and Spain had lent their support to the Empire.

This, the so-called 'Thirty Years' War', had become a meat-grinder at the heart of Europe. It wasn't just the military combat

ABOVE:
SMALL BEGINNINGS
Fort St George, on India's Coromandel Coast, was the trading post around which the city of Madras – now Chennai – would take shape. It represents the start of English settlement, and eventually conquest, in South Asia.

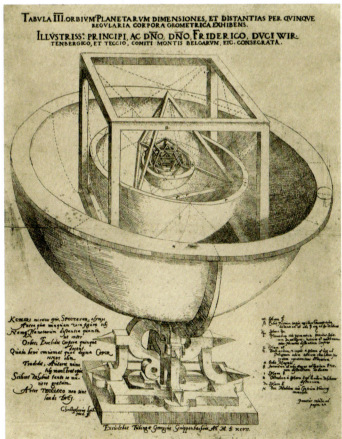

LEFT:
PLANETS ON PARADE
Kepler elegantly modelled the movement of the planets around the sun. He described their elliptical orbits in his *Mysterium Cosmographicum* ('The Cosmographic Mystery'), first published 1596, revised and much-expanded in 1625.

OPPOSITE BOTTOM:
PILGRIM PIONEERS
Plymouth Rock, at Plymouth Massachusetts, marks the place at which the Pilgrim Fathers landed and set up their colony. Things were difficult at first, and the first Thanksgiving was celebrated in 1621 with great relief. By the end of the seventeenth century, Plymouth Colony had several thousand inhabitants, while similar settlements were springing up nearby.

deaths, which numbered hundreds of thousands on both sides; or the soldiers dead from diseases (well over a million). In a war of scorched earth and city sieges, civilians were extremely vulnerable. Exemplary massacres were carried out to encourage co-operation. Add in the epidemics and famines fostered by the breakdown of civil society and you get truly terrible casualties: around 8 million overall, historians believe.

Finally, in 1648, the Peace of Westphalia was signed. A compromise-agreement, it felt like a defeat for a Holy Roman Empire that had reigned unchallenged. The treaty was negotiated in parallel with the Peace of Munster. This brought an end to the

BATTLE OF FLEURUS, 1622
Well-drilled squares and lines collapse into chaos as a Spanish force gives the Protestant army of Duke Christian the Younger of Brunswick a severe mauling at this encounter in the Netherlands. Pieter Snayers specialized in painting panoramic battle scenes like this one – a handy accomplishment to have in the Europe of the Thirty Years' War.

LEFT:
CRUEL CONQUEST
Fort Belgica was an important base for the Dutch East India Company in the Banda Islands, Maluku, Indonesia, the world's sole source of nutmeg in the seventeenth century. The Islands' conquest (1609–21) had involved scenes of genocidal slaughter.

OPPOSITE:
MANCHU MASTER
Dorgon was never actually emperor of China: technically he was regent for his nephew, Fulin, a little boy. The young 'Shunzi Emperor' resented his uncle and when he died in 1650, stripped him of his titles retrospectively, but Dorgon's historic contribution could not be undone.

BELOW:
DIVINITY OR DUNG-HEAP?
The fall from the top-floor window of Prague's Hradcany Castle should have killed the papal envoys. Pious Catholics were in no doubt that God had intervened to save them. Protestants had a more prosaic answer: their landing had been cushioned by a dung-heap at the bottom of the tower.

Eighty Years War between the Netherlands and Spain, the latter recognizing an Independent Dutch Republic. Released from its Spanish captivity, the Dutch Republic enjoyed a boom, and a cultural golden age that lasted almost 90 years.

ABSOLUTE DISASTER

In 1625, meanwhile, James I/VI had died, to be succeeded by his son Charles I (1600–49), a firm believer in the 'divine right of kings'. The king, he believed, owed no accountability to any human law but only to God, on whose behalf he ruled.

This absolutism set him on a collision course with his Parliament which, in addition to naturally wishing to protect its own authority, was predominantly Puritan. Charles wasn't a Catholic but he was married to one (Henrietta Maria of France); his authoritarianism recalled that of the Roman Church and many felt that the achievements of the Reformation were at stake.

Eventually, things broke down completely and civil war broke out, pitting the Parliamentary 'Roundheads' (their heads were shaven, for their helmets) against the (flamboyantly coiffed and coutured) 'Cavaliers'.

Defeated at the Battle of Naseby (1645), the king was captured and tried and, in January 1649, executed for treason.

Oliver Cromwell (1599–1658), the Parliamentary leader who had designed and the 'New Model Army' which had won the war, appointed himself 'Lord Protector' of what was no longer a kingdom but a 'Commonwealth'. Cromwell's death in 1658 wasn't deeply mourned. People had found his puritanical regime well-

AGE OF REASON

RIGHT:
THE DEVIL'S WORK
England's self-appointed Witchfinder General, Matthew Hopkins, sent around 300 women to their deaths. Weirdly, the witch hunts of the seventeenth century were centred on self-consciously progressive, Protestant countries. Scotland's James VI (James I of England) was conspicuously enlightened – but paranoid about witchcraft.

nigh unbearable and welcomed the 'Restoration' of the monarchy with the return of the flamboyantly free-and-easy Charles II from exile in 1660.

THE 'SUN KING'

If the Treaty of Westphalia had brought setbacks for Spain and the Holy Roman Empire, these had been a boost for the France of Louis XIV. He was still only eight, but before too long the Boy King would become the self-styled 'Sun King'. Largely dispensing with advisers and any real form of government, he ruled his country by decree. Like England's Charles I, he believed in the 'divine right of kings'. He summed up his constitutional position: 'L'État, C'est Moi' – 'The State, it is I'. Louis made no distinction between his own personal glory and that of France: his self-promotion transcended mere vanity. It was only fitting that, in 1668, he should give orders for a splendid palace to be built outside Paris at Versailles. Conceived as a showcase for French wealth and power, designed by Lois le Vau and Jules Hardouin-Mansart, it was stunning in magnificence and scale. His Gobelins Manufactory in Paris became famous for its sumptuous tapestries.

In 1682, Louis had a land named after him when René-Robert Cavelier, Sieur de la Salle, a fur-trader travelling by canoe, found his way down from the Great Lakes to the Mississippi via its tributary, the Illinois River. He called the lands of the Mississippi Basin La Louisiane, claiming them for France. Since the area drained by the Mississippi stretches from the Appalachians to the Rockies, this was no insignificant bit of land.

RUSSIA LOOKS WEST

Another absolute monarch, Peter I (1672–1725) became Russia's czar at the age of 11. His half-sister Sophia, then his mother, acted as his regents till, in 1694, aged 22, he managed to take power in his own right.

In 1696, he won his first military victory, taking the Black Sea port of Azov from the Turks. Not only did this serve notice of Russia's arrival as a power: it identified the country with the

RIGHT:
PROTECTOR OF PURITANISM
Oliver Cromwell seemed to sum up Puritanism in its stereotypical virtues and vices. On the one hand, a man with iron principles. On the other, a fanatic, unbending – at best joyless, at worst exulting in the slaughter of the Catholic Irish (1649).

OPPOSITE:
MOMENTOUS ACTION
Charles I's beheading, from a Dutch pamphlet. The action was the ultimate affront to the monarchical principle. Conservative interests around Europe were outraged. Even the Dutch Republic was divided, some aristocrats sympathizing with the Stuarts while the mercantile elite generally supported Parliament.

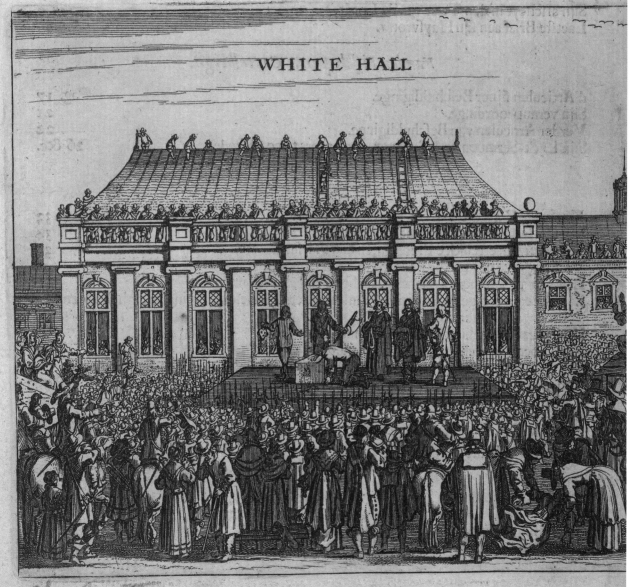

Engelandts Memoriael,
Tot Eeuwige gedachtenis.

Verhalende de Proceduren, Declaratien, Beschuldigingen, Defencien, Vonnissen, Laetste woorden en Executien, van

De Vice-Roy van Yrlandt, *Onthalst den* 22 *Maey*, 1641.
De Bisschop van Cantelbury, *Onthalst den* 10 *Ianua.* 1645.
Den Koningh van Engelandt, Schotlandt, en Yrlandt, *Karolus Stuart*, d'eerste van dien Name, *Onthalst den* 30 *Ianuarij*, 1649. *Ouden-Stijl.* Alle binnen Londen ge-executeert.

In desen lesten druck vermeerdert en verbetert, als op de volgende zijde te sien is.

Alles naer de Copyen van LONDEN.

t'Amsterdam, By Joost Hartgerts, Boeck-verkoper bezijden het Stadhuys, 1649.

cause of the Christian West. That same year Peter set out on an extended tour in western Europe, observing everything from etiquette to the arts, taking in public lectures, visiting factories and shipyards – even training as a carpenter. Back in Russia he tried to inculcate Western ideas and attitudes. He started with symbolic gestures, ordering his boyars or nobles to shave off their beards, and encouraging the introduction of French fashion (and language) in high society. Soon he was bringing in foreign craftsmen and scientists, and promoting education on an unprecedented scale. He built a modern navy and reformed Russian institutions: the army, the civil service, the Orthodox Church.

Not that his admiration for all things Western prevented his picking quarrels with his European neighbours – notably with Sweden, then the main power in the Baltic. The 21-year 'Great Northern War' reflected his resolve not only to aggrandize Russia but to reorient it geopolitically: access to the Baltic meant a 'window on the West'. By 1703, he could found a fort at the mouth of the River Neva, looking out across the Baltic; by 1712, Russia had a new capital there, St Petersburg.

AGE OF REASON

OPPOSITE LEFT:
LEADING FROM THE FRONT
Gustavus Adolphus leads his troops to triumph at Breitenfeld (1631), the first important Protestant victory of the Thirty Years' War. Not just a powerful monarch but a dashing military leader, Gustavus Adolphus made Sweden one of Europe's foremost powers and was recognized as the prime defender of the Protestant faith.

OPPOSITE BOTTOM:
MONUMENT TO MISRULE?
There's no doubt that Louis XIV had built himself a spectacular 'statement' residence at Versailles, but what it said became increasingly controversial. By the late eighteenth century, it was widely seen as standing for the obscene wealth and luxury in which a parasitical nobility now lived.

LEFT:
THE 'SUN KING'
Louis XIV was firmly convinced that he ruled by 'divine right'. God might indeed have chosen a lot worse. There's no doubting Louis' intelligence, his capability or his commitment, but his achievements would be taken to justify the absolutism of much lesser monarchs.

AGE OF REASON

LEFT:
THE MONKEY MARKET
The first such speculative bubble known, 'Tulipmania' tore through the Netherlands in the 1630s, when a single bulb might sell for many times the average income of a working man. An appropriate subject for Jan Brueghel the Younger's *Satire of the Tulip Mania* (1640s).

ABOVE:
COSSACK CONQUEROR
In 1582, Yermak Timofeyevich led an expedition against the Khanate of Sibir, in what would come to be called 'Siberia'. Fantasy-portraits like this one testify to both the paucity of known facts about him and his hold on the Russian imagination.

An intimidating, even thuggish, presence, Peter stood over 2 m (6.56 ft) tall and was noisy and aggressive. He had little interest in the arts or scientific enquiry for their own sake. Or in what we might see as civilized morality. Tens of thousands of Russian serfs and Swedish prisoners-of-war had been worked to death in the construction of St Petersburg. Peter's law of 1721 helped jump-start Russian industry by allowing entrepreneurs to buy serfs like slaves from rural landowners: while advancing the economy, it showed contempt for 'human rights'.

RESTORATION

England had meanwhile been suffering tragedy at home, the Great Plague (1665–6), another bout of bubonic plague, killing almost 70,000 people in London alone. Later in 1666, an oversight in a bakery in Pudding Lane caused the Great Fire of London. The resulting devastation did at least allow the city to be rebuilt and to some extent refurbished, notably

AGE OF REASON

RIGHT:
IMPERIAL ENCROACHMENTS
Sugar plantations and refineries line the coast of Pernambuco in 1647. Brazil had been allotted to Portugal under the 1494 Treaty of Tordesillas, but the Protestant Dutch didn't feel any deference to the Pope. They made repeated attempts to establish themselves around Recife, but were dislodged after the Battle of Guarapes in 1654.

BELOW:
'THE PLAGUE DOCTOR OF ROME'
Paulus Fürst's satirical engraving sends up the charlatans who preyed on people's fears – though at this time the most reputable practitioner was no more capable than the basest fraud. Grotesque as it appears, this doctor's outfit is not necessarily unrealistic. The 'beak' would be filled with 'purifying' plants and herbs like lavender. Pleasant smells were thought to banish plague.

with the new St Paul's Cathedral and other churches designed by Sir Christopher Wren (1632–1723). Abroad, England had continued to extend its interests, establishing a trading post in Sierra Leone in 1663 and an East India Company colony at Bombay (Mumbai), India. 1670 saw the establishment of the Hudson Bay Company in northern Canada. (What had been viewed as wilderness in much of North America had become super-productive since the vogue for furs.)

In 1686, the English scientist Isaac Newton (1643–1727) had done his bit for scientific enlightenment with the publication of the *Mathematical Principles of Natural Philosophy*. Most famous for describing its author's 'discovery' of gravity, in its wider purpose – establishing that the laws of the heavens were the same as those of earth – it struck a blow against old-style superstition.

Another modernizing move was the country's stepping away from monarchical absolutism. The 'Glorious Revolution' of 1688 saw the divine-right-believing Catholic James II (and James VII of Scotland) overthrown in favour of the Protestant William of Orange, who as Stadtholder or 'Steward', had been in charge of the Dutch Republic. James made a fight of it but was defeated in Ireland at the Battle of the Boyne in 1690, a triumph celebrated by the militantly Protestant 'Orange Order' in Northern Ireland and in Britain ever since.

For most in modern Britain, though, the Revolution's real, enduring significance has been William's agreement to reign 'constitutionally', in keeping with the wishes of his Parliament.

'BOUGHT AND SOLD'

Scotland was spinning into crisis now, its great families having largely bankrupted themselves investing in the Darien Scheme (1698–1700). It was a point of pride, its backers argued, that a proud and independent European country like Scotland should have overseas colonies as England, France and other nations did.

Unfortunately, it had been first come, first served: the best site Scots could find for their get-rich-quick colony was what turned out to be an infertile and disease-ridden corner of Panama. Approximately 2,000 settlers died and a quarter of Scotland's liquid capital was lost.

As was just about any option the country had to continue as an independent entity. Scotland's elite had little alternative but to agree to the Act of Union (1707), which created a single kingdom of 'Great Britain'. It isn't clear quite how controversial this decision was when it was made, but there's little doubt that it came to seem shabby to many Scots in retrospect. For the poet Robert Burns (1759–96), writing in 1791, it was only too clear that Scotland had been betrayed by its ruling class: 'We're bought and sold for English gold –/ Such a parcel of rogues in a nation.'

WAR AFTER WAR

The seventeenth century ended with Western victory in the Great Turkish War of 1683–99. The outcome had been uncertain for a while, the Turks coming close to capturing Vienna, but eventually they'd suffered a serious defeat. The eighteenth century began with Louis XIV still on the throne of France, and very much a master. His apparent early intentions of bringing Europe under French control hadn't really materialized, though, so he was feared less than he had been before.

BELOW:
MODEST ORIGINS
Woolsthorpe Manor in rural Lincolnshire was home to one of history's greatest scientists. Isaac Newton was born and brought up here, narrowly escaped a life as a farmer here, and came back here to study when Cambridge University was closed by the plague.

OVERLEAF:
THE GREAT FIRE OF LONDON
On 2 September 1666, fire broke out in a bakery on Pudding Lane, a little way north of the Thames in London. Soon the whole city was going up in flames. The conflagration raged for three whole days; entire streets were destroyed or left unsafe; the old St Paul's Cathedral was burned down. The Monument erected after the fire was inscribed with a message claiming that Catholics had started the fire, in a fit of 'Popish frenzy' against 'this Protestant city', but this was removed in the mid-nineteenth century.

AGE OF REASON

ABOVE:
CELEBRATORY CERAMIC
A dish commemorates King William III and his co-monarch Mary II. (Mary was the partner with the claim on the English Crown.) As a ruling couple, they were iconic of English Constitutionalism – and, less edifyingly, of anti-Catholic prejudice.

RIGHT:
BULLET-RESISTANT ARMOUR
This samurai armour is a rare example of the *morohada-nugi-dō gusoku* type from the early Edo period (17th century). Warfare in Japan changed dramatically throughout the 16th century, with the introduction of firearms and the utilization of larger contingents of troops. This necessitated significant changes in armour design, including the introduction of bullet resistant materials, such as this cuirass.

OPPOSITE:
VICTORY AT VIENNA
1683 saw Vienna besieged by the forces of Sultan Mehmed IV, the culmination of three centuries of Ottoman pressure on the Holy Roman Empire. On 12 September, the Christians broke the siege, securing a major strategic and symbolic triumph.

AGE OF REASON

RIGHT:
TOUR DE FORCE
Marlborough's conduct of the Battle of Blenheim (13 August 1704) was masterly. Throwing his foe off guard with feints, he smashed directly through his centre. The quickness of his thinking and the ease with which his forces executed it on the ground were something new in military history. For all the mercurial manoeuvring, though, the fighting was all too real: 31,000 soldiers were killed or wounded.

BELOW:
BARCELONA BESIEGED
With the mass of Montjuïc rising to the west, we see the still-walled city of Barcelona by its old port. In British hands, the Catalan capital is now (April 1706) being encircled by a Franco–Spanish army. Within weeks, a British fleet will arrive to lift the siege.

In 1700, however, King Charles II of Spain died, leaving his crown to Louis' grandson, Philip, Duc d'Anjou. The Emperor Leopold I had no wish to see Spain wrested from his Habsburg relations and objected. He found support in England, Prussia and the Netherlands, none of whom had any desire to see Louis' France extending its influence at their expense. Portugal threw in its lot with Louis.

The result was the so-called 'War of the Spanish Succession'. Fighting raged for 13 years, a spin-off conflict ('Queen Anne's War') opening up in France and England's North American colonies in Canada. The war ended in mutual exhaustion, brought to a close with the signing of the Treaty of Utrecht (1713). Louis had lost, but his France appeared as formidable as ever.

SHARES IN SLAVERY

The beginning of the eighteenth century saw the Atlantic Slave Trade at its height. One provision of the Treaty of Utrecht was the awarding of Portugal's right to ship slaves from Angola to the Americas to England's South Sea Company. This was widely viewed as a good thing. Cruel as of course it was, the slave trade was sanitized for Europeans by the fact that its most inhuman practices took place at a far remove. The way the 'Triangular Trade' worked was that ships left European ports carrying commodities to Africa, traded them there for slaves, then loaded their human cargoes up to cross the Atlantic (the 'Middle Passage') to the Americas and exchanged them for cotton, sugar and other raw materials to bring back home. No one in Liverpool, Bristol or Nantes had to confront the reality of what the traffic involved; still less the private investor in his townhouse or village home.

Add in the enduring appeal of something for nothing and it becomes clear why shares in the South Sea Company were bought so enthusiastically – and eagerly traded as their price began to soar. As dishonest brokers and corrupt politicians 'talked them up', shares rose tenfold in price. Far beyond their realistic value, given that the recent war had left the economies of the colonies depressed. In 1720, the price collapsed completely, leaving many once-wealthy families ruined.

In 1723, Johann Sebastian Bach (1685–1750) became Director of Church Music in Leipzig – a high point in the career of a composer whose cantatas and oratorios were to revolutionize

BELOW:
WITCHES' BROUHAHA
The European witch-hunts came to America with the Salem Trials of 1692. After Mrs Ann Putnam testified to her 'torture' by witches' spells, her daughter Ann Jr. denounced 62 people, including several of her friends.

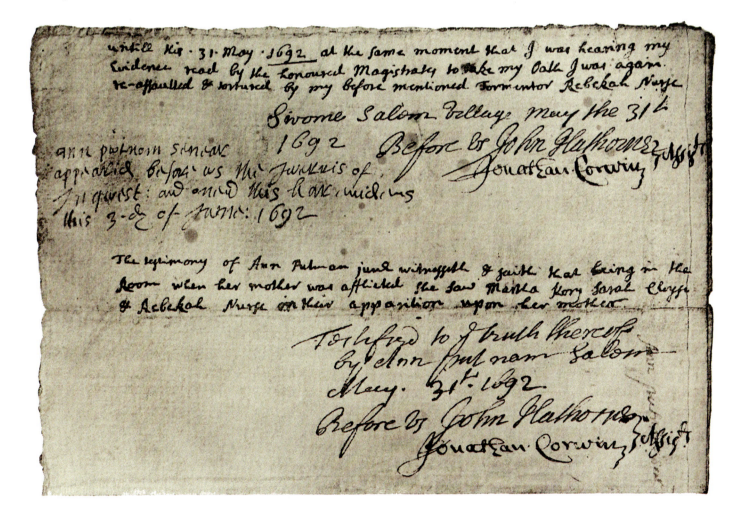

AGE OF REASON

SHOWDOWN AT VIGO BAY
The advantage swung back and forth in the early months of the War of the Spanish Succession, the victories of France's Duc de Vendôme offset by the capture of forts along the Meuse by John Churchill, Duke of Marlborough. At Friedlingen, Bavaria, in October 1702, Prince Louis William of Baden-Baden lost to the Duc de Villars but prevented him from linking up with his Bavarian allies. Just days later, in Galicia's Vigo Bay, George Rooke's Anglo-Dutch expedition captured the Spanish treasure fleet and sank its French escort – 15 warships strong.

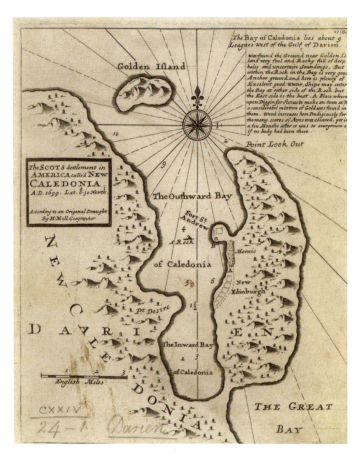

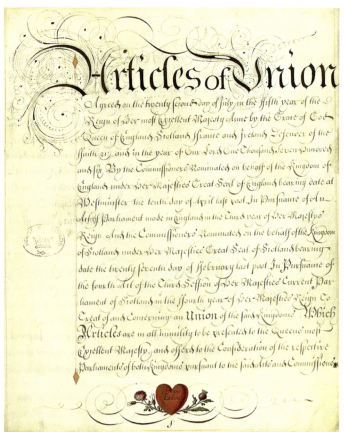

ABOVE:
NEW CALEDONIA
An upbeat map presents an exciting prospect. Darien, its proposers said, was 'door of the seas' and 'key of the universe'. It turned out to be an uncultivable, uninhabitable sink of disease. By the time the project failed, it had swallowed up some 20 per cent of Scotland's available money, leaving the country staring into an economic abyss. Union with England might yet have been refused, but was clearly the line of least resistance for a Scots 'elite' now facing bankruptcy.

ABOVE RIGHT:
SIGNED AWAY
The Articles of Union (1707) abolished Scotland as an independent kingdom, though arguably as the price of admission to a stronger, more dynamic Britain. By some measures Scotland certainly gained as an industrializing United Kingdom grew in wealth and imperial power, but things would look different in a Britain in retreat.

RIGHT:
TUSSLE OVER TRADE
In 1663, the Dutch East India Company captured Cochin (now Kochi in Kerala, India) from the Portuguese. It was the centre of the regional pepper trade, and a real prize.

ABOVE:
STAYING POWER
Only seven when enthroned in 1661, the Kangxi emperor, third ruler of the Manchu dynasty, was ultimately to reign for 61 years. He is celebrated for the prosperity and peace he brought to China, but also for his military victories over the Russians and the Dzunghar Mongols.

ABOVE:
PRIZED PORCELAIN
The Ming dynasty is especially celebrated for the excellence of its ceramic art; for breathtaking pieces like the ewer here. Its elegant curves, with pear-shaped body and slender neck, are shown off to thrilling advantage by the bravura of its glazing in cobalt blue and gold.

church music and whose keyboard works would form a foundation for the later piano repertoire. With his fellow-German George Frideric Handel (1685–1759) and their Italian contemporary Antonio Vivaldi (1678–1741), he is seen as an originator of 'Baroque' music.

TREMORS

The year 1722 was the end of an era in China, where the Kangxi emperor died. He'd been the most illustrious ruler of the Qing dynasty. It was the end of an era in Iran as well, an Afghan invasion toppling Soltan Hoseyn and bringing the Safavid Empire to a close.

England had a shock in 1745 when Charles Edward Stuart (or 'Bonnie Prince Charlie') landed in the Scottish islands, hoping to raise an army in the Highlands. His father, son of James II, had pretensions to be Britain's king, hence his nickname of the 'Old Pretender', and Charles's of the 'Young Pretender'. Support for the exiles had remained strong among Scottish 'Jacobites' (from the Latin name for James, *Jacobus*). The question was whether this could translate into a successful rising. For a time, the answer appeared to be 'yes', Prince Charlie's Highlanders taking Perth and Edinburgh. But they waited in vain for a popular insurrection in those cities. Marching out of the city to Prestonpans, they defeated an army sent by the government, then headed south, via Carlisle and Manchester. Again, they weren't successfully stopped, but neither was there any sign of popular support. They got as far as Derby when Charlie's Highland chiefs voted to turn back. Government forces were soon pressing at their heels. On 16 April 1746, they were cornered at Culloden (outside Inverness) and badly defeated. Bonnie Prince Charlie spent several months on the run in the Highlands before a French ship rescued him. The Duke of Cumberland ('Butcher Cumberland') waged a bloody campaign to put down the remaining Jacobites in the Highlands.

Perhaps as many as 40,000 people were killed when, in 1755, the Portuguese capital of Lisbon was largely levelled by a tremendous earthquake. The scale of the tragedy rocked the West – and provoked much moralizing and philosophizing, between those religious fanatics who saw the catastrophe as

PICTURE OF PROSPERITY
A workaday scene, but it was on this humdrum bustle of trade and commerce that the Dutch Golden Age was being built. Contacts are being made and business done. At right, by the river, in Johannes Lingelbach's painting, is the weigh-house for the market; a splendid city hall is under construction to the left.

ABOVE:
BACH'S BARS
The 'Gavotte' from French Suite No. 5 in the original manuscript of Johann Sebastian Bach, among the greatest composers of all time. But also a composer of his own time: Bach's career saw him serve as *Konzertmeister* at Weimar's ducal court and as *Cantor* and *Kapellmeister* at a succession of prestigious Lutheran churches in prosperous German cities, the patrons for his famous choral works.

OPPOSITE:
SOUTH SEA BUBBLE
After the bursting of the 'South Sea Bubble', London's pamphlet press bought stock in *Schadenfreude*. But the ruin of thousands of the country's wealthiest families inevitably had consequences for the economy as a whole, which was badly damaged in both the short and longer term.

God's punishment for a sinful world and those freethinkers who felt it discredited the whole idea of God as a caring creator.

Almost as shocking, in England at least, was the episode of the 'Black Hole of Calcutta', which took place the following year. Soldiers serving Siraj ud-Daulah, nawab or ruler of Bengal, having captured the East India Company's Fort William in what is now Kolkata, India, crammed up to 146 prisoners into a tiny dungeon. Many British and Indian soldiers and civilians suffocated and died. Reported by an outraged British press, the episode helped reinforce assumptions that India's 'natives' were essentially 'savage' and Britain's colonial project in the subcontinent a 'civilizing' one.

A more convincing claim to a civilizing role might have been made by the Society of Jesus, who'd worked hard to protect indigenous communities from the depredations of the settlers. Committed, strong and independent-minded, they had always taken their duties as missionaries very seriously – even when these clashed with what the colonial authorities might have wanted. Accused of fomenting rebellion, the Jesuits had been expelled from the Portuguese territories of Brazil, Angola and Mozambique (1760); seven years later, they'd been expelled from Spanish America as well.

TO THE VICTOR THE SPOILS

It was, accordingly, a cause for great rejoicing in England in 1757 when news came through of Robert Clive's army defeating the French at the Battle of Plassey. This victory effectively broke the power of the French in India. Within four years their headquarters at Pondichéry (Pondicherry) would be taken.

By this time, Anglo-French colonial competition in what are now the USA and Canada had spiralled into serious conflict: many Native American peoples joined the 'French and Indian War' (1754–63) on either side. Not only this, but as the

AGE OF REASON

The Bubblers Mirrour, or Englands Folly.

OPPOSITE:
COFFEE AND COMMERCE
Coffee came to England in the middle of the seventeenth century. The first coffee houses were opened not long after. They were popular in promoting an atmosphere of conversation and conviviality without the inflammatory impacts of alcohol. As places where ideas could be exchanged, they quickly became key to intellectual life. And to business, the origin of the modern stock exchange.

ABOVE:
BATTLE OF CULLODEN (1745)
Heroes cut down by red-coated villains. The iconic status of the '45 says much about how even the most educated of us can end up reading history, finding narratives of inspiration in grim realities, romance in realpolitik. Whatever they may have told themselves, Scotland's gallant clans were fighting for Stuart absolutism – and helping France's Louis XIV make mischief for his English enemy.

conflict widened into what is known as the 'Seven Years' War' (1756–63), it swept up most of Europe's other countries. It had expanded to encompass theatres not only in Europe but also in West Africa, Latin America, India and the Philippines. Britain's main ally had been Prussia, becoming an important military power under the despotic Frederick the Great; France's were Austria, Spain and (for a while) Russia. The result was close, but Britain and Prussia came out on top.

SEEING THE LIGHT

France could on the other hand claim to have brought the world into the modern age. Begun in 1751, the *Encyclopédie* ('Encyclopaedia') eventually ran to 28 volumes and was completed in 1772. Whether it actually contained all knowledge didn't really matter: the important thing was that it saw all knowledge as being available to science and logic and consequently recordable in books.

Led by Denis Diderot, the Encyclopédistes – the group of writers who'd produced this work – had wished to rid the world of mumbo-jumbo in all its forms. And France was full of mumbo-jumbo, they believed. Between the Church, with its spirituality of superstition, and the monarchic state – reactionary and repressive – this had meant a denial of freedom and all possibility of progress.

Their fellow-*philosophes* ('intellectuals') agreed. 'Man was born free,' Jean-Jacques Rousseau (1712–78) had written, 'but is everywhere in chains'. Chains, he didn't have to add, of his own forging. '*Écrasez l'infâme*' – 'obliterate the infamy' – wrote François-Marie Arouet (1694–1778), better known as 'Voltaire'.

There had been others elsewhere … In Scotland the philosopher David Hume (1711–76), and Adam Smith (c. 1723–90), who had pretty much inaugurated economics as something like a science. In England, along with scientists like Isaac Newton, there'd been philosophers like John Locke

AGE OF REASON

(1632–1704), who had tried to put regular thinking on a more scientific footing.

Locke argued for empiricism – the view that we could only know what we could perceive with our senses. In England, too, the early feminist Mary Wollstonecraft (1759–97) had appealed to reason to back her view that women were rational beings and should be educated as such. In Germany, Immanuel Kant (1724–1804) had (in his *Critique of Pure Reason*, 1781) argued that, while we could indeed only know what we could perceive through our senses, our imagination played a part in our perceptions.

There's no real doubt, though, that it was in France that the Enlightenment not only attained its greatest height but became most obviously identified as an attitude to life.

RIGHT:
A NEW WAY OF THINKING
'Out of the crooked timber of humanity, no straight thing was ever made.' Immanuel Kant opened the door to Romantic ideas of subjectivity by calling into question our capacity to perceive our world in a purely objective way. Reason could only be as reliable as the individual doing the reasoning; science was limited by human limitations. Our perceptions help to shape the world we see.

BELOW:
AN ORDERLY COMMERCE
Savi, Benin, was one of several centres for the slave trade in the eighteenth century. The 'factory' here has separate compounds for French, Portuguese and English traders. Savi had been capital of the Kingdom of Whydah till its conquest by Dahomey in 1727. Over a million enslaved Africans would be shipped to the Americas from this and nearby ports.

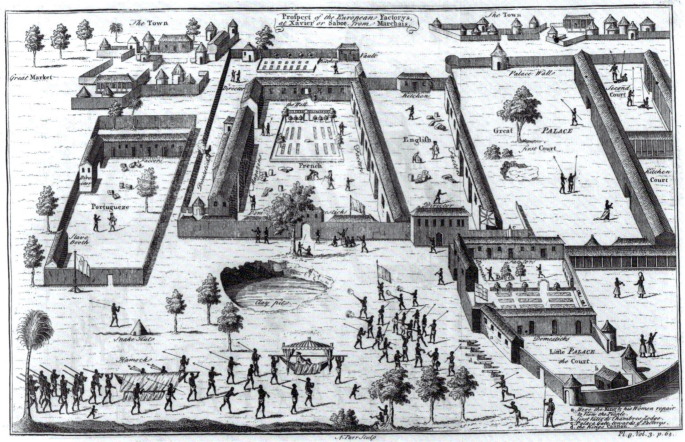

AGE OF REASON

LEFT:
NOT JUST A BOOK …
The *Encylopédie* was a revolution in its own right. Big as it was, it was less about the content than the intellectual approach; the empowerment it represented for the thinking individual. Diderot wanted people to have access to learning. As important, he wanted that access unmediated by the Church and its related institutions – so a secular equivalent to Luther's vernacular scriptures.

THE RUSSIAN VERSAILLES
Peter the Great had Peterhof Palace built in the early eighteenth century as his official residence outside St Petersburg. It was directly inspired by the Palace of Versailles. His plans for a relatively modest country house were scrapped after a visit to France in 1717 revealed to him the sort of splendour in which an eighteenth-century despot could expect to live.

CONQUEST AND REVOLUTION
1760 – 1850

Among the most important sponsors of Diderot and his *Encyclopédie* was the Russian Empress Catherine II, 'the Great' (1729–96). More genuinely interested in ideas than Peter I had ever been, Catherine shared her predecessor's ruthless streak and seized power from her weak and stupid husband Peter III (1728–62). The last straw was his capitulation to Frederick the Great's Prussia in 1762 in negotiations around the ending of the Seven Years' War.

CATHERINE THE CRUEL
Personally abusive, sometimes violent, Catherine was comfortable with the most savage corporal punishment, though enlightened in her rejection of the death penalty, for any crimes. But she didn't flinch from going to war. Her main duty, as she saw it, was the protection and expansion of Russia's territory. In this she was successful. She extended the Empire to encompass Crimea, much of

OPPOSITE:
SILK AND STEEL
'The Sovereign is absolute,' said Catherine II of Russia, unabashedly despotic in her rule. But in unexpected ways enlightened – and generally more complex, even contradictory, than her forthright manner might have led observers to believe.

RIGHT:
THE CHARGE OF THE MAMLUKS
No longer the slave-soldiers of the Middle Ages, the Mamluks were now an elite unit of France's Imperial Guard. As Goya's (1746–1828) famous painting shows, they had intimidating associations of oriental barbarity for European populations, especially that of a post-*Reconquista* Spain.

the Caucasus, White Russia (Belarus), Lithuania and parts of Ukraine.

It was partly to colonize these new territories that Catherine established the so-called 'Pale of Settlement'. Russia's Jews were relocated there and no longer allowed to live or trade in areas outside. Not just prisoners, they were hopelessly restricted in their economic possibilities. They made what they could of a life in impoverished *shtetls* or small towns.

Catherine showed more concern for the welfare of Russia-proper, setting up banks and finance houses to boost a tottering economy. She also undertook programmes of public health. Leading by example, in 1768 she had an English doctor, Thomas Dimsdale (1712–1800), inoculate her against smallpox – this pioneering treatment involved giving the patient the disease in

LEFT:
PROPHET OF ROMANTICISM
'Man was born free, but is everywhere in chains.' Jean-Jacques Rousseau (1712–78) saw civilization as inherently repressive; law and convention as corrupting humanity's natural nobility and virtue.

BELOW:
A COLLISION OF CULTURES
'Discovery' came at a cost – at times to the explorers, as Captain Cook found here. More often – and more enduringly – to the indigenous peoples who found their homelands 'explored' and, thereafter, were subjected to centuries of colonial exploitation and oppression.

ABOVE:
A POLISH PATRIOT
In 1794, Tadeusz Kosciuszko (seen reading, swearing his commitment; 1746–1817), led an uprising to free the Polish–Lithuanian Commonwealth from Russian control. Though unsuccessful, his rebellion inspired a wider world which had fallen in love with the ideal of freedom but grown discouraged by France's Reign of Terror.

one of its mildest strains. It was still risky: not till 1796 would another English doctor, Edward Jenner (1749–1823), find a way of vaccinating against smallpox by dosing with milder cowpox.

SCIENTIFIC ENDEAVOURS

In 1766, the French navigator Louis-Antoine de Bougainville (1729–1811) set out from Nantes to circumnavigate the globe. His was a scientific expedition. With him was the botanist Philibert Commerçon (whose valet turned out to be a woman in disguise: Jeanne Barret, the first woman known to have sailed around the world). They stopped at Tahiti, the Tuamotus and Samoa.

The South Pacific was the scene of a sort of 'space race' at this time. Trailing Bougainville by just two years, Captain James Cook (1728–79) of Britain's Royal Navy sailed the HMS *Endeavour* to the South Pacific in 1788. With him were scientists hoping to observe a forthcoming Transit of Venus (the passage of the planet across the face of the Sun) which was going to be most clearly visible from there. This first voyage took the *Endeavour* round Cape Horn to the Pacific and on to Tahiti. Here the expedition's scientific leader Joseph Banks oversaw the recording of astronomical observations.

Meanwhile its artists (notably Sydney Parkinson; c. 1745–1771) recorded the ways of the Pacific Islanders, while botanist Daniel Solander (1733–82) collected a wealth of undiscovered plants. They sailed south to New Zealand before heading west to Australia, landing at what Cook called 'Botany Bay' for the richness of the specimens it afforded Solander.

CONQUEST AND REVOLUTION

The *Endeavour* then rounded the Northern Cape and passed through the Torres Strait to New Guinea and Indonesia.

It returned to England in 1771. Along with a shipload of specimens, Banks had brought back a young Polynesian man named Omai. The scientist hoped to study the effects of civilization on the 'primitive' mind. Instead, Omai became an exhibit, though fashionable London was full of admiration for his 'natural' grace and courtesy. People were well primed by their reading in Rousseau, who had lamented 'civilized' humanity's corruption by its own conventions, contrasting it with the pure-heartedness of the 'noble savage'.

THE LAND THAT NEVER WAS

In 1772, Cook led a second voyage, this time commanding HMS *Resolution* and accompanied by a second ship, the aptly named *Adventure*. The expedition was charged with trying to find *Terra Australis* – not Australia but an as yet undiscovered southern continent whose existence had been proposed since ancient times. The desire to find this land was based on the entirely theoretical grounds that it would somehow 'balance out' the vast landmasses of the northern hemisphere.

They didn't find it, of course – though they would have found Antarctica if they'd ventured even a little further (Cook did discover South Georgia and the South Sandwich Islands). That cold wasteland was not quite what the *Terra Australis* tradition had anticipated, though.

THIRD TIME UNLUCKY

Omai went with Captain Cook on his third voyage, to be returned home. The trip began in 1776 and was intended to make further explorations in the Pacific. Cook discovered Hawaii before striking north along the western coast of North America, including Oregon, Washington and British Columbia. Putting in at Nootka Sound, Vancouver Island, Cook and his crew spent time with the local people before pushing on to Alaska and the Bering Strait.

OPPOSITE:
GUNNED DOWN
An atrocity in itself, the 'Boston Massacre' (1770) was still more momentous in its symbolism, making it clear to the colonists where they stood in the British hierarchy of respect.

BELOW:
VACCINATION ANXIETIES
Cows erupt from the arms of country people after Edward Jenner has vaccinated them with cowpox. James Gillray's (1756–1815) cartoon (1802) seems smugly supercilious now, but the popular fears he mocks weren't wholly bogus. Few felt comfortable about willingly contracting a disease.

CONQUEST AND REVOLUTION

RIGHT:
GEORGE AND THE GENIUS
An eight-year-old Wolfgang Amadeus Mozart (1756–91) performs for Britain's George III (1738–1820), 1764. He'd grow up to be the foremost composer of his age. Poised, elegant and regular, his 800-odd compositions brought the 'classical' music of the late-eighteenth century to its height.

BELOW:
MAN OF THE PEOPLE
'Lay then the axe to the root, and teach governments humanity,' said Thomas Paine (1707–1809) in his influential call to revolutionary arms, *The Rights of Man* (1791). Like Rousseau, he trusted to 'the natural dignity of man'. It was state oppression that turned citizens against each other.

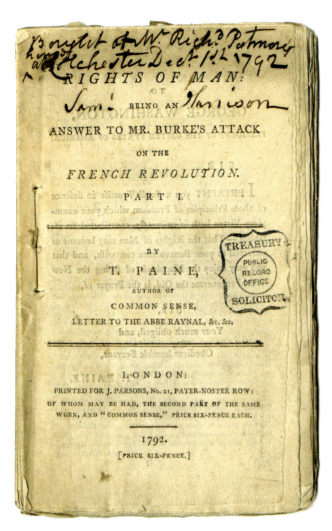

Their goal was to find the fabled Northwest Passage from the 'other' – in other words, the Pacific – side. Navigators had long believed (or hoped) that there might be a way around the 'top' of North America to the Pacific, avoiding the storm-whipped waters off Cape Horn. (There was, of course: it just happened to be snow- and icebound and extremely dangerous, as too many explorers were to find.)

Having no success, Cook headed back south to Hawaiian waters, finally putting in to rest at Kealakekua Bay in January 1779. Here, on 14 February, Cook clashed with a group of local warriors. He was killed, in confused circumstances, on the beach.

First and foremost, Cook's explorations make an exciting and colourful story but they also show the Enlightenment working itself out in real time. Old superstitions – like those of *Terra Australis* and the Northwest Passage – were being debunked. Even if newer ones, like that of the 'noble savage', were becoming established in their place.

THE INCAS AGAIN

'Noble' or not, those descendants of the Incas still living under Spanish rule in Peru were increasingly angry, as a string of insurrections showed. They resented being conscripted for labour by the authorities and being overtaxed. In 1781, however, they fell under the spell of the charismatic leader named José Gabriel Condorcanqui (1738–81).

OPPOSITE:
FOUNDING PRINCIPLES
'Life, Liberty, and the pursuit of happiness,' said the Declaration of Independence, were the 'inalienable rights' of every individual. Government existed only to protect these rights. America saw itself as a utopia of freedom, though its slaves would surely have seen things differently.

Or, rather, as he called himself, Túpac Amaru II, claiming descent from the last Inca king, who'd risen unsuccessfully against the Spanish in 1532. Túpac promised to rebuild the old Inca Empire. He undoubtedly gave the Spanish a scare but his rebellion was put down and he was pulled apart by four horses – one lashed to each limb – in Cuzco's city square.

AMERICA UP IN ARMS

Of more lasting significance was the revolt of the Thirteen Colonies Britain now had on North America's Eastern Seaboard, from Massachusetts all the way down to Georgia. It had become clear to the colonists that Britain needed them more than they needed Britain. By the 1740s, they had taken 25 per cent of Britain's export trade. The government taxed them on everything from sugar to printed publications, claiming the revenues were needed for their governance and defence.

The colonists had no voice in these matters. Even so, their tax burden rose through the early reign of George III (1760–1820). Boycotts failed. When one was tried in Boston in 1765, the British sent troops in to occupy the city. When, in 1770, passers-by jeered and threw stones at British soldiers in the street, the 'Redcoats' opened fire and five colonists were killed.

In 1773, the British introduced a tax on tea in America. At that year's 'Boston Tea Party', when a group of colonists dressed as Native Americans stormed a ship in Boston harbour and tossed its cargo of tea overboard, it was to shouts of 'No taxation without representation!'

Generalized anger found a focus in the *Pennsylvania Magazine*, published by the English radical Thomas 'Tom' Paine. Falling foul of the authorities at home, he'd come out to Philadelphia where, however, he'd continued to speak out against what he saw as an oppressive British state. (The book he's best remembered for, *The Rights of Man*, would not appear until 1791, but he was busily agitating all this time.) It was in Philadelphia that, in 1775, the colonists asserted their rights at the First Continental Congress. Instead they got the 'Intolerable Acts', restricting their freedoms further.

A REVOLUTIONARY WAR

The settlers had long organized militias to defend against Native American attack. These now formed a ready-made 'Continental Army'. Led by George Washington (1732–99), they besieged Boston. General Howe's attack at Bunker Hill (17 June) brought a British victory – but failed to stop the siege. The city was taken in March 1776, and on 4 July the Second Continental Congress issued the United States Declaration of Independence. ('We hold these truths to be self-evident, that all men are created equal …')

RIGHT:
COURAGE AND COMMITMENT
George Washington's crossing of the Delaware already had its place in the founding mythology of the USA when Emanuel Leutze (1816–68) came to represent it in 1851. But this exhilaratingly iconic painting seemed to sum up the spirit of the American Revolution.

By September, though, General Washington had lost New York and had to retreat in haste through New Jersey and escape across the Delaware River. The celebrated 'Crossing of the Delaware' was undertaken on Christmas night. However, Washington subsequently returned to capture a force of German mercenaries fighting for the British at Trenton, New Jersey. He followed through by defeating Lord Cornwallis's (1738–1805) English army at Princeton.

The following summer saw a succession of victories culminating in a crucial one at Saratoga on 7 October.

THE FRENCH CONNECTION

Louis XVI of France (1754–93) offered his assistance. Any British discomfiture suited him. Despite his help, and that of idealistic French volunteers like Gilbert du Motier, the Marquis of Lafayette (1757–1834), they were soon on the back foot again. The British regrouped and took their capital, Philadelphia, in September 1777. Washington and his (now much reduced) Continental Army hunkered down for a grim winter at Valley Forge. Britain was losing focus, though. Washington broke his army back up into smaller militia-type detachments and Generals Clinton (1730–95) and Cornwallis became bogged down in a guerrilla war. Finally, Cornwallis was ordered to retreat to the coast and fortify a base for a Royal Navy rescue force. He withdrew to Yorktown, Virginia, on Chesapeake Bay.

Cornwallis's withdrawal had been orderly; he felt no undue alarm. But his commander Clinton wasn't so much confident as complacent. Assuming his comrade was secure against what seemed a very small besieging army, led by Lafayette, he left him to fend for himself.

But the rebels had reinforcements ready. Not just further colonists, but a French force led by the Comte de Rochambeau (1725–1807), just landed at Rhode Island. France's Caribbean fleet was headed up the coast in their support. Emboldened, the rebels marched down from New England as if to attack New York, then swerved around that city and continued south. Soon, with Lafayette's army, there were almost 17,000 men around Yorktown, pounding it relentlessly with heavy guns.

IGNOMINY … AND INDEPENDENCE

Even now, Cornwallis expected support. The Royal Navy was on its way, indeed. But France's warships were waiting for it when it arrived. Battle was joined just outside the bay on 5 September.

BELOW:
VIRGIN TERRITORY
Better known now as Sydney Harbour, Port Jackson was named by Cook in honour of George Jackson, a Lord Commissioner of the Royal Navy. European explorers saw the realms they were 'discovering' as empty, blank, unmapped, unknown. Indigenous cultures were effectively invisible to them.

LEFT:
FROM IDEALISM TO ACTION
The traffic in revolutionary thought that took place between France and England's American colonies was personified by Gilbert du Motier, the Marquis de Lafayette. Schooled in the radical thought of France, he'd been tried in the fire of America's Revolutionary War before coming home to help lead the overthrow of the French monarchy.

It was a scatty affair, both fleets being short-crewed, while sandbanks hampered the formation of lines. The outcome was inconclusive – but that didn't matter to the French, or the Americans. The British fleet was forced to continue north. Cornwallis, marooned with his men, under ferocious bombardment, had no alternative but to surrender. The American War of Independence had been won.

The details still had to be thrashed out. Many would have to wait for the Constitutional Convention of 1787. And even then some would prove intractable. Slavery was a sticking point – and not just in the South, though that part of the country was most reliant on slave labour: the freedom to own slaves was a big part of what many felt they'd fought for. Thomas Jefferson (1743–1826), main author of the Declaration of Independence, was a slaveowner; so was Washington, leader of the fight for 'freedom'.

Tom Paine still denounced as 'wickedness' the trade in 'MEN (an unnatural commodity!)', but he was increasingly distrusted as a firebrand. Many of the 'revolutionaries' were damping down their rhetoric – and Americans' expectations. No one asked the slaves (though many had implied a position by fighting for the British in the recent war). As in ancient Athens, slaves weren't citizens – any more than women were.

OFF WITH THE OLD …

Nothing if not persistent, Britain was starting on its 'second empire'. In 1788, the first shipload of convicts arrived in Botany Bay, where a penal colony was to be established. It got off to a difficult start: despite the name that Cook had given it, the soil here was far from fertile, there was little water and the trees were too hard for felling. A new site was chosen at Sydney Cove. The modern city started here: as – despite the presence across the continent of so many Aboriginals – did what became the modern nation of Australia.

It was long a place of sadness. Not just for its dispossessed indigenous inhabitants but for the 'colonists' – who of course weren't there by choice. 'My dear wife', wrote one transported man: 'belive my hart is almost broken to think I must lave you behind …' But for a British state beset by urban crime on the one hand and agrarian unrest on the other – especially in Ireland – the system was a crucial safety valve.

NEW NATION, NEW TOWN

By now, a New Town was being built in Edinburgh. The project was driven by a desire to catch what optimism there was following on from the Acts of Union and to will it into existence where it couldn't be found. Scotland, Union supporters said, had contributed disproportionately to the Enlightenment precisely because it had a place in the Union. Initial plans to lay the new development out in the shape of the UK's 'Union Jack' flag proved impractically complicated, but the simplified version was still beautiful and imposing.

Edinburgh's New Town is up there with Bath, now a prestigious spa and social hub, as an example of 'Georgian' architecture – classical in conception, serene in style. The late-eighteenth and early nineteenth centuries would see a succession of King Georges. The period was a high point for culture and creativity, but it's for its architecture that it's best remembered now.

OPPOSITE:
FUN FOR THE FEW
Fragonard's (1732–1806) famous 1767 painting *The Swing* evokes both the beauty and the decadence of the life available to the tiniest elite under France's *Ancien Régime*. Meanwhile, the masses were afflicted by mounting poverty and famine – and growing steadily in anger, year by year.

RIGHT:
TAKING THE CAKE
Seen here walking in woods at Versailles with two of her children, Marie Antoinette (1755–93) lived far removed from the realities of eighteenth-century France. She wasn't actually uncaring, though: there's no truth in the story that, told that the starving poor could get no bread, she responded 'Let them eat cake'.

CONQUEST AND REVOLUTION

CONQUEST AND REVOLUTION

ABOVE:
'OUR CAUSE IS JUST'
'The God who gave us life, gave us liberty at the same time.' Thomas Jefferson embodied all the highest principles of America's 'Founding Fathers' – and shared the blind spot several had when it came to owning slaves.

LEFT:
THE STORMING OF THE BASTILLE
The events of the French Revolution rolled themselves out over several months. But if we had to choose a snapshot moment when (as the cliché has it) 'history was made', it would have to be the Storming of the Bastille on 14 July 1789.

THE KING AND THE PEOPLE

The radical ideas of intellectuals don't necessarily represent the thinking of the people. So it was with France's *philosophes* and their critique of the *Ancien Régime* ('Old Order'). As the century wore on, though, discontent had risen steadily among a populace bled dry by taxes and afflicted by crop failures and famine. Despite the burdens it was placing on its people, meanwhile, the Crown was facing bankruptcy.

Not surprisingly, given the extravagance with which the royals lived in Paris and Versailles – we get a glimpse of this in the famous paintings of Jean-Honoré Fragonard. And see the splendour of Versailles to this day – including, decadently, the picturesque country village Marie Antoinette had built specially so she could play at being a humble shepherdess.

In May 1789, his financial crisis forced the king to call his 'Estates General' – a legislative assembly his absolutist predecessors had preferred to do without. Its three 'estates' were the nobility, the clergy and the 'commoners'. Their deputies were summoned to Versailles to approve Louis' emergency measures.

CONQUEST AND REVOLUTION

LEFT:
UNCONQUERABLE
'Thou hast great allies:/Thy friends are exultations, agonies,/And love, and Man's unconquerable mind.' As the English poet William Wordsworth (1770–1850) appreciated, revolutionary leader Toussaint Louverture (1743–1803) was exemplary even in defeat; a new kind of underdog-hero for the Romantic age.

OPPOSITE ABOVE:
COLONIAL CRITIC
A teenage crewman of Captain Cook, George Vancouver (1757–98) grew up to continue his explorations – notably up North America's northwestern coast. Quicker than most of his countrymen in appreciating the evils attending colonialism, he took pains to establish good relations with indigenous peoples.

OPPOSITE BELOW:
MONARCHY NO MORE
On 21 January 1793 Louis XVI goes to the guillotine set up permanently in the Place de la Révolution (now Place de la Concorde). The blade drops, neatly severing his neck, and the executioner holds his royal head up to the jeering crowd.

The king gave elaborate welcomes to the First and Second but snubbed the Third. The deputies of the Third Estate occupied the assembly hall, inviting the others to join them there. The aristocrats, and the more conservative clergy, refused; the others came along. Weeks went by in stalemate; no legislation could be passed in all this chaos.

THE MONARCHY IN MELTDOWN

On 14 July 1789, a long, hot summer of rioting in Paris culminated in the Storming of the Bastille – the fortress in which political prisoners were kept. The ordinary soldiers refusing to put down the rebellion, but rather joining their brothers and sisters on the streets, Louis XVI's authority collapsed.

That year's 'August Decrees' abolished the hereditary privileges of the nobility – including their feudal rights over their peasantry. Drafted by Lafayette and friends (including Thomas Jefferson, one of America's 'Founding Fathers'), the Declaration of the Rights of Man and of the Citizen offered equality to every citizen under the law. In October, a women's protest march made its way out to the Palace of Versailles and demanded that the royal family return with them to Paris. Whether fearful or conciliatory, the king agreed.

RIPPLES OF REVOLUTION

News of France's revolution quickly travelled around the world, causing consternation in some places and exultation in others. Saint-Domingue (Haiti) fell into the latter category. There, a freed slave, Toussaint Louverture, led a slave revolt that turned into a wholesale revolution. A complex figure, Louverture had for a time owned slaves himself and on occasion allied with the French against rival campaigners for his cause. (In the end, he would be captured on Napoleon's orders in 1802 and die

in a French prison the following year, but he's known today as 'Father of Haiti'.)

France itself was ambivalent. Here, as in America, some were reining in their liberationist rhetoric. *Liberté, égalité, fraternité* (Liberty, Equality, Fraternity or Brotherhood) didn't extend to the enslaved. All were concerned at the shortages of commodities the Haitian unrest had caused and the renewed disorder this was causing on the streets of France's cities. (France would eventually get round to abolishing slavery in 1794.)

THE KING ON TRIAL

Even now, the country remained a monarchy, though Louis and his queen, Marie Antoinette, were effectively imprisoned in their Paris residence, the Tuileries Palace. In June 1791, the royal family tried to slip out by night and escape to safety but were recognized and forced to return.

France faced foreign enemies. In February 1792, Austria and Prussia agreed to intervene to protect the French monarchy. Their forces would be defeated that September at the Battle of Valmy. In August, though, fearing the gains of the Revolution might be snatched away, the radicals had stormed the Tuileries Palace and arrested the king. A National Convention replaced the Estates General as the new Republic's legislative assembly. That December, Louis XVI was tried for 'conspiracy against public liberty' and condemned to death. In January 1793, he was taken to the guillotine. Marie Antoinette followed him a few months later.

CONQUEST AND REVOLUTION

CONQUEST AND REVOLUTION

ABOVE:
POETIC JUSTICE
An architect of the Terror, Georges Danton (1759–94) drove the September Massacres of 1792, in which over a thousand political opponents were summarily executed. Ironically, it was when he tried to rein in the violence that he was denounced as a traitor and sent to the guillotine himself.

LEFT:
ROBESPIERRE OVERTHROWN
On 4 June 1794, Robespierre was unanimously elected President of the National Convention. Over a thousand were sent to the guillotine in the weeks that followed. Former supporters turned against him and on 27 July the same National Convention which had elected him had him arrested and sentenced to death.

TERROR IN CHARGE

They were only the most famous of the more than 40,000 men and women who were to go to their deaths on the orders of the Revolutionary Tribunals. Radical leaders like Jean-Paul Marat (1743–93) and Maximilien Robespierre (1758–94) sought to galvanize the rage of the country's *sans-culottes* – literally, 'without breeches': the ragged poor who felt they had nothing to lose if France collapsed, and much to gain.

Faction fighting flared, the 'Girondins' supporting the Revolution but deploring the 'Reign of Terror' which the more radically republican 'Jacobins' had introduced under the auspices of the ironically named 'Committee of Public Safety'. A certain amount of 'radical chic' posturing went on, the Jacobins often cutting their hair short in the style of (Republican) Roman busts.

But this tribalism could be more serious: Marat's assassination (in his bath) by the Girondin-leaning Charlotte Corday in 1793 showed how quickly things were spinning out of control.

As Robespierre increased his influence, even sometime-supporters were alarmed at the extent of his ambition to obliterate the old world and build a new one. A Republican Calendar took as its start date the proclamation of the French Republic in September 1792. The months were renamed to rid them of any religious or royal associations. There were still 12, but they had 10-day 'weeks' (with 10-hour days). Robespierre even reinvented religion, replacing the Church with a cult of the 'Supreme Being'. Notre Dame Cathedral was renamed

LEFT:
ABOLITIONIST EMBLEM
Josiah Wedgwood's (1730–95) factories made this ceramic medallion in the 1790s. It was worn to show abolitionist support. The slave's kneeling posture and pleading manner seem too meek to many nowadays, but reassured the well-meaning white middle-class consumers at whom the medallion was aimed.

BELOW:
MUTUAL INCOMPREHENSION
As far as Captain James Wilson and these Protestant missionaries were concerned, the ornate speeches of the Tahitian priests marked their acceptance of British authority – political and spiritual. The priests appear to have believed they were just welcoming foreign visitors.

LEFT:
THE SPINNING JENNY
Invented in the 1760s, Hargreaves' 'spinning jenny' was just one of a series of innovations which were making textile manufacture more productive at this time. This early version was driven by hand: the real gains of the 'Industrial Revolution' came when machines like this were progressively adapted to steam power.

the 'Temple of Reason'. By July 1794, powerful people in the Revolution felt they'd seen enough. Robespierre himself was sent to the guillotine.

COLONIAL CONTINUITIES

Developments in France would reverberate for quite a while. In the meantime, though, life went on around the world. Colonial conquest (and reactions to it) were a common theme. In 1790, the captain of the American trading vessel *Eleanora* quarrelled with a Hawaiian community, called them out in their canoes to meet him, then opened up with his cannon, killing around a hundred. That same year, US soldiers backing settlers in what is now Indiana were defeated by an 'Indian Confederacy' led by Miami and Shawnee fighters.

The 'voyages of discovery' went on. In 1792, Captain George Vancouver sailed up Puget Sound, claiming it for Britain. That same year saw the establishment of a 'Province of Freedom' in Sierra Leone. This was a settlement for freed slaves from America, sponsored by Britain as a reward for their support during the War of Independence. To local tribes, though, their new neighbours were outsiders, colonists: they launched repeated raids, and the settlement struggled to survive.

In 1793, George, Earl Macartney was sent to China by the British to discuss possible trading links. His refusal to 'kowtow' to the Emperor Qianlong (1711–99) – this involved showing obeisance by kneeling and repeatedly striking the forehead against the floor – saw him sent on his way empty-handed. If the Englishman's response was arrogant, the emperor's demands were unrealistic if China hoped to have successful relations with the outside world.

Elsewhere, colonialism was being resisted widely, though by no means always successfully. The Hawkesbury and Nepean Wars (1794–1816), fought between local Aboriginals and English settlers and soldiers in the Australian interior, west of Sydney, ended with the indigenous population being dispossessed. This was of course to be the general trend, though at the Battle of Fallen Timbers, in northwest Ohio, in 1794, local tribes defeated US Army troops.

Western rule didn't have to be imposed by force. The presence of English missionaries in Tahiti from 1797 would see its people lose their independence even if it saved their souls. But much of the time, military force was used. Since the 1760s, the British had fought a series of wars against the southern Indian Sultanate of Mysore. The Fourth Anglo-Mysore War, in 1798–9, brought victory to the British and strengthened the hold of the East India Company on the subcontinent.

THE ADVENT OF INDUSTRIALISM

Having an overseas empire gave Great Britain great prestige, but it wasn't just 'bragging rights' that were at stake. It was increasingly important for the country to have access to raw materials for its industry and markets for its manufactured goods.

The 'Industrial Revolution' had been under way for some time now. It had gathered momentum slowly since, in 1709, at Coalbrookdale, Shropshire, Abraham Darby had built a coke-fired blast furnace for making iron. Three years later, Thomas

CONQUEST AND REVOLUTION

Newcomen (1664–1729) had invented an early steam engine, used to pump water from flooded coal mines.

These early breakthroughs had fostered further developments. From 1764, James Hargreaves' (1721–78) 'Spinning Jenny' had been winding raw cotton into usable yarn. James Watt's (1736–1819) steam engine of 1776 was a vast improvement on Newcomen's. As important as Samuel Crompton's (1753–1827) Spinning Mule (1779) was, Richard Arkwright's (1732–92) introduction of the whole factory system, using steam power to drive spinning and weaving equipment (like Edmund Cartwright's power loom) was more vital still.

There was always a cost, of course, each new technology rendering previously important skills redundant. Hence the protests of the 'Luddites' as the industrialization of textile manufacture took hold in earnest in the new century. In a spate of attacks from 1811, they broke into factories and smashed the machines. Named after Ned Ludd, the (quite possibly mythical) hand-weaver who had started the craze, they feared the new technology was destroying jobs.

STOPPING THE SLAVE TRADE

Cotton was brought from India or, increasingly, from the slave-worked plantations of the American South. The new but rapidly growing urban working class consumed large quantities of slave-grown sugar. All sections of society smoked tobacco and many drank rum. There's no doubt that the Industrial Revolution in Britain was to some extent 'built on slavery', though it's harder to say quite *how* important it was.

Throughout the 1790s, though, an 'abolitionist' movement had been taking shape, led by religious groups like the Quakers, and by individual philanthropists and politicians like William Wilberforce (1759–1833) as well as industrialists like pottery magnate Josiah Wedgwood. In 1807, the Slave Trade Act outlawed the trade in slaves throughout the British Empire. (Though not their ownership, which wouldn't be abolished until 1833.)

BELOW:
RIGHTS AND WRONGS
In 1840, the first World Anti-Slavery Convention was held in London to press for the 'universal extinction' of slavery. Women were admitted only as spectators, a decision which helped to bring attention to other injustices that also needed attending to.

LEFT:
'KING LUDD'
Ned Ludd as the London papers saw him. His floaty gown and headgear obviously 'other' him, underlining his look of Celtic savagery, but may have some hazy roots in real fact. Cross-dressing was a common feature of popular uprisings in many cultures, a coded way of calling for the prevailing order to be overthrown.

As important, the Royal Navy appointed itself policeman of the ban, stopping ships of all nationalities and obstructing the trade throughout the first half of the nineteenth century. By the end of that time slavery had pretty much died out.

REVOLUTIONARY WARS

France's revolutionary regime had always known that the crowned heads of Europe wouldn't like what they had done. They'd already had to see off the Austrians and the Prussians at Valmy. But paranoia suited them. They were unfazed by the formation of a First Coalition against them in 1793, though, with the combined strength of Britain, Austria, Spain, Prussia and the Kingdoms of Sardinia and Naples, it should have been quite scary.

The confidence of the French was justified: the defeat of an Austro-British army at Tourcoing (May 1794) left the First Coalition in disarray and, by 1795, France appeared secure. But war was a way of life now in France; the first resort of a regime which preferred seeking enemies abroad to tackling difficulties at home.

CONQUEST AND REVOLUTION

Despite the distractions, those difficulties hadn't eased. Inherently unstable, France's new democracy see-sawed between mob-rule and tyranny. As the Convention struggled to keep order, its leaders leaned in the latter direction, replacing it with a five-man 'Directory'. This too failed to stay on top of things, in 1795 facing a coup from which it had to be saved by an up-and-coming military officer.

Corsican by birth, Napoleon Bonaparte (1769–1821) had come to prominence as a young artillery commander at the Siege of Toulon (1793), after that city's bid to throw off the Republican government – with British backing. Promoted to

BELOW:
COUNTER-REVOLUTION
In 1793, French Royalists in the southern city of Toulon tried to start a fightback against the revolutionary regime. They had support from British and Spanish forces and might have fared far better had it not been for the courage and quick-wittedness of the young Napoleon Bonaparte.

the rank of general by a grateful Directory, from 1796 he fought a triumphant campaign against Austria in Italy. Austria was brought to terms in 1797, though it was back in the fray the following year as a member (with Britain, Russia, Portugal, Sweden and the Ottoman Empire) of the Second Coalition.

CROPPY BOYS

However much may have divided them, France's kings and revolutionary leaders shared the desire to make any mischief they possibly could for Great Britain. An ideal opportunity presented itself in 1796 when the Society of United Irishmen (formed in 1791) asked for French assistance in overthrowing British rule in Ireland.

They were 'United' in including both Protestants and Catholics – hitherto (as subsequently) a damaging faultline in Irish nationalist politics. It had been assumed (as, again, it would be later), that Protestants had a 'natural' affinity to British rule. But, being mostly more privileged and educated than their Catholic countrymen and -women, they were also more likely to be abreast of the intellectual currents of the time. The United Irishmen's leadership, all Protestants, had been inspired by the example of America, and then of course of France itself,

ABOVE:
'THE FINAL CONCLAVE'
'Shaking scythes at cannon,' in the later poet Seamus Heaney's words, Ireland's peasant rebels were cut down themselves; 'the hillside blushed', saturated with their blood. Defeat at Vinegar Hill brought the United Irishmen's insurrection to a bitter end.

and hoped to overthrow the rule of Britain's Crown in Ireland. Supporters who wore their hair short in emulation of the Jacobins earned Republicans an enduring nickname, 'Croppies'.

A planned French invasion of 1796 was foiled by a storm. This near-miss caught the imagination of the Irish people. By the beginning of 1798, the United Irishmen had 280,000 members. France, by contrast, had started to lose interest.

'SHAKING SCYTHES AT CANNON'

When the rebellion broke out in late May in County Kildare, it became clear that Irishmen weren't really all that united: the response, countrywide, was rather patchy. Whilst the Society was strongest in Ulster and around Dublin, those were also the areas the British had locked down most firmly, so the uprising failed to get off the ground. It fared much better in rural areas, but there the Catholic peasantry had its own agenda: less high-mindedly secular; more interested in local disputes with landlords. Even so, they fought heroically, braving well-armed infantry and mounted militias with only old-fashioned pikes (essentially spikes on poles) and agricultural scythes.

The climax came in June 1798 at Vinegar Hill, in County Wexford, where some 16,000 rebels were defeated, with the loss of around 1,200 lives. It was mopping up thereafter, though a brave campaign of guerrilla warfare continued till the rebellion was finally put down in mid-October. Overall, up to 50,000 rebels and 3,000 soldiers and loyalist civilians had been killed.

IN THE SHADOW OF THE PYRAMIDS

Napoleon had a free hand now. The Directory didn't feel it could challenge him. In 1798, he decided to invade Egypt. The move made sense, in fairness. Though its canal had yet to be built, Suez was already vital to Britain's communications with its Indian empire. So the British supported the Ottoman Turks, Egypt's then-rulers. Whilst the Royal Navy failed to stop the French landing outside Alexandria, the victory of their charismatic admiral, Horatio Nelson (1758–1805), at the Battle of the Nile (August 1798), thwarted their efforts to bring up the reinforcements they needed. In 1799, moreover, British naval gunners helped push the French back at the Siege of Acre, preventing them from conquering Syria. Back in France, by summer 1799 the Directory had fallen out of favour. Napoleon made a quick dash home to take advantage. Appointing himself consul (effectively dictator), he conducted a cosmetic plebiscite to lend the process a democratic air. Returning to Egypt at the end of 1799, he supervised the evacuation of French troops after what hadn't actually been the most successful of campaigns.

Despite his dictator's role, he remained a field commander, leading his reorganized army to dazzling victories at Marengo (1800) and Hohenlinden (1800). In 1802, with Austria once more forced to surrender, Britain agreed its own reluctant peace at Amiens.

RIGHT:
BROODING GENIUS
Ludwig van Beethoven (1770–1827) took 'classical' forms like Mozart's and supercharged them with emotion, bringing music into the Romantic age. His symphonies, piano sonatas and string quartets had an unprecedented intensity; his opera *Fidelio* (1805) was a profoundly powerful call for freedom.

BELOW:
AN EXOTIC ESPRIT
An architectural invasion of England's south coast by the memory of the Mughal emperors or a boastful celebration of British expansionism in India? Brighton's Royal Pavilion can reasonably be seen as both. It was built between 1787 and 1823 as a seaside summer residence by England's King George II.

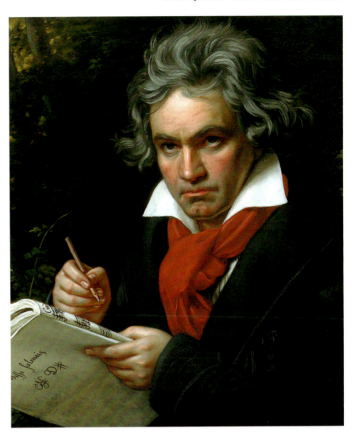

CONQUEST AND REVOLUTION

LEFT:
A HISTORIC MOMENT
'From the heights of these pyramids,' Napoleon had told his men, 'forty centuries look down on us.' They were to witness a crushing French victory over an Ottoman Mamluk force. Only very distantly: it was something of a reach for the French commander to call this 'The Battle of the Pyramids', since they were something like 14 km (9 miles) away.

CONQUEST AND REVOLUTION

RIGHT:
IMPERIAL EGOTIST
No one else was august enough to crown him emperor so Napoleon took on the job himself. The absurdity might have been more amusing had he seemed a little less invincible: not for another decade would he be finally overthrown.

Both sides broke this treaty, the French by interfering in Switzerland, the British by seizing Malta. When a Third Coalition brought Britain into alliance with Austria, Russia, and others, an unperturbed Napoleon crowned himself emperor in December 1804. (This move so disgusted his sometime-admirer, the great German composer Ludwig van Beethoven, that he renamed the 'Bonaparte Symphony' he'd been working on the *Eroica Symphony*.)

AMERICA ENLARGED

The year before, the USA had almost doubled in size at a stroke, without firing a shot, simply by buying 'Louisiana' from the French. President Thomas Jefferson had made the deal: the territory had been a snip at $15 million but the French had been too distracted by their military commitments to care too much.

Jefferson promptly sent out the explorers Meriwether Lewis and William Clark to scout out his purchase. Specifically, they'd sail up the Missouri to its source and seek a convenient route over the Rockies to the Pacific.

ALL AT SEA

Napoleon next decided to invade England, assembling 180,000 troops on France's northern coast. This was almost as many soldiers as the British Army had in total (about 200,000, to France's 2.5 million), but they were useless if they couldn't get across the Channel. The Royal Navy controlled the English Channel so successfully that Napoleon's force was stuck on shore in France.

Sea-power was evidently going to be key to defeating Napoleon, so vast were his armies and so dazzling his generalship. Victory over the French at Finistère in July 1805 and Nelson's triumph a few months later at Trafalgar (tragically, he fell during the battle) ensured that the advantage remained with Britain and its Coalition allies.

Just as well given that, on dry land, Napoleon still appeared invincible. On 2 December 1805, he won his culminating victory (over an Austro-Russian army) at Austerlitz. Austria was again forced out of its coalition. Its armies were too depleted for it to join the Fourth Coalition, now hastily formed by Britain with Prussia, Russia, Saxony and Sweden. Events followed the familiar pattern: Britain won vital victories at sea, but the Coalition was quickly trounced on land. For Prussia, which prided itself on its military prowess, defeat at Jena (October 1806) was a humiliation.

Spain co-operated with France's invasion of Portugal in 1807, allowing Napoleon's army free passage through its

CONQUEST AND REVOLUTION

RIGHT:
CHEAP AT THE PRICE
Napoleon had toyed with the idea of expanding France's colonial presence in North America but finally decided that it mattered more to consolidate the country's power in Europe. As costly as the Louisiana Purchase was for so young a nation as the United States, it was to prove an immeasurably good deal over the longer term.

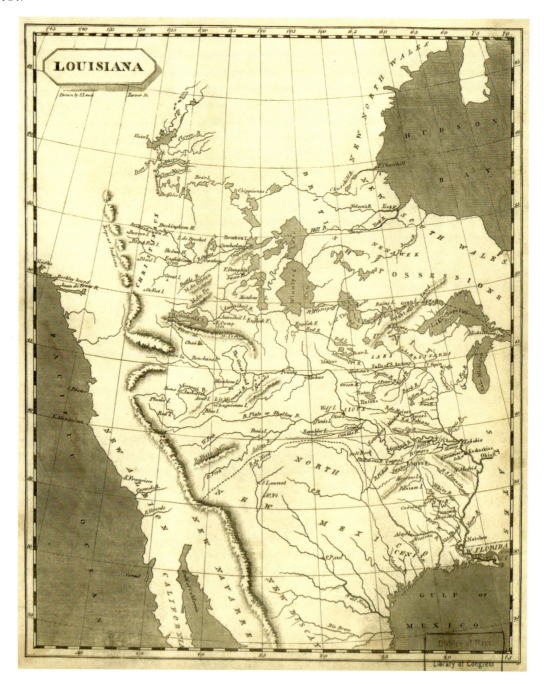

territory. He repaid the favour by occupying Spain itself. The Peninsular War (1807–14) resulted, a long and dirty conflict fought largely by guerrillas on the Spanish side, with help from British forces. (The ugliness of this struggle was unforgettably captured in Francisco de Goya's etching series *The Disasters of War* – not just a historical revelation but, in its searing truthfulness, an artistic breakthrough.)

In May 1809, Britain's Arthur Wellesley (1769–1852; later the Duke of Wellington) expelled the French from Portugal at the Battle of Grijó. It was by no means a rout, however. Indeed, a lengthy stalemate ensued. Britain's attempt to open a second front in Central Europe in a Fifth Coalition with Austria failed in the face of now-familiar defeats.

THE TIDE TURNS

The year 1812 was a turning-point. Wellesley was already back on the offensive in Iberia when Napoleon invaded Russia in June that year with the greatest invasion force so far seen. But the lack of roads and an already overstretched supply line were already posing problems a few days in. In the heat and rain of the Baltic summer, the going was swampy, the atmosphere unhealthy: thousands of men were sick with flu.

By the time Napoleon's troops reached Smolensk on 16 August, they were long past the point at which Napoleon had assumed the czar would sue for peace. Rationally, this might have been the obvious course for Alexander I to take. Instead, the Russians sat back and took their punishment – saved the

French the trouble of laying waste their land, indeed, burning enormous acreages in a literal 'scorched earth' strategy. Still the French came on, albeit in mounting anxiety and exasperation.

WINNING … WHAT?

The climactic engagement they'd been looking for finally came at Borodino, west of Moscow, where on 7 September a quarter of a million men clashed and tens of thousands lost their lives. Napoleon won the day and, the natural order of things apparently re-established, advanced in triumph on Moscow to take charge. Over 100,000 troops entered the outskirts of the city on 14 September. They found the place in flames, set alight by its own people.

The French waited for the czar's surrender but it never came. He and his court had withdrawn to the east to sit out the occupation. After five weeks, with autumn well advanced, Napoleon realized he would have to withdraw his army in order to survive.

BELOW:
FAR FROM HOME
With their complex coalitions, the Napoleonic Wars brought troops from many nationalities to battlefields in many countries. Here, at Somosierra, Spain (1808), Polish *Chevau-Légers* (light cavalry) make a heroic charge against a Spanish artillery battery, opening the road for Napoleon's infantry to press forwards.

A HIDEOUS RETREAT

'General Winter' now took the field. By the beginning of November the country was icing in. The French were burdened down by booty – from jewellery to carriages. Abandoned along the roadsides by frightened and exhausted men, larger objects impeded those coming behind. Ladies' silks and furs were pressed into service to provide warmth. Said one survivor: men looked 'like ghosts dressed up for a masquerade'. 'The roads were like glass,' another said. 'The horses fell down, and could not get up. Our worn-out soldiers no longer had strength to their arms. The barrels of their muskets were so cold that they stuck to their hands … we had to eat the horses that fell down on the ice.'

Dogs and cats were killed and eaten – and the soldiers' fallen comrades. Of the half million men who'd mounted the invasion, only 30,000 made it home. This was great news for Napoleon's enemies, who felt optimistic enough to form a Sixth Coalition. Under unrelenting pressure in Spain, where Britain was still fighting alongside the local guerrillas, Napoleon was defeated in Germany at the Battle of Leipzig (October 1813). The French were finally driven out of Spain in April 1814. By then Napoleon had been forced to abdicate and had been sent to Elba, an island off Italy's western coast. The monarchy had been restored, with the late king's brother on the throne as Louis XVIII (1755–1824).

CONQUEST AND REVOLUTION

CONQUEST AND REVOLUTION

ABOVE:
EAGLE ALTERCATION
French troops of the 4th Line Regiment look on in consternation as a Russian Imperial Guard cavalryman brandishes a regimental standard he's just captured in the ferocious back-and-forth at Austerlitz (1805). They would have the last laugh, though: this was arguably to be Napoleon's greatest victory.

LEFT:
TRAGIC GLORY
The Royal Navy's 1805 triumph off Cape Trafalgar, southwest Spain, strengthened the Coalition's hold at sea, thwarting Napoleon's plans to mount an invasion of England across the Channel. But the loss of the victorious British commander, Admiral Nelson, was a major blow.

Elsewhere, 1812 had also seen the publication of *Childe Harold*, a rambling narrative by the British poet George Gordon, Lord Byron (1788–1824). An outrageously colourful character himself, Byron embodied the Romantic spirit in which he wrote. Truth to feeling, as against adherence to form, was key to the Romantic sensibility, which swept Europe over the years that followed.

THE 'WAR OF 1812'

The repercussions of the 'Napoleonic Wars' reached well beyond Europe. The USA saw its shipping harassed by both sides. By the British because they were striving to stop supplies reaching France and felt the (recently 'British') Americans should be on their side; by the French (in the so-called 'Quasi War') because they felt America owed them gratitude for their support in its independence struggle.

America, for its part, believed the British had been making mischief for it (from Canada) by encouraging the rebellion of Chief Tecumseh's Shawnee-led 'Northwest Confederacy'. Fighting had broken out around Ohio in 1811. Tecumseh had actually refused British backing, but America was unconvinced. (And, indeed, the *intention* to interfere had assuredly been there.)

CONQUEST AND REVOLUTION

INDOMITABLE
Russia's wounded commander, Pyotr Bagration (1765–1812), continues to direct his army as he lies wounded on the battlefield at Borodino. A refusal to admit defeat was key to his country's eventual triumph over Napoleon in 1812 – just as it would be against Germany in World War II.

CONQUEST AND REVOLUTION

Having defeated the Confederacy at Tippecanoe (November 1811), the Americans pressed their advantage. Reasoning that, the British being so overstretched in Europe, their 5,000 troops in Canada were vulnerable, President James Madison (1751–1836) decided that his country might as well just help itself to Canada. Unfortunately, his volunteers were no match for the seasoned professional soldiers Britain had in Canada.

By August 1814, moreover, the end of the war in Europe allowed the British to beef up their forces considerably. After defeating the Americans at Blandensburg in August 1814, a British army marched on Washington, burning down its public buildings, including the White House and Capitol.

Moving on to do the same to Baltimore, it was held at Fort McHenry. Hostilities continued but, as the weeks went by and things settled down into an exhausted stalemate, both sides started to think better of the conflict.

LATIN LIBERATION

The Caribbean had already witnessed a revolution in Haiti, but similar conditions prevailed in Latin America at large. In 1810, a Catholic priest in Dolores, Guanajuato, Miguel Hidalgo (1753–1811), raised his 'Cry of Dolores', calling for Mexican Independence. (For now, at least, he proposed a 'Mexican

BELOW:
COMEBACK TOUR
Crowded round by his supporters, Napoleon prepares to embark for his escape from Elba (February 1815). His rampage through Europe in the months that followed gave his enemies a nasty scare, but proved his last imperial hurrah.

Empire' – a constitutional monarchy with some worthy Spanish military officer for emperor.) While he failed in his endeavour, and was executed in 1811, he set the war for independence unstoppably in motion.

South America had its rebels, too. Francisco de Miranda (1750–1816) had a revolutionary résumé that included the USA and France. Now he wanted to free his Venezuelan homeland. In 1806, he launched a rebellion against Spain. It grew slowly and saw many setbacks but by 1810, the Spanish had been successfully expelled. They were back in force soon after to overthrow this 'First Republic', and Miranda was forced to come to terms.

Angered at this capitulation, one of his officers, Simón Bolívar (1783–1830), had taken up the fight. Forced to flee initially, he'd

ABOVE:
PATIENT VICTOR
'In the midst of winter … invincible summer.' Mikhail Kutuzov (1747–1813) was supreme commander of Russian forces in 1812. He was behind the scorched-earth strategy which, while apparently giving Napoleon's invasion forces endless ground, left them overstretched and ultimately helpless, far from home.

returned with an army 17,000-strong and installed a provisional government in Caracas. The people had hailed this Second Republic with unbounded enthusiasm, bestowing on Bolívar the honorary title of *Libertador* ('Liberator'). Within a year, though, the Spanish had regrouped and the Republic was under pressure once again. Forced to flee to the Caribbean islands, Bolívar found sanctuary in British-run Jamaica where in 1815 he wrote his famous 'Jamaica Letter'. This set out his vision for a federation of free and equal states stretching from northern Mexico to southern Chile, where Spain's Latin American empire had been till now.

SETBACK, BOUNCEBACK

The following year, with the help of Haitian freedom-fighter Alexandre Pétion (1770–1818), Bolívar led a small expedition back to Venezuela. His 300 men were mainly officers: the hope was that they'd gather patriotic volunteers in their thousands.

CONQUEST AND REVOLUTION

RIGHT:
THE LIBERATOR
'Our sole mission is to break the chains of servitude,' said Simón Bolívar in 1813. How successful he would ultimately be in his overarching project is debatable but he became a hero – and a revolutionary role model – for Latin America in later times.

This didn't really happen: between fear of Spain and suspicion of the rebels, the people in the countryside were too wary.

Bolívar withdrew to Guyana, thwarted. At this point, though, he had an offer of help from Britain – nominally Spain's ally, and unsympathetic to Bolívar's democratic ideals but tempted by the prospects of cheap raw materials and fresh markets for their manufactured goods. They got more meaningful ideological support from the USA who, still championing New World revolution, sent a diplomatic mission in June 1818.

Bolívar's reinforced republican army was able to retake some of the towns that had been lost before; in 1819, he turned his attentions to New Granada, which encompassed the entire area of present-day Panama and Colombia. Bolívar led his 2,000 troops over the Andes, where they won a series of victories over the Spanish. That August they gained their culminating triumph at the Battle of Boyacá, after which the road to Bogotá was clear. Bolívar was given a hero's welcome.

BELOW:
STILL SPANISH
Baroque-style churches like the Temple of Santo Domingo in southern Mexico's Oaxaca gave a distinctive look to a lot of city centres in Latin America. Long after independence, the clergy here – and the attached convent – helped keep up the cultural 'Spanishness' of such places.

In December, he proclaimed the Republic of Gran Colombia. A federation, it extended over 2 million sq km (0.8 million sq miles) – or rather it would, because not all its territories had yet been liberated. While modern-day Venezuela, Colombia and Panama had been recovered, the fight for Ecuador went on.

In 1820, a political crisis in Spain forced Madrid to compromise, recognizing Gran Colombia's independence. With the help of Bolívar's most successful general, Antonio José de Sucre (1795–1830), it was soon to be joined by Ecuador.

FREEDOM FOR PERU

That left Peru as the last bastion of Spanish rule in South America, though the Spanish viceroyalty of that name extended far beyond the borders of the modern state to include much of Bolivia and Chile. (Up until 1776, when the viceroyalty of Río de la Plata had been established pretty much on the eve of independence, Spanish rule had also included Uruguay, Paraguay and Argentina.)

Bolívar and General de Sucre advanced on Peru from the north, whilst the Argentinean general José de San Martín (1778–1850) led an army from the south. Bolívar was besieging Callao when, in December 1824, what turned out to be the decisive

battle was fought. De Sucre led the little force which met 9,000 Spanish soldiers on the pampas outside Ayacucho and put them to flight. In August 1825, Peru became an independent nation; 'Upper Peru' was renamed Bolivia after its liberator.

No sooner was it established, though, than the new state started to disintegrate, pulled apart by regional rivalries and factional squabbling. In hopes of imposing order, Bolívar proclaimed himself dictator, but this drew (understandable) allegations of Napoleonesque megalomania. He did indeed show signs of being simultaneously idealistic and power-hungry, a problem that would dog Latin American politics into modern times.

In 1830, Gran Colombia broke up into the separate states of Venezuela, Colombia and Ecuador. Bolívar resigned all his offices in disgust and declared he was leaving the country, but died of tuberculosis, aged 47, before he could.

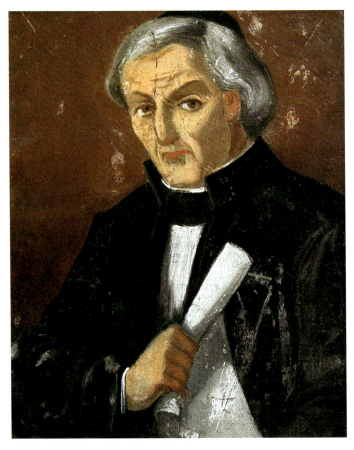

RIGHT:
PATRIOTIC PRIEST
Miguél Hidalgo has justly secured a place in the pantheon of Latin American liberation heroes. Primarily a plea for fair administration, his 'Cry of Dolores' wasn't quite as revolutionary as it sounds, maybe, but its call for 'Death to the *Galupines*!' (Spanish settlers) was inflammatory indeed.

BELOW:
A VITAL VICTORY
Boyacá brought Bolívar the decisive victory he needed to set him on the road to Bogotá and the way to independence for New Granada.

CONQUEST AND REVOLUTION

ABOVE:
AN EPIC ADVENTURE
The Argentinean general José de San Martín leads his 'Army of the Andes' over the mountains. Their heroic advance was to be the second prong of a joint invasion of Peru which saw Bolívar and De Sucre advancing on the Spanish stronghold from the north.

BONAPARTE BACK

In March 1815, just as Europe's leaders were relaxing, Napoleon escaped from Elba and returned to France – to a hero's welcome. For the 'Hundred Days' that followed he was back in charge. While the Coalition allies mobilized, he mustered 200,000 seasoned, loyal troops. He marched them into Belgium (then part of the United Kingdom of the Netherlands) to prevent British and Prussian forces linking up.

The Duke of Wellington moved south from Brussels, meeting the left wing of France's army on 16 June. Holding their attack, they fell back to a ridge above the Brussels road. Wellington's force faced Napoleon's full army – stronger and more experienced, with twice as much artillery. But Wellington set up fortified outposts in farms on the ridge and established his own artillery and sharpshooters there.

He kept his main force below the skyline so the French bombardment was wasted, moving his men up only when the French infantry advanced. Despite devastating musket volleys, Napoleon's troops kept coming till they were forced back by Wellington's heavy cavalry. The French cavalry now charged – again and again; but the British formed squares and held firm. Even so, Napoleon had gained the upper hand.

Except that Field Marshal Blücher's (1742–1819) 50,000-strong Prussian army was approaching fast. While the main French army tried to hold them back, the Imperial Guard tried one last time to break the British line. Wellington's men stood firm and the French fled: 25,000 of them were killed and 8,000 captured. Now truly finished, Napoleon was sent to St Helena, in the South Atlantic.

Meanwhile, in the South African interior, King Shaka (c. 1787–1828) and his Zulu nation had been on the rise, the most irresistible military force the region had ever seen. His campaign of conquest was called *mfecane*, 'the crushing'. Its

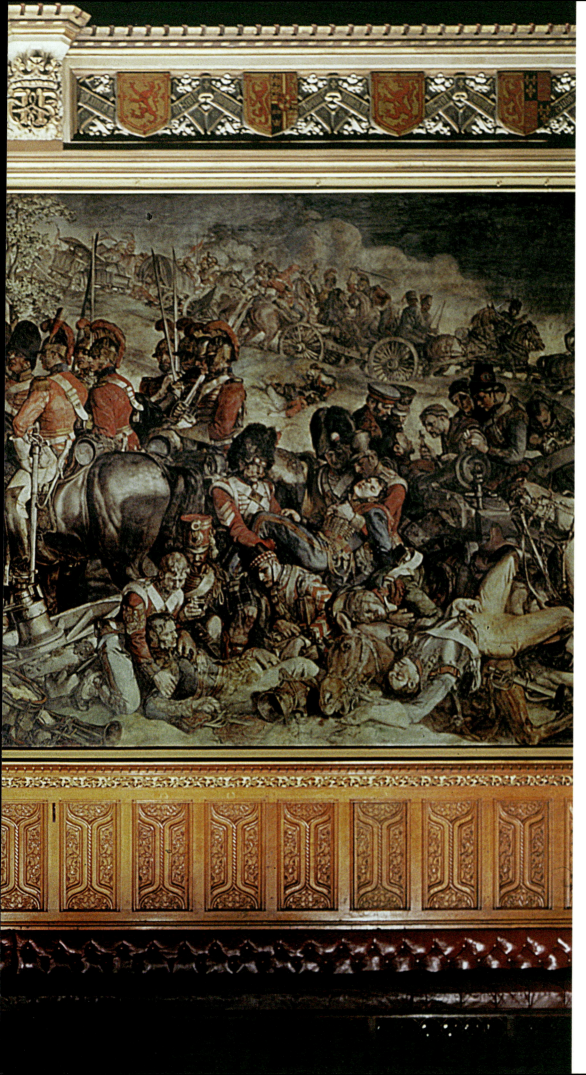

A JOB WELL DONE
Britain's Duke of Wellington (right) and Prussia's Field Marshal Blücher meet and shake hands amid scenes of carnage after their victory at Waterloo in 1815, in this monumental wall painting by Irish painter Daniel Maclise, now displayed in the Palace of Westminster, London. That Napoleon had at last been beaten was a huge relief to the nations of the Seventh Coalition.

impact rippled far beyond the actual area of the fighting, as displaced population groups came into collision with others, causing innumerable secondary conflicts.

TECHNOLOGY IN TRAIN

This was an age of invention. In 1821, British scientist Michael Faraday (1791–1867) invented the electric motor. He followed up a decade later with the transformer and the dynamo. In 1827, Frenchman Nicéphore Niépce (1765–1833) made what's thought to have been the first photograph – though he called his technique 'heliography'.

Another Frenchman, Louis Thimonnier (1793–1857), came up with the earliest known sewing machine in 1830 – though the first one to find success in domestic use was invented by the American Elias Howe (1819–67) in 1845. Also from the USA came the first 'electric telegraph', which was invented in 1832 by Samuel Morse (1791–1872); his famous code came six years later. In 1834 came Jacob Perkins' (1766–1849) refrigerator.

In September 1830, the Liverpool–Manchester Railway was opened, the first passenger railway in the world. The proceedings began with a tragedy: the statesman William Huskisson was killed when he fell under an advancing engine.

Despite this, the day still ended up a triumph. George Stephenson's (1781–1848) locomotive, the *Rocket*, was cheered to the skies by festive crowds. Not only would the railway allow bulk transportation and mass tourism; it would radically alter people's sense of space and social geography.

What sort of sense of space and social geography did the people of Japan have, cut off from the world throughout the Edo period? The country's aristocracy were additionally cut off from the life of the country. They basically wore stunning clothes and socialized.

Ordinary people worked hard, but the cultural tone was set by this elite who, in their idle privilege, appeared disconnected from everyday life, as though adrift in a 'floating world'. The name *Ukiyo-e* ('art of the floating world') was given to the distinctively delicate woodblock prints which recorded their gracious lifestyle in all its elegance and colour.

IMPERIAL 'PROTECTION'

In 1823, a couple of slow-burn issues started. February saw the first of a lengthy series of 'Ashanti Wars' between Britain and its former partners in the slave trade, the Asante Kingdom, over control of the coastal strip of the Gold Coast (modern Ghana).

CONQUEST AND REVOLUTION

OPPOSITE:
LOCOMOTIVE LAURELS
Stephenson's *Rocket* is hailed as the victor (out of 10 contenders) at the Rainhill Trials, southeast of Liverpool, October 1829. It was chosen to pull the train on the new Liverpool & Manchester Railway when it opened the following year.

RIGHT:
HAZY BUT HISTORIC
'Heliography' just meant 'drawing with the sun', which was how Joseph Nicéphore Niépce saw his photographic technique, invented in 1822. This *View from the Window at Le Gras* (1826) is the first known camera photograph.

BELOW:
SMALL BEGINNINGS
This elegant little device, Michael Faraday's first electric motor, was the start of a whole new arm of engineering. With innumerable applications, in everything from transport to industrial manufacturing, it was one of the most important inventions ever made.

The British Empire had taken upon itself the protection of the local Fante and Ga people in the face of small-scale imperialism on the Asante's part. Britain was badly mauled before beating the Asante back into the interior. A second war of 1863–4 would prove inconclusive. Britain won the third (1873–4) convincingly, burning the Asante capital Kumasi. After further wars (1894–6 and 1900), the Asante's territory would be absorbed into Britain's Gold Coast colony.

Talking of small-scale imperialism, US President James Monroe (1758–1831) proclaimed the 'Monroe Doctrine'. His country, he said, would be the protector of its hemisphere. Any intervention from Europe would be viewed as an attack on the USA. The threat, from what remained a new and insignificant nation wasn't taken seriously. It would be remembered, though, as the century wore on and America became powerful enough for Monroe's warning to have real force.

RUSSIA IN REACTION

On 26 December 1825, Russia was shaken by a revolt against the accession of the reactionary Nicholas I (1796–1855) as czar. The rebels favoured the late czar's younger brother, Konstantin, though he'd privately ruled himself out of the succession. The so-called 'Decembrists' were defeated and executed or sent into exile in Siberia. Nicholas was as reactionary as they had feared, but also less competent, mismanaging the economy and

CONQUEST AND REVOLUTION

dragging Russia into a succession of futile wars, culminating in Crimea.

EXPLORING AUSTRALIA

Explorers had continued to fill in the blanks in the world map. The modern criticism that they were preparing the way for colonial exploitation can't readily be dismissed, but if they were imperialists, they were mostly unconscious ones.

The Scottish explorer Mungo Park (1771–1806) certainly seems to have been motivated by a spirit of scientific enquiry. He'd drowned while exploring the Niger in 1806. In Australia, in 1829, Charles Sturt (1795–1869) set out from Sydney to explore the Darling Basin, finally reaching the Murray River, which he traced down to the sea. He set out into the deep interior for his Central Australian Expedition of 1844–6. Stricken by scurvy, heat and dehydration, he was fortunate to make it back alive.

Robert O'Hara Burke (c. 1820–61) and William John Wills (1834–61) weren't so lucky. In 1860, they left Melbourne to cross the continent from south to north. They took camels rather than horses. Even so, only four out of 20 men made it to the Gulf of Carpentaria. Nine dropped out in the early stages; then seven died, three (including Burke and Wills themselves) on the return journey. Only one – John King – limped safely home, but the expedition had achieved its object.

VICTORIAN VALUES

In 1837, Queen Victoria (1819–1901) ascended the British throne. Despite the terrible social problems that accompanied the rise of industrial capitalism and the exploitation and atrocities attendant on building one of the greatest empires of the modern era, her reign tends to be looked back on in Britain as something of a golden age.

The electoral franchise had been widened in the Great Reform Act of 1832 to include middle-class property-owners. Demand grew for the working class (or working-class men at least) to get the vote. Millions signed petitions calling for a

LEFT:
OVERWEENING AMBITION?
Monroe was the Mouse that Roared; by the 1950s, the USA would be bossing (sometimes bullying) the world. Bernhard Gillam's (1856–96) 1889 cartoon shows America somewhere in between, warning off European interests trying to take charge of the Panama Canal.

OPPOSITE:
MESSAGE MAN
Inventions apart, Samuel Morse was a painter of real ability (he was admitted into Britain's Royal Academy). Less endearing features included his virulent anti-Catholic and anti-immigration feeling. His later years were troubled, his patent prompting lengthy legal wrangling, but his telegraph undoubtedly changed the world.

CONQUEST AND REVOLUTION

AN IMPROBABLE REVOLT
The 'Decembrists' weren't your usual revolutionaries. As seen by Georg Wilhelm Timm (1820–95), their 'revolt' looks like a military review. Rightly so, because they were actually patriotic (and comparatively conservative) officers driven to mutiny by the prospect of Nicholas I as czar.

ABOVE:
FUJI AFLOAT
Hokusai's (1760–1849) *The Great Wave off Kanagawa* (1831) is the most celebrated example of the extraordinary artistic outpouring that accompanied Japan's *Ukiyo-e* period. It is not just beautiful but mysterious (whose are the boats?) and witty, a painterly pun making Mount Fuji into a little wave.

OPPOSITE:
A NEW KIND OF HERO
This was the age of the engineer, but none would surpass the achievements of Isambard Kingdom Brunel (1806–59). He built bridges, railways and tunnels (including one under the River Thames) as well as a succession of record-breaking steamships.

'People's Charter'. Chartists held mass protests. Some ended in violent unrest.

Since the start of the Industrial Revolution, workers had tried to organize to improve their conditions, but this had been outlawed by a series of 'Combination Laws'. In 1832, however, a group of farmworkers in Tolpuddle, Dorset, formed what's seen as being the first trade union. The 'Tolpuddle Martyrs' were transported to Australia for their pains, but have had iconic status in the labour movement ever since.

Capitalism was cruel. As the German thinker Karl Marx (1818–83) pointed out, it was inherently exploitative, the factory owner helping himself to the 'surplus value' of his employee's labour; the landlord living idly on his rent. In his *The Communist Manifesto* (1848), Marx would advocate for a class war of the industrial proletariat against the bourgeoisie. The workers had 'nothing to lose but their chains', he ringingly proclaimed.

There's no doubt that, for many millions, both in Britain and the other industrializing countries (the USA, Germany and France weren't too far behind now), work-hours were long, pay poor and living conditions often squalid, sometimes (as cholera epidemics swirled) downright dangerous. But another aspect of the Victorian mentality was a conscientious desire to improve things: laws were passed prohibiting child labour, limiting working hours, imposing safety standards and trying to provide safe water supplies and sewage removal.

THE GREAT HUNGER

This was the sensibility that kept up pressure on the state to keep cracking down on the slave trade, even if it wasn't quite so anxious about the indigenous peoples of the empire.

Or about the Irish who, from 1845, were hit by a disastrous famine, caused immediately by the failure of the potato crop two years running. Eight million Irish lived almost entirely on potatoes while they reared the livestock and grew the grain their Anglo-Irish masters stayed rich exporting. *Phytophthora infestans* – the potato blight – may have represented a

catastrophe but, given the fact that food was exported in massive quantities throughout the famine, it couldn't be said to have been the cause of so many deaths. Neither landlords (with some exceptions) nor the British Parliament were ready to give Ireland relief, while its people starved. Over a million died of hunger and associated sicknesses; a similar number were forced into emigration, mostly to the USA. Less quantifiable was the loss of a longstanding culture, and the near-disappearance of the Irish language in the Famine's aftermath.

PUSHED AND PULLED

But then mass emigration was a feature of nineteenth-century life. A spin-off of Greece's War of Independence (1821–9), in which Greeks fought to throw off the overlordship of the Ottoman Turks, the Odessa Pogrom of 1821 claimed the lives

RIGHT:
THE ADVENTURER
He may indeed have been, as a former lover called him, 'mad, bad, and dangerous to know', but Byron was absolutely adored by his own age. Thomas Phillips' (1770–1845) portrait (c. 1835), fittingly flamboyant, shows him in Albanian dress, in honour of his love of travelling – and his service with the Greeks in their War of Independence against the Ottomans.

BELOW:
A TORRENT OF TEXTILES
Calico is printed in a cotton mill in Lancashire, England, in the 1830s. Plentiful water, coal from the northern mines and slave-grown cotton from the southern USA placed Lancashire's textile industry in the very vanguard of England's Industrial Revolution.

ABOVE:
CLAMOURING FOR A VOICE
Thousands of Chartists gather on London's Kennington Common, in April 1848. Welcome as they had been, the reforms of 1832 had only encouraged the demand for the electoral franchise to be widened further.

of 14 Jews. (Jews were believed by Greek expatriates to have sided with the Ottoman authorities in the Crimean city, and to have mocked the Orthodox Patriarch when he was abused by the Turks.) Jews began leaving in a trickle then; it became a flow as the century wore on. Most of the emigrants would end up in the USA.

As would many of those streaming out of southern Italy, though a sizeable minority went to Argentina and Uruguay. Many Chinese emigrants went to work on the fruit and sugar plantations of Hawaii as indentured labourers, as did Indians to Guyana and the West Indies, Mauritius, East and Southern Africa. Along with this sort of 'push' migration there was 'pull' migration like that of the thousands of European and Chinese workers attracted to America at the time of the 'Gold Rush' in California (1848–55) and New South Wales and Victoria, Australia (1851). Prospectors – mostly disappointed – often stayed on after the excitement ended to take up a range of labouring jobs.

EXPLORATORY ADVENTURES

Africa was still substantially unexplored from a European perspective. Large parts were actually well-known: the Maghreb and Egypt in the north had been on their mental map for many centuries; Cape Province in the south had been settled since 1652; but vast areas of the interior were familiar only to its indigenous inhabitants.

It wasn't exactly exploration, but the Boers blazed a trail. These Dutch-descended settlers, in South Africa's Cape Province since the seventeenth century – had since 1806 had to live under British rule. They were tiring of what they saw as their unwarranted interference in their lives (not least in according citizens' rights to their slaves in 1828). In 1835, loading their families and belongings into their ox-wagons, they left their farms and made the 'Great Trek' into the interior, across the Vaal River to 'Transvaal'.

LEFT:
INGENIOUS ADA
Byron's daughter Ada Lovelace (1815–52) lived more quietly than her father but was every bit as extravagantly talented in her way. Using a mechanical calculating machine previously invented in the 1820s by Charles Babbage (1791–1871), a family friend, she foresaw the expansion of computing beyond the realm of pure calculation.

OPPOSITE ABOVE:
OFFBEAT ATTITUDES
The originator of *On the Origin of Species* went to Edinburgh University to study medicine but played truant, investigating marine life in the Firth of Forth. Driven more by curiosity than by conventional ideas of success or scientific conformity, Charles Darwin was ready to rethink his discipline from scratch.

OPPOSITE BELOW:
INTO EXILE
A million emigrants left Ireland in the Famine for North America, Australia and elsewhere; emigration became an established tradition in that country. As did the existence of a vast diaspora, with a deep and enduring suspicion of the British state.

FROM EXPLORATION TO EVOLUTION

At sea, the centuries-old search for the Northwest Passage went on. Sir John Franklin (1786–1847) mapped much of North America's northern coastline from the 1820s. But his final expedition ended tragically, his ship iced in off King William Island, during the winter of 1846–7. What happened to Franklin and his crew will likely never be known, though rumours of murder and cannibalism circulated and speculation has continued ever since.

In 1831–6, British naturalist Charles Darwin (1809–82) took a round-the-world voyage with the Admiralty's survey vessel, HMS *Beagle*. Stops in Brazil, Argentina, the Galápagos Islands and Australia opened his mind to the immense variety of biological life. Like him, Alfred Russel Wallace (1823–1913) was drawn to the idea that this variety had emerged by some sort of evolution: Wallace went up the Amazon to research this further. It was, however, Darwin who, in his *On the Origin of Species* (1859) came up with a convincing theory of how such evolution might have taken place, through a process of 'natural selection'.

There were other scientific advances too. In 1847, Scottish surgeon James Young Simpson (1811–70) first used chloroform as an anaesthetic, performing an incalculable service to generations of patients since. In 1869, Dmitri Mendeleev (1834–1907) developed his Periodic Table of the elements, imposing order and logic on the hitherto hit-and-miss science of chemistry. Late as it may seem, medical science was only

ABOVE:
STRIKING OUT
Up to 14,000 Boers made the 'Great Trek', leaving Cape Colony in wagon trains to find fresh homelands out of reach of British interference. They travelled in several successive waves, between 1835 and 1846.

BELOW:
FORTY-NINERS
The Gold Rush of 1849 drew an estimated 300,000 people to California, most from further east in the USA but some from far beyond. Few were to make their fortunes, and the euphoria quickly faded, but the boom helped kick-start California's conventional economy.

now questioning the old idea that diseases were the result of 'miasmas' – toxic mists. The 'germ theory' that was the basis of modern healing was in development by Louis Pasteur (1822–95), who in 1877 perfected the idea of vaccination. The idea of inoculation was a century old, but this was still a major step.

THE WAR FOR DRUGS

By the 1830s, Britain's addiction to Chinese tea was proving deeply destructive to China because its merchants were paying for the product in opium shipped from India. Or, rather, smuggled, since opium had been illegal in China for a century or more. Six million Chinese were addicted, the emperor's efforts to control the crisis thwarted by the British merchants.

BELOW:
ROMANTIC VISION
New times, new subjects: J.M.W. Turner's (1775–1851) *Rain, Steam and Speed – The Great Western Railway* (1844) couldn't possibly have been painted a few decades before. Not just the trains but the perspectives they opened up hadn't been available; nor the noise, the smoke, the sensory overload …

When he asked London to step in, he was ignored, then – when in 1831 he took action, seizing 20,000 crates on Guangzhou docks – found himself facing a punitive expedition of 16 British warships, with 4,000 men, who sank ships, destroyed coastal batteries and slaughtered civilians. The emperor was forced to hand Hong Kong to the British as a colony. China had entered its 'century of humiliation'. A second 'Opium War' ensued when China again tried to take action in 1856, and the indignities weren't going to stop there.

'UNEQUAL TREATIES'

Nor than they would for Japan, after Commodore Matthew Perry turned up in Tokyo harbour with a flotilla of ships in 1853 and, in essence, ordered the country at gunpoint to open up to US trade. Like Britain, an industrialized America needed markets for its manufactured goods so weaker countries had to be forced into 'free' trade. The Shogunate had no alternative but to comply, after seeing what had happened to China. So a Treaty of Amity and

CONQUEST AND REVOLUTION

LEFT:
TYRANNICAL TERMS
Beautifully presented bullying. Signed in 1842, the Treaty of Nanking (Nanjing) brought the First Opium War to an end but was the start of a 'century of humiliation' for the Chinese at the hands of the West.

BELOW:
PROTESTING TOO MUCH?
Elaborate ceremony surrounded the signing of the Treaty of Nanking, with extravagant expressions of friendship for the future. No one was fooled, however: the agreement was a devastating blow to Chinese pride and gave Britain a near-complete carte blanche for colonial exploitation.

OPPOSITE:
LAST-STAND CITY
Standing at the mouth of the Yangtze River, at its junction with the Grand Canal, Ching-Keang Foo was one of China's most important seaports. Its garrison held out heroically against the British in 1842.

Commerce with the USA was 'agreed' in 1858. Similar treaties with Britain, Russia, the Netherlands and France followed. Over the next few decades, the Western powers made what tactful historians have called 'unequal treaties' with all the Far Eastern countries.

LOSING GAME

Not everything was going the imperialists' way, as Britain found out in Afghanistan. In 1839, it had embarked on the First Afghan War with the utmost confidence. It ended in ignominious defeat – and a tragic waste of life.

From a colonial-development perspective, Afghanistan seemed little better than a wasteland, but it was at the centre of the 'Great Game' of power between Britain and Russia. The fear of growing Russian influence had prompted the British East India Company to invade. Afghanistan's Emir, Shoja Shah (1780–1842), had been toppled by Dost Muhammad (1793–1863), and the Company was concerned that he would build bridges with their Russian rivals.

Sir Willoughby Cotton's (1783–1860) expedition made light of rugged terrain and difficult conditions. By the end of April, they had captured Kandahar. In July they took Ghazni. Then it was on to Kabul: the capital fell on 6 August. Dost Muhammad fled, and Shoja Shah was restored.

Cotton learned how little it meant to hold the administrative centre of what had never actually been a centralized nation-

state. Despite this, a complacent Company replaced this tough commander with the elderly William Elphinstone (1782–1842). In 1841, Akbar Khan (1816–47) called a general revolt. Under sustained attack with winter approaching, Elphinstone finally appreciated the predicament his troops were in and gave the order to retreat. They were dogged every step of the way by tribesmen: over 16,000 were ultimately killed. Only one British soldier and a handful of sepoys (Indians, fighting for the British) made it back to Jalalabad.

In 1857, the British Raj (imperial state) in India itself was shaken when thousands of sepoys mutinied, many civilians rising up against the Raj as well. The causes were complex, but the immediate provocation for the soldiers' rising seems to have been the introduction of the new Lee–Enfield rifle. Its cartridges (which had to be bitten open before firing) were greased with either beef tallow or pork fat, which are forbidden to Hindus and Muslims respectively.

At the rebellion's height Delhi and Cawnpore (Kanpur) were besieged, but regiments of British and loyal sepoy troops were brought in and eventually restored order. Not, however, for a year and a half, nor before 8,000 British soldiers and civilians had been killed – and 10 times that number of rebel sepoys.

India had been an arm's-length possession of the British Empire, administered by the East India Company, which had some autonomy from the state. Now it was taken directly under the control of the government in London as an imperial possession of the British Crown.

REVOLUTION RENEWED

The rise of an educated, urban middle class had helped drive the religious Reformation three centuries before. That rise had only gathered momentum since. And received fresh impetus with the advent of industrialism. Between Britain's constitutional monarchy and its electoral reforms, the middle class had enjoyed reasonable representation, but in mainland Europe this hadn't been the case. Building tensions burst out in revolution in 1848.

They began in France, where bourgeois frustrations were compounded by the desperation of a poorer populace after a succession of failed harvests had brought food shortages. In February, they all rose up and overthrew Louis Philippe's (1773–1850) monarchy. The struggle was then on between the two wings of the Revolution – the bourgeoisie and the working-class leftists. Able to call on assistance of the military, the former won, proclaiming the Second Republic that November.

In the various states of Germany, people were fired up by France's Revolution, and by the thought that they might be

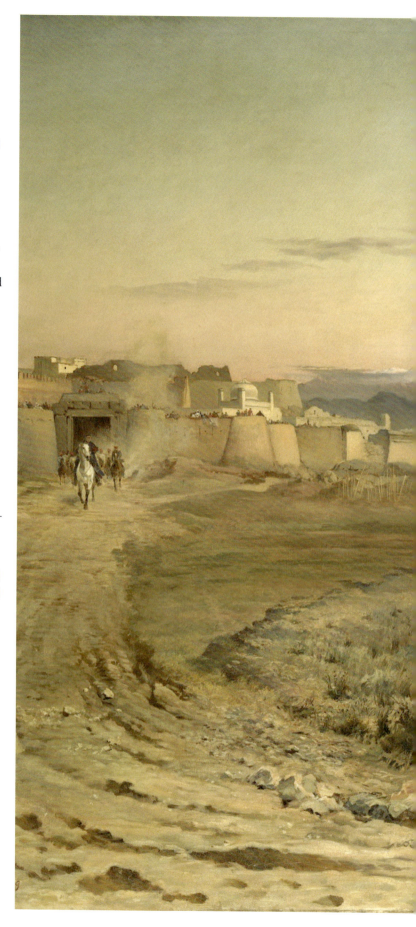

RIGHT:
REMNANTS OF AN ARMY
Assistant-Surgeon William Brydon makes it back to Jalalabad after Britain's defeat in the First Afghan War. The idea that Western colonialism was prompted by a spirit of self-sacrifice was widely accepted. 'The White Man's Burden', England's poet Rudyard Kipling (1865–1936) would call it later.

CONQUEST AND REVOLUTION

ABOVE:
A DUSTY ANSWER
The 'March Demands' of 1848 (for freedom of the press; freedom of assembly; a written constitution and wider democratic representation in an all-German parliament) were rejected by the authorities in no uncertain terms. Here, Frederick William IV's troops put down the rebels in Frankfurt.

united in a single state. Since 1834, the *Zollverein*, a customs union encompassing the whole country, had shown the way things might be. The 'March Demands' were essentially that there should be a parliament for all Germany and that its emperor – envisaged as being Prussia's Frederick IV (1795–1861) – should rule constitutionally. Backed by Habsburg Austria, Frederick refused to have his powers curtailed and the rebellion was violently suppressed.

In Austria itself, the middle class won all the reforms it wanted – at the expense of the working-class radicals who got no concessions. The middle class was rattled when the workers took to the streets and threw up barricades in the 'May Unrest' – and quietly relieved when a reactionary state cracked down.

Austria was an empire with non-German territories in Bohemia, Hungary, Romania, Croatia and parts of Italy. Its conflicts weren't just about class, by any means. All these peoples yearned for independence for their nations. Whilst in Bohemia the Revolution was quickly suppressed, Hungary's Lajos Kossuth (1802–94) won autonomy for his country, though he failed to anticipate that other nationalities living within its territories (Slovaks, Croats, Serbs, Transylvanian Romanians …) would want the same.

THOUGHT AND ACTION IN ITALY

Italians hoped for freedom within a unified nation. In 1831, the poet Giuseppe Mazzini (1805–72) had founded the *Giovine Italia* ('Young Italy') society to bring about that aim. He popularized the slogan 'Thought and Action'. Elected in 1846, Pope Pius IX seemed sympathetic to the idea of stepping back from the rule of the so-called Papal States (then a major part of central Italy) and introduced democratizing reforms. At this time forming the

Kingdom of Two Sicilies under King Ferdinand II (1810–59), Naples and Sicily agitated for – and won – a constitution.

In Milan, meanwhile, the rising of the 'Five Glorious Days' of 1848 forced Austria's Field Marshal Radetzky (1766–1858) into an undignified withdrawal. King turned rebel in Piedmont, Charles Albert of Piedmont-Sardinia (1798–1849) led an independence war against Austria. In Rome, the Pope had got more than he bargained for in his alliance with the radicals, whose extreme wing now rose up and overturned his rule.

Early in 1849, Mazzini proclaimed the Republic in Rome, but by this time France had come to Pope Pius's support and Radetzky had regrouped in Lombardy. The Italians were finally defeated at that March's Battle of Novara. Within hours, Charles Albert had abdicated in favour of his son, Victor Emmanuel II (1820–78), who was forced to come to terms with Austria. By November, the Pope was back in place, his reformist moment passed, the Roman Republic over. In Venice, the rebels held out till August 1850, but were finally forced to capitulate to the Austrians.

The dream wouldn't die; it was kept going culturally in part by the newspaper *Il Risorgimento* ('Resurgence') which, founded by Piedmont's Count of Cavour in 1847, gave its name to the whole Italian independence movement.

As in 1798, European revolution rippled into Ireland: 1848 saw 'the Battle of Widow McCormack's Cabbage Patch'. Forty-odd rebels, roused to action by the journalist William Smith O'Brien, marched through Tipperary and fought with a group of policemen outside a farmhouse. O'Brien's 'Young Ireland' movement failed farcically, but helped inspire the Fenians – named for the warrior-band of the ancient Irish hero Fionn mac Cumhaill. Their efforts to bring about Irish freedom would also prove unavailing, but they'd keep the idea of armed resistance alive.

BELOW:
FIGHTING FOR THE FLAG
Parisians defend a barricade in the Rue Soufflot, in the shadow of the Pantheon. Louis Philippe had been deposed in February: there followed a revolution-within-a-revolution as working-class radicals fought on against the forces of a now-ascendant bourgeoisie.

CONQUEST AND REVOLUTION

CONQUEST AND REVOLUTION

VIENNA IN FLAMES
Emperor Ferdinand I was forced to flee and his troops to storm their own city after it was taken over in a people's uprising in October 1848. A mixed crowd of workers, students and disaffected soldiers, the revolutionaries fought pitched battles against the forces of law and order, even lynching Austria's Minister of War.

AGE OF EMPIRE
1850 – 1914

In France, the name Napoleon still had cachet. The great man's nephew, Louis Napoleon Bonaparte (1808–73), used it to get himself elected president in 1848 then try to abolish the country's democratic Constitution three years later. Having failed, he seized power in a coup, then, following a family tradition, staged a phony plebiscite to have himself crowned emperor by inheritance. (Hence skipping straight to Napoleon III – the second would have been the first emperor's son.) He stayed in power by making France a police state.

In all but democratic principles, Napoleon III was relatively enlightened, backing business but also improving conditions for the poor. It was during his reign (1854–70) that George-Eugène Haussmann (1809–91) carried out a spectacular renovation of Paris, furnishing the capital with broad, sweeping boulevards, spacious squares and elegant apartment blocks. Thus Napoleon III enjoyed considerable support. Especially as he was a 'lucky' leader, involving France in the Crimean War of 1853–6, allying with Britain against Russia and Ottoman Turkey. This war is mainly remembered now for the terrible conditions its soldiers were forced to fight in, the ravaging effects of disease under these circumstances,

OPPOSITE:
'MOST WONDERFUL'
'We are living through a period of most wonderful transition …' said Queen Victoria's consort, Prince Albert (1819–61). Staged in a specially constructed 'Crystal Palace' of glass, his Great Exhibition of 1851 showcased Britain's industrial achievements and the imperial power it now wielded in the world.

ABOVE:
AN AGE OF INVENTION
Innovation snowballed, each new invention creating new demands and prompting new responses. Developed by John Boyd Dunlop (1840–1921), the pneumatic tyre began by revolutionizing the bicycle (itself a recent invention) but would later make possible the age of the motor car.

and the role of pioneer nurses like Britain's Florence Nightingale (1820–1910) and Mary Seacole (1805–81) in easing the sufferings of the sick and wounded. But it was also significant in weakening the losers – the Russians and the Ottomans – storing up trouble for both empires in the decades ahead.

RISORGIMENTO REVIVED

A bit-part having been played on the Allied side in Crimea by the Kingdom of Sardinia-Piedmont, its king, Victor Emmanuel II (1820–78), and his prime minister, Cavour (1810–61), could call on Napoleon III for his support. He gave it, in return for western Savoy and Nice – till then Italian – and in 1859 helped the Piedmontese drive the Austrians from northern Italy, defeating them at Magenta and Solferino. The French emperor then double-crossed the Italians by trying to hold on to Lombardy.

Further south, though, the freedom struggle was finding its own momentum under the leadership of Giuseppe Garibaldi (1807–82). A longstanding agitator, condemned to death after a republican rising in Piedmont in 1834, he had fled the country and spent several years participating in liberation struggles in Latin America. Returning in 1848, he had led the defence of the

LEFT:
NURSING PIONEER
Jamaica-born Mary Seacole brought traditional skills she had learned from her mother to bear in her work with the sick and wounded, alongside those of Western medicine. She set up hospitals in the Caribbean and Central America before going to the Crimea in 1855.

BELOW:
A HEALTHCARE REVOLUTION
Austere, but clean and airy, a ward in Florence Nightingale's hospital in Scutari, Turkey, provided a much healthier environment for the sick and wounded as they convalesced. Nightingale's reforming work put nursing on something more like a modern footing.

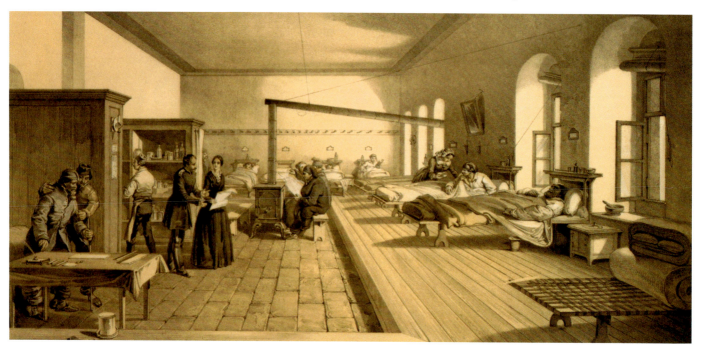

ABOVE:
MAN OF DESTINY
Wearing his signature red shirt, bowed beneath the nation-builder's burden of responsibility, Garibaldi cuts a heroic figure in Vincenzo Cabianca's (1827–1902) painting (1870). No one had done more to inspire Italy's Risorgimento.

Roman Republic in 1849, before being exiled again to return to Italy in May 1854. With a thousand followers, his so-called 'Red Shirts', he landed in Sicily, proclaiming himself dictator in the name of Victor Emmanuel II. Within days, though heavily outnumbered, they'd defeated the army of King Francis II of the Two Sicilies (1836–94) and by early June had captured Palermo. In mid-August, they crossed over to the southern Italian mainland and on 7 September 1860, they took Naples. Patriots flocked to Garibaldi's banner, and by the end of September, *I Mille* ('The Thousand') were 20,000 strong.

In March 1861, with Garibaldi's support, Victor Emmanuel II became King of Italy, though he didn't rule anything like the whole of the peninsula. In June 1862, Garibaldi landed in Sicily again, promising to free Rome from papal rule. They marched under the slogan *Roma o Muerte* ('Rome or Death'): for most, in truth, it was to be neither since they were intercepted and dispersed by a Piedmontese army.

In 1864, Napoleon III took the Papal States under his protection. Attempts by the Italians to liberate them were unsuccessful. But French forces had to be withdrawn after the outbreak of the Franco-Prussian War and Italian troops were able to take Rome. On 26 January 1871, it became the capital of the Kingdom of Italy. Victor Emmanuel II moved into the Quirinal Palace, hitherto the summer residence of the Pope. Italy was finally a nation.

NO COMPROMISE

In 1861, however, the USA had split in two, following the election of Abraham Lincoln (1809–65) as president the year before. Fearful of his intention to abolish slavery, the Southern states had seceded and set up their own 'Confederacy'.

MONSTROUS ARRIVAL
The first locals who saw Commodore Perry's ships steam into Tokyo Harbour thought them 'giant dragons puffing smoke'. This representation of the USS *Powhatan* comes from a more cynical, satirical place but still sums up the shock of this first, coercive contact with the West.

AGE OF EMPIRE

ANAESTHETIC ADVANCE
The 1840s brought the first surgical operations in which ether was used. The picture is a pioneering work in itself, a daguerreotype made in 1847 by the Boston studio of Southworth & Hawes. (They photographed a re-enactment because of J.J. Hawes' fear of blood.)

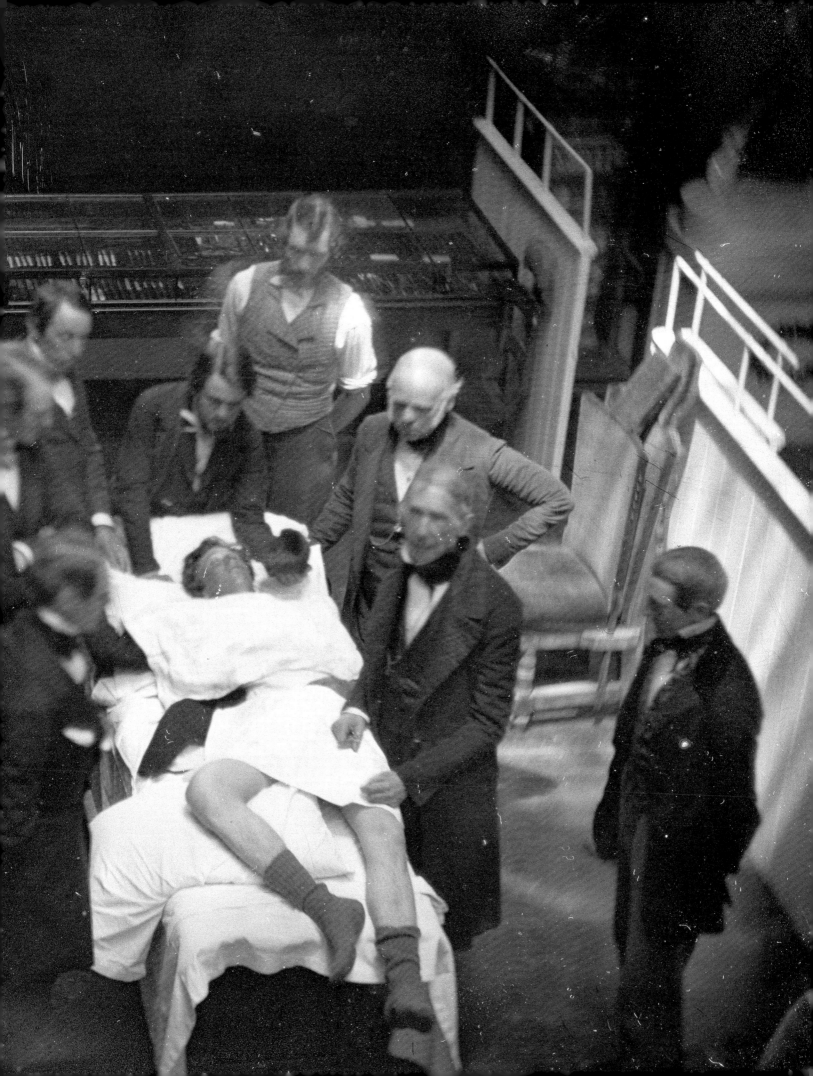

ABOVE:
A PLEA FOR PEACE
'The Chief Magistrate derives all his authority from the people.' Abraham Lincoln's Inaugural Address of 1861 called for calm and patience to prevail in a USA that was spiralling into civil war.

Slavery had long been illegal in the North but the South had been exempt under the Missouri Compromise of 1820. Lincoln had made it clear that, as far as he was concerned, there was no justification for this compromise continuing. South Carolina formally wound up its connection with the USA on 20 December. Georgia, Florida, Alabama, Mississippi and Louisiana – and, a little later, Texas and Virginia – followed suit.

Slaveholding had been the sticking point, but there was a general culture clash between the North (a land of big, industrialized cities and small, family-run farms) and the South, its overwhelmingly agrarian economy dominated by slave-worked plantations. Northern horror at the institution of slavery had been stoked by the publication (in 1852) of Harriet Beecher Stowe's novel *Uncle Tom's Cabin*.

One radical abolitionist, John Brown, had tried to trigger a general uprising of America's slaves, in October 1859 attacking the US Armory and Arsenal at Harpers Ferry, Virginia. The assault had failed, and Brown and his men had been taken prisoner. Sentenced to hang, he'd became an abolitionist martyr. His cause had acquired unstoppable momentum. Lincoln's election had made conflict between North and South inevitable.

THE FIGHTING BEGINS

The North certainly had the advantage when it came to mobilizing men in large numbers. And the South had an early setback with the decision of Kentucky and Missouri – two states whose support it had counted on – to enlist instead with Union cause. Virginia was divided, its small farmers favouring the Union, its great landowners the Confederates. It was here, in

Richmond, indeed, that the Confederacy established its capital, with its own government headed by President Jefferson Davis (1808–89).

The South only had 11 states to the Union's 24. The population of the North states was approximately 22 million; the free population of the South just 9 million (its 3 million slaves were potentially a threat). And if the South had tradition on its side, the North had more material advantages: its iron and steel production dwarfed that of the agrarian South. The South hoped Britain would support it, for the sake of its textiles industry. But Britain offered only its neutrality. Napoleon III also held back, leaving the South no international allies. But people were buoyed up by euphoria on both sides, volunteers flocking to enlist – at least at first. Later, conscription would be necessary; the South would end up having to call up all men between the ages of 17 and 50 – finally, it would have to conscript its slaves.

Richmond and Washington were only 150 km (93 miles) apart. Most of the fighting took place in between, in the open countryside of Virginia. The North attacked first, but on 21 July was badly defeated at Bull Run. Fortunately, the Southern troops failed to press their advantage. Lincoln placed General George McClellan in overall command of the Union army. He sat the winter out, advancing towards Richmond in the spring, only to find his way barred by the South's star general, Robert E. Lee. With Washington under attack by the force of Confederate general, Thomas Jonathan 'Stonewall' Jackson, McClellan couldn't get the reinforcements he needed.

THE SOUTH IN A STRANGLEHOLD

Lincoln had ordered a naval blockade of the southern ports, a decision vindicated as it became clear the war was going to last some time. General Ulysses S. Grant blocked in the ports from the landward side. Its cotton exports cut off, the South found its funds dwindling. The stranglehold was tightened when, in April 1862, the fleet of Union Admiral David Farragut forced its way into the Mississippi and captured New Orleans. Sailing on upriver, Farragut besieged the town of Vicksburg but failed to take it. Yet the Confederates couldn't find a breakthrough. Instead, at Antietam, in Maryland, that September, the Union won an inconclusive victory.

At the start of 1863, Lincoln issued his 'Emancipation Proclamation'. All slaves in Southern territories conquered by the North would be considered free. His own principled position apart, the president wanted to make mischief, prompting local uprisings within the Confederacy and boosting the recruitment of runaway slaves to Union forces. Almost 200,000 joined up between 1863 and 1865.

The North was defeated at Fredericksburg in December 1862, then again at Chancellorsville the following May. On 1–3 July 1863, however, Robert E. Lee was unable to prevail against a Union army

BELOW:
DEMOCRACY AT STAKE
'We here highly resolved that these dead shall not have died in vain … and that government of the people, by the people, for the people, shall not perish from the earth', said Lincoln in November 1863, four months after the Battle of Gettysburg.

HOPELESS HEROICS
Led by Major General George Pickett, 2,000 Confederate infantrymen attacked the centre of the Union line at Gettysburg in what became known as Pickett's Charge. The Union troops wavered but did not break, and ultimately won the day.

AGE OF EMPIRE

RIGHT:
COMING TO TERMS
'We must consider its effect on the country as a whole,' said General Robert E. Lee to calls for the Confederates to fight to the bitter end. Here (seated left), he meets Union General Ulysses S. Grant in the Appomattox Court House to offer his surrender.

led by George G. Meade at Gettysburg, Pennsylvania. There were almost 50,000 casualties in this battle, which sealed the fate of the Southern states. It didn't help the Confederacy's cause that, within a couple of days, Ulysses S. Grant had finally secured the surrender of Vicksburg. The Union's possession of the Mississippi split the South right down the centre.

SCORCHED EARTH

Grant marched his men to assist a Union army beset by a Southern force at Chattanooga, Tennessee. Victory there in September 1863 freed him up to head south to deal with Lee.

His subordinate, General William Tecumseh Sherman, was meanwhile developing a new way of waging war, divesting his army of all unnecessary ballast to make them more mobile, and more forceful. He swept through Georgia laying waste the land and setting fire to the already conquered city of Atlanta before heading for the coast at Savannah. His forces devastated a corridor some 400 km (250 miles) long and 80 km (50 miles) wide before ravaging the Carolinas in the same way. Though widely condemned, his scorched-earth policy certainly sapped Southern morale.

But the speed of Sherman's march was exceptional. Overall, indeed, thanks to innovations in weaponry, the war had become increasingly static. The rival armies had each other pinned down by sheer firepower, leading to trench warfare of a sort to become familiar in World War I.

'OUR FEARFUL TRIP IS DONE'

Lee was uncomfortable with this way of fighting, but running out of room to manoeuvre, with Sherman's force advancing from the devastated south and another led by General Philip Sheridan from the west. He dug in around Richmond, conscious that once it fell, the Confederacy would be finished. Soon enough it was. On 9 April 1865, Lee signed his surrender at the courthouse of Appomattox, Virginia.

The war had mobilized 3 million men, 2 million on the Northern side – of whom 360,000 were now dead. The South had lost a quarter of a million men. As in Crimea, more had died through disease than battle wounds. The tragedy wasn't over yet. On 15 April, the Confederate-supporting actor John Wilkes Booth dashed into Lincoln's box at the theatre and shot him dead.

Lincoln's successor Andrew Johnson was frankly racist and had bitterly criticized the freeing of the slaves. But this was already a done deal. Even in Texas, which had dragged its feet, the slaves had formally been freed on 19 June (hence 'Juneteenth') 1865, completing the emancipation process. Johnson still bent over backwards to accommodate the South through the 'Reconstruction' period that followed, a time in which corruption became endemic and the white supremacist Ku Klux Klan harassed African Americans to discourage them from asserting their new-found rights.

The re-United States got a little bigger in 1867 when it bought the Russian territory of Alaska.

AN EPHEMERAL EMPIRE

Among the odder acts of Napoleon III had been his invasion of Mexico in 1862. The Americans had been too busy with their civil war to have their minds on the Monroe Doctrine, so Napoleon had deposed the Liberal President Benito Juárez (1806–72) and installed the Austrian Archduke Maximilian (1832–67) as the Emperor Maximilian I. His hope had been that Maximilian, while owing an obvious debt to France, would succeed in bringing Mexico's warring Liberals and Conservatives together.

It wasn't to be. Republicans in the countryside resisted his reign from the start and Maximilian's efforts to take tough action, executing thousands, only alienated the people further. In 1867, the USA intervened in support of Benito Juárez and Maximilian was sent before a firing squad.

REVOLUTIONS AND RESTORATIONS

In Spain, 1868 saw a 'Glorious Revolution'. Like England's, it ushered in a constitutional monarchy. But 1868 also brought the beginning of the first war of Cuban independence – or the Ten Years' War, because it wasn't over for a decade. And even then it wasn't really over, given that Spain still had its colony. The rebels did win a vague commitment to the abolition of slavery on the island but this wouldn't be fulfilled for a few years. Rocked by radical unrest, Spain's Amadeo I (1845–90) had abdicated in 1873 but by the following year the monarchy had been restored, and a new, more conservative, political tone been set.

Revolution and restoration met in Japan's Meiji Restoration (1868). Leading figures rose up to overthrow a Tokugawa regime they felt was caving too readily to foreign interference. In modern terms, this was a 'rebranding': the role of the emperor had never actually been abolished, but Mutsuhito (or Meiji; 1852–1912) made a discreetly ceremonial role into a more public one.

A new French revolution was heralded in 1872 by Claude Monet's (1824–1926) painting, *Impression, Sunrise*. A symphony in light and colour, showing the sight of the scene as it struck the artist's eyes, rather than as a drawn-and-outlined composition, it gave its name to a whole artistic approach which was to be crystallized (with works by fellow artists like Edgar Degas [1834–1917], Camille Pissarro [1830–1903], Pierre-Auguste Renoir [1841–1919] and Alfred Sisley [1839–99]) at the 'Impressionists' exhibition, 1874.

SMALL WORLD

For transport, 1869 had been a red-letter year. In May, having worked their way east- and westward respectively,

BELOW:
THE DAWN OF MODERN ART
A seemingly undirected array of dabs and streaks somehow evoked an early morning view of the port of Le Havre. Monet's *Impression, Sunrise* was like no painting anyone had ever seen before – yet somehow simultaneously exactly as the world actually appeared.

ABOVE:
MODERNIZING MEIJI?
Mutsuhito's imperial authority is summed up in a scowl in this 1873 portrait by Uchida Kuichi (1844–75). Historians differ on whether the Meiji Emperor drove his country's modernization or just watched it passively. Japan was certainly transformed completely during his reign.

RIGHT:
GATEWAY TO THE EAST
The opening of the Suez Canal was celebrated at Port Said with considerable pomp. The event was genuinely epoch-making, cutting almost 7,250 km (4,500 miles) from the East–West sea route, not just boosting freight traffic but also facilitating colonial exploitation more broadly.

America's Central Pacific and Union Pacific Railroads met at Promontory Summit in Utah to complete North America's first transcontinental railroad. A few months later, after a decade's construction and much longer being planned by France's Ferdinand de Lesseps (1805–94), the Suez Canal was opened. Cutting journey times – and making the voyage significantly safer – this did much to shrink the world and bring the East and West into closer contact. It also opened up East Africa to exploitation by the European countries.

The canal's impact wasn't necessarily direct or immediate. Resentment against Western interests had been well-established for decades before an angry Chinese mob attacked French diplomats and missionaries in the Tianjin Massacre of 1870. The arrival of a new wave of Spanish priests and administrators in the Philippines alienated the existing elite, encouraging an independence movement in the longer term.

The world seemed even smaller when in 1876 the Scotsman Alexander Graham Bell (1847–1922) invented the telephone.

AGE OF EMPIRE

TRANSATLANTIC COMMUNICATION
Deck of the SS *Great Eastern* (painted by Robert Charles Dudley, 1866), a cable-laying vessel. One of the nineteenth century's great technological achievements was to lay a telegraphic cable beneath the Atlantic, allowing messages to speed back and forth between North America and Europe in minutes, rather than 10–12 days by steamer.

AGE OF EMPIRE

RIGHT:
END OF EMPIRE
'Mexico', Porfirio Díaz was notoriously to say, was 'so far from God, so close to the United States'. But it was pushed around by other powers too. Including France, which imposed the Emperor Maximilian I on the country. Maximilian met a cruel fate – but no more so than many thousands of his Mexican subjects. His greatest achievement was probably to have his death depicted in a series of paintings from 1867 to 1869 by the great French Impressionist painter Édouard Manet (1832–83).

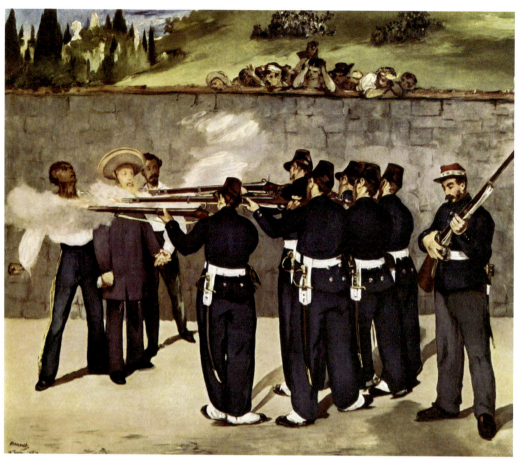

LEFT:
LIGHTBULB MOMENT
The Enlightenment had been all very well, but with his incandescent lightbulb (1878), Thomas Edison (1847–1931) had literally lit up the world; the culminating moment of a century that had seen a technological transformation of everyday life.

OPPOSITE:
ARMS RACE
No corner of modern life had been left untouched by innovation. Military technology was changing particularly fast. This French cannon represented a remarkable advance on earlier models – though they were to be surpassed by Germany's artillery in the Franco-Prussian War (1870–1).

(The following year America's Thomas Edison introduced a vibrating diaphragm which improved it greatly. The year after that, he'd help light up the world with his electric bulb.)

In 1880, De Lesseps had the idea for a Suez-style canal over the Isthmus of Panama, reasoning (rightly) that this would be a boon for global trade. Running 80 km (50 miles) through tropical rainforest, with some significant inclines, it would prove much more challenging to construct. It wasn't even to be started for another generation (in 1904) and wasn't opened until 1914.

The world was to be brought together to some extent with the resurrection of the ancient Olympic Games. The first modern version, held (appropriately) in Athens in 1896, involved competitors from 14 nations, competing in nine different sports. Over the decades, it was to expand. First, in 1900, with the addition of female competitors; then in a massive increase in its scope. (The first Winter Olympics would be held in 1924.)

FROM PARIS TO PARAGUAY

The year 1870 brought the outbreak of the Franco-Prussian War. Prussian forces invaded France and laid siege to Paris. The Emperor Napoleon III was taken prisoner and, with the collapse of his Second Empire, France's Third Republic began. The disputed province of Alsace–Lorraine was ceded to Germany. Paris's humiliating surrender sparked wider unrest in France. Angry radicals in the capital responded by establishing a workers' republic, the Paris Commune. This was suppressed after several weeks of vicious fighting.

Conservative Germany, by contrast, was buoyed by Prussia's victory. Prussian statesman Otto von Bismarck (1815–98) declared the inception of a Second Reich. Germany was unified under the authority of William I – formerly King of Prussia but now officially 'Emperor'; as Bismarck himself was to be the country's chancellor.

Anything European countries could do, independent former-colonies could do as well, for better or worse. This had been shown in 1870 when Argentina, Uruguay and Brazil had checked Paraguayan expansionism with their victory in the War of the Triple Alliance. Starting in 1864, this conflict had cost half a million lives.

SEMI-CITIZENS

A more peaceful struggle had begun in 1869, when Elizabeth Cady Stanton (1815–1902) and Susan B. Anthony (1820–1906) founded America's National Woman Suffrage Association to campaign for voting rights for women. The war for America's democratic soul was to go on for decades – and would have an important racial front as well. Not until 1876 did the Fourteenth Amendment grant the freed slaves full citizenship. An important step, though some ambiguity remained about their right to vote, an issue that would be wrangled over for generations.

It was unclear too on the citizenship-status of Native Americans. Several peoples were still fighting, quite literally, for their freedom. In 1876, the Great Sioux War – fought over access to the mineral-rich Black Hills, which were sacred to several native peoples – reached its climax at Little Bighorn, Montana. This engagement became iconic as a Native American victory and the scene of General W. Custer's fateful Last Stand, but the war was ultimately won by the USA.

In so far as citizenship was envisaged for Native Americans it was seen as conditional on self-cancelling assimilation. In 1894, leaders of Arizona's Hopi nation would be imprisoned on Alcatraz for resisting the forcible removal of their children

LEFT:
UNAVAILING VALOUR
French heroes hang on grimly at the Gate of Longboyau against an overwhelming attack by German infantry (1870). French fortunes at the Battle of Buzenval (1871) sum up the story of the Franco-Prussian War. Alphonse de Neuville's (1835–85) painting throws an epic lustre on defeat.

to state boarding schools. White resentment in the South was appeased by the blind eye Washington turned to discriminatory Jim Crow laws (a Jim Crow was a male crow, or of course in pejorative slang, a Black person) in the Southern states. These laws, officially enforcing racial segregation, were backed up informally by harassment from white supremacist groups.

Speaking in Atlanta in 1895, the African American intellectual Booker T. Washington (1856–1915) attracted much attention with what became known as the Atlanta Compromise. By a determined campaign of self-improvement, education and career advancement, Washington argued, African Americans would win white America over to their acceptance. Later leaders would see this as naive. How much remained to do became evident the following year when the case of Plessy vs Ferguson reached the US Supreme Court, which ruled that racial segregation was constitutional.

In 1893, New Zealand became the first country in the world to give its women the vote. Elsewhere, they would have to wait some time.

COLONIAL MISMANAGEMENT

A generation on from Ireland's Great Hunger, a still more severe and widespread famine hit southwestern India in 1876–8. Again, the effects of a natural disaster (in this case a drought on the Deccan Plateau) were compounded by official mishandling. Again, the afflicted area continued to export food while its people starved. The casualties were worse than they had been in Ireland, though, between 5 and 10 million people dying.

Not that Britain admitted blame. The following year it made Queen Victoria (1819–1901) 'Empress of India'. Though really just a ratification of the imposition of direct rule after the Rebellion of 1857, the ceremony has come to seem at best tone-deaf.

But British rule would appear benign beside that of the International African Association founded in 1876 by Belgium's King Leopold II (1835–1909). Purportedly a charitable foundation, its primary purpose was his own enrichment.

Leopold's personal imperialist project would appear utterly incredible if it weren't that Cecil Rhodes (1853–1902) had also acted as a colonialist one-man show, with Britain's backing. A mining magnate, he grew fabulously rich after founding De Beer's Mining Company in 1880 and was elected Prime Minister of Cape Colony two years later.

An avowed Anglo-Saxon supremacist, he saw Britain's destiny as ruling large tracts of Africa. Licensed by London, he'd go on to carve out a whole country ('Rhodesia') to the north of Cape Colony. (Northern Rhodesia would one day win its independence as Zambia ; Southern Rhodesia as Zimbabwe.)

LAST STAND HILL
Markers on the slopes of Last Stand Hill show where men of the US 7th Cavalry fell. General Custer's marker bears a plaque in black. A desperate day for the US Army, the Battle of Little Bighorn in 1976 represented the high point for the Lakota Sioux in their war to protect their way of life and the beginning of a longer, tragic arc of defeat and dispossession.

RIGHT:
CONTESTED LEGACY
Born a slave in 1856, Booker T. Washington would in 1901 have dinner with Theodore Roosevelt at the White House, the first African American to meet a US president on equal terms. Inspirational as his rise had been, his status as a role model was increasingly to be questioned by those who criticized his message of co-operation and compliance.

The discovery of diamonds along Cape Colony's northern edge in 1869 had caused conflict with the Boers there until the British simply took possession of the disputed area, compensating the Boer administration with financial payments. But Britain's attempt to annex Transvaal was defeated in the First Boer War, between 1880 and 1881.

THE SCRAMBLE FOR AFRICA

The idea of Africa as 'Dark Continent' dates back only to the 1870s. True, it was largely unexplored, but this was so for much of the world. The 'dark' designation self-servingly suggested a need for civilizing 'light'. Africa was duly on the agenda at the Berlin Conference of 1884–5. Bartering between the European powers here set off the Scramble for Africa.

Britain's claim on South Africa could hardly be disputed; nor could her hold on Egypt and the Upper Nile, though Germany was granted a chunk of East African territory in between. South West Africa (now Namibia), Togo and Cameroon also fell to Germany. Britain also had key footholds in West Africa, though France was the dominant power here. From 1890, Britain had a protectorate in Zanzibar. Portugal retained her longstanding possessions in Angola and Mozambique, whilst territorial scraps were thrown to Spain and Italy.

King Leopold II's bid for Belgium and his 'claim' was recognized. In the years that followed he would create a colonial holocaust. Millions died at the hands of Leopold's troops over the decades, many severely tortured and mutilated first.

Rhodes's flamboyant adventurism went on meanwhile. In 1886, gold was found in Transvaal and British prospectors streamed in. They had no right to be there but to Rhodes the obvious way of legitimizing their position was to make this British territory by force. He had already funded imperial expansion into Bechuanaland – and of course 'Rhodesia'. In 1895, he backed the Jameson Raid (led by one Captain Jameson) – a daring but foolhardy attack on Transvaal by freelance desperadoes. This was supposed to provoke an English settler uprising, which would allow a more 'official'

BELOW:
EMPIRE BUILDER
Cecil Rhodes, as he liked to see himself, an English colossus – and exemplar of Anglo-Saxon supremacy – bestriding the African continent from Cape to Suez. In real life, Rhodes grew rich and powerful enough to have a whole country named after him. Now he's seen as representing all that was wrong with the nineteenth-century colonial era.

RIGHT:
INTO THE ABYSS
Published in London in 1901, *Fortunes Made in Business: Life Struggles of Successful People* showed how the myths of colonialism and capitalism went hand in hand. Men like Rhodes were lionized for the 'life struggles' they'd allegedly endured; men like these miners at Kimberley, South Africa, supposedly owed them the utmost gratitude.

British intervention. Rhodes had to resign when the enterprise collapsed ignominiously.

SLAUGHTER IN THE SUDAN

Egypt by now was a semi-detached province of the Ottoman Empire, its viceroy or khedive looking to London as much as to Istanbul. By 1882, he was seriously alarmed at events up the Nile Valley in Sudan. Here, the teacher Muhammad ibn Abdallah (1843–85) had announced he was the Mahdi (a Messiah-like redeemer prophesied in certain traditions of Islam).

General Charles Gordon (1833–85) went to Khartoum to restore order but, his presence only inflaming the situation, he was ordered to withdraw. Instead, he decided to mount a heroic defence of the city. By March he had his way: he was actually under siege. A popular clamour in Britain led to the dispatch of a relief expedition from Egypt, but in January 1885 – just a couple of days before help arrived – the rebels stormed the city. Gordon got his heroic end, cut down by the attackers.

Fury erupted at home and Lord Herbert Kitchener (1850–1916) began a long and arduous campaign to take back Sudan – a point of honour now. The battles of Omdurman (1898) and Umm Diwaykarat (1899) were both victories for Britain's Maxim gun (an early machine gun) and heavy artillery. Fewer than 50 British soldiers died in the former, as against 10,000

AGE OF EMPIRE

OLD VERSUS NEW
The reforms of the Meiji era in Japan were naturally resisted by the traditional elite. By none more resolutely than by the country's Samurai warriors, who would have no place in any modern army or social structure. In 1877, the Samurai of the Satsuma Domain (now Kagoshima) rose in rebellion. After eight months of ferocious fighting they were defeated.

ABOVE:
BENZ'S BABY
No one could have guessed, presented with this spindly, insubstantial-looking tricycle, the impact that the motor car would have. Not just as a means of transport, but as a status symbol, a cultural icon and a force in everything from industry to urban planning. Dating from 1886, this Benz Patent-Motorwagen model is kept as a museum piece in India.

Sudanese tribesmen; the latter saw three Britons killed and 1,000 Mahdists killed or wounded. Sudan was declared a 'condominium', jointly ruled by Britain and Egypt, but the former was very obviously in charge.

Italy's plans for an African empire weren't going quite so well. In 1895, its forces were defeated at Adwa and it was forced to recognize Ethiopian independence in the Treaty of Addis Ababa.

Asia was in Western sights as well. Francis Younghusband's trip to Tibet on behalf of Britain in 1904, though labelled 'exploration', was primarily about opening the country up to trade; secondarily about beating the Russians there under the rules of the 'Great Game'.

Not that all the empire builders were European. Japan, by now beginning to recover from earlier humiliations, was thriving economically and in expansionist mood. In 1894–5 it went to war with China over possession of Korea. Victorious in this First Sino-Japanese War, Japan took Taiwan as well.

ASSEMBLING AN EMPIRE

A Second Cuban Independence War began in 1895. This widened when, in 1898, the USS *Maine* – there to protect US interests – blew up in Havana harbour. Whilst the explosion was almost certainly accidental, it suited America to see it as Spanish sabotage. The Spanish-American War subsumed the independence struggle and quickly won it, albeit at the cost of increased Cuban reliance on its northern neighbour. America got Guam, the Philippines and Puerto Rico as colonial possessions whilst what in Spain was called the 'Disaster' precipitated political panic and cultural soul-searching.

Separately, the USA annexed Hawaii, whose indigenous royal family weren't (in the view of American pineapple magnates) looking out sufficiently for the interests of international business. It was taken as read that Westerners knew best: in 1896, an Anglo-French treaty had established the borders between (British) Burma and (French) Laos, though the independence of Siam (Thailand) was to be respected.

CHANGE IN CHINA?

Modernity had meanwhile been catching up with Qing China. In 1894, Sun Yat-sen (1866–1925) founded his Chinese

AGE OF EMPIRE

Nationalist Party (Kuomintang). That same year, Japan invaded Korea, triggering the Sino-Japanese War. Despite its size, China was no threat to an industrialized Japan with a powerful fleet and modern weaponry. It was forced to recognize Korean 'independence' (as a client of Tokyo) and hand Formosa (Taiwan) over to the Japanese. In 1897, German forces seized Kiaochow Bay, Shiantung, China, ostensibly in retaliation for the murder of two missionaries, though they quickly established a trading post there.

Many felt a need for change. In 1898, a groundswell of reformist feeling (the Hundred Days Reform) seemed set to

LEFT:
PERIODIC PIONEER
The son of an Orthodox priest from western Siberia, Dmitri Mendeleev (1834–1907) went on to become one of the greatest scientists of the nineteenth century. It is to him that we owe the Periodic Table of the Elements (1869), a cornerstone of modern chemistry, along with advances into a range of other disciplines, from meteorology to hydrodynamics.

BELOW:
MOMENTOUS MEETING
The coming-together of the Central Pacific and Union Pacific Railroads in Utah opened the door to transcontinental travel in the USA. In 1876, a train would make the trip from New York to San Francisco in just 83 hours – the journey would have taken weeks by stagecoach or on horseback.

bring China a constitutional monarchy, but was suppressed by the Dowager Empress (the late-emperor's widow) Cixi (1835–1908). Even so, China continued to be pushed around by foreign powers. In 1898, its Manchurian port of Lushun was taken by the Russians and renamed Port Arthur, while Britain bullied the country into granting it a 99-year lease on Kowloon, the mainland territory across the straits from Hong Kong. Without it the island colony would have been unviable.

In 1899, the Boxer Rebellion broke out. Members of the Cult of Righteous and Harmonious Fists attacked foreigners, killing several hundred businessmen and Christian missionaries (and more than 30,000 Chinese converts). An Eight-Nation Alliance including Britain, Russia, the USA, France, Japan, Austria-Hungary, Italy and the German Empire all sent troops to northern China to put the rising down. The allies sustained several thousand casualties themselves but cut down the rebels in their tens of thousands.

BEATING THE BOERS

A Second Boer War started in 1899. Invading Cape Colony, the Boers besieged the towns of Ladysmith, Mafeking and Kimberley. In this static situation, though, they were a sitting target for the biggest British army ever sent abroad (almost 200,000). The Siege of Ladysmith was finally lifted on 27 February 1900. Amidst jubilant celebrations back in Britain, Mafeking was relieved on 18 May, whilst Transvaal's capital, Pretoria, was taken on 5 June.

But the Boers just melted away into the hills to continue a guerrilla war that better suited them. Britain reacted ruthlessly, with a scorched-earth policy, creating its own small forces of mounted troops to counter the Boer raiding parties. Trains were used to whisk men and munitions around the country. And – controversially – Kitchener, the British commander, confined over 100,000 Boer civilians in 'concentration camps'. Thousands died in disease-ridden conditions here.

Eventually, in 1902, the Boers were forced to sign the Treaty of Vereeniging, giving up their territory – though they were granted a degree of autonomy five years later. In 1910, South Africa became a self-governing dominion, comprising Cape Colony, Natal, Transvaal and the Orange Free State.

'VOTES FOR WOMEN'

Women's struggle for representation had continued in many countries. In 1897, Millicent Garrett Fawcett (1847–1929) brought Britain's different groups together to form the

OPPOSITE:
GERM THEORY
Louis Pasteur's (1822–95) microbiological researches were to make him one of the founders of germ theory – a crucial scientific advance. More practically, the process of 'Pasteurization' (a method of killing microbes with gentle heat) he developed would help shape food technology into the twentieth century. He would also have a lasting impact on the field of medicine.

ABOVE:
SITTING BULL
The leader of the Lakota Sioux is shown here in 1883 – two years after his final surrender. The ferocity with which Sitting Bull had resisted encroachment on the Great Plains would soon be vindicated as settlers' wagon trains streamed westward and the bison herds were hunted to extinction.

National Union of Women's Suffrage Societies (NUWSS). By 1903, though, some feminists felt the NUWSS's commitment to peaceful, lawful methods meant that, realistically, it was doomed to fail. Hence Emmeline Pankhurst's (1858–1928) formation of the Women's Social and Political Union (WSPU), dedicated to direct action with the motto 'Deeds, not words'.

Its members stood up to address the public in city parks and fairgrounds. Even so, progress was slow, so when in 1905 Emmeline's daughter Christabel and another suffragist, Annie Kenney, were arrested for disrupting a Liberal Party meeting, they chose to go to prison rather than pay a fine. A succession of 'suffragettes' were then imprisoned after attention-grabbing protests – from breaking shop windows to chaining themselves to railings outside public buildings. One, Emily Wilding

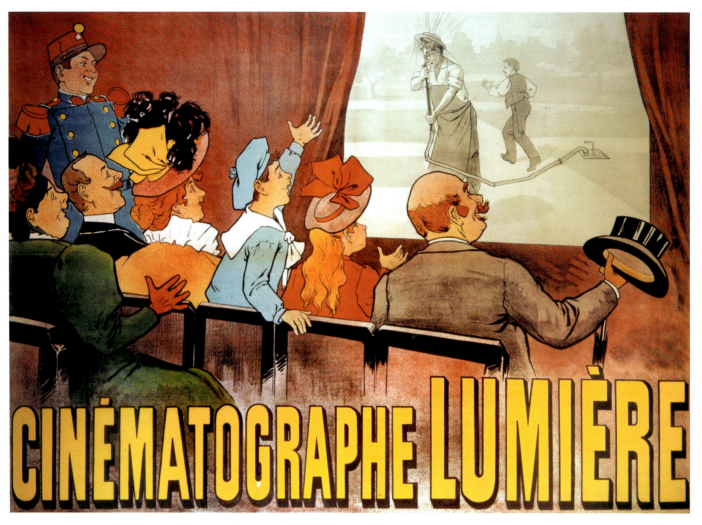

ABOVE:
THE FIRST FILMS
The French Lumière brothers, Auguste and Pierre, developed their Cinématographe in the 1890s: an integrated system, it both recorded and projected moving pictures. As this poster shows, this period saw rapid change in the commercial arts more generally, mechanical reproduction methods fostering an innovative aesthetic of art nouveau.

OPPOSITE:
ON THE LINE
On 19 October 1892, inventor Alexander Graham Bell completes preparations for the first phone call from New York to Chicago. The conversation between the cities' mayors was stilted and ceremonial, but it still marked the start of a new era in communications.

Davison, even threw herself to her death beneath the hooves of the King's racehorse in the Derby of 1913.

Some suffragettes continued their protests in prison, going on hunger strike. Several were force-fed. Women's contribution to the war effort in 1914–18 not only as nurses but on the home front may have helped sway political opinion. By the time the war ended, opposition to women's suffrage was softening, though not till 1928 would all adult British women have the vote. American women had won this right by 1920, though discriminatory practices often prevented Black and Native American women – along with their menfolk – from exercising it.

AN AGE OF INNOVATION

The nineteenth century had seen enormous changes. Some crucial ones came as it approached its end. In 1885, Chicago's Home Insurance Building was constructed around a steel frame, making it arguably (though there are other claimants) the world's first 'skyscraper'. The following year, in Germany, Karl Benz (1849–1944) and Gottlieb Daimler (1834–1900) just about dead-heated with a 'vehicle powered by a gas engine' – a car. In 1888, the Scottish inventor John Boyd Dunlop opened the way to softer rides for everyone by developing the first pneumatic tyre. Ten years later, Rudolf Diesel (1858–1913) gave his name to a new kind of internal combustion engine. Everything was in place for the automobile age.

Flight was always going to take longer, but even so it came quite soon. In 1903, Orville and Wilbur Wright made the first mechanically powered flight at Kitty Hawk, North Carolina.

Few were aware, and even fewer, perhaps, able to understand, but in 1905 the physicist Albert Einstein (1879–1955), a German Jew working in Switzerland, came up with his Special Theory of Relativity. Meanwhile, in Vienna, another

AGE OF EMPIRE

AGE OF EMPIRE

ABOVE:
LADYSMITH BESIEGED
The Second Boer War posed different challenges to its contending foes. If British forces struggled in the scrubland of the Veldt, the Boers – the quintessential guerrillas – were ill-equipped to mount a large-scale siege. That they managed to pin down the might of the British as long as they did is testimony to their determination.

RIGHT:
SIGMUND FREUD, 1903
Technological progress was bringing men and women unprecedented mastery over their environments, saving labour, banishing the darkness, warming the cold. Even so, it struck Sigmund Freud, they were as subject as ever to their psychologies, to desires and fears of which they weren't necessarily aware of themselves. Freud posited a theory of the psyche that has become the foundation for much of modern psychology and psychotherapy.

OPPOSITE:
SUN YAT-SEN
Kuomintang leader Sun Yat-sen wasn't just the first revolutionary to free China from imperial rule: he wore what Westerners know as the 'Mao Jacket' (shown here) before his Communist successor did. Sadly, his democratic rule was overthrown by a Nationalist rival.

Jew had since the 1890s been delving into the depths of the human psyche. Sigmund Freud (1856–1939) suggested that our conscious thoughts and actions were strongly influenced by subconscious motives of which we weren't aware.

BLAMING THE JEWS

Did the sense that Jews knew other people better than they knew themselves prompt the fear that many felt for them, despite their objective vulnerability in much of Europe? Deepening economic woes within the Russian Empire would no doubt have fuelled a rise in antisemitism even if this hadn't been fostered by a Czarist state looking to distract attention from its failures. Pogroms, a problem for decades, had flared up again after the assassination (by socialist revolutionaries) of Alexander II in 1881.

In 1894, the Dreyfus Case began in France. The Jewish-descended army officer Alfred Dreyfus was accused of selling secret documents to Germany. Found guilty, he did five years' hard labour on Devil's Island in French Guinea. When new evidence appeared to clear him and implicate a non-Jewish superior, it was suppressed; and new documentation forged to further incriminate Dreyfus. His retrial, from 1899, divided France, bringing antisemitism out into the open. He was proven innocent – but not officially exonerated till 1906.

In the face of what appeared to be an intractable problem, increasing numbers of European Jews had been wondering about the possibility of emigration to a place of safety. It made sense for many to try to fulfil the traditional Passover prayer 'Next year in Jerusalem …' with a return to their ancestral homeland in the Middle East. This goal was taken up by Theodor Herzl's Zionist Movement (though in 1903 it would briefly consider a British offer of an area of Uganda).

In the meantime, the persecution in Europe went on. Grew worse, indeed, between 1903 and 1906, when, in a wave of 600-odd pogroms, hundreds of Jews were killed and thousands of homes and businesses burned down. This time, too, the outbreaks were discreetly stirred by the state, whose agents wrote up the main conspiracy theories in the *Protocols of the Elders of Zion* (1903). Purporting to be a plan for world domination drawn up by leaders of the international Jewry, this document has been comprehensively debunked but remains a central text for antisemitism worldwide.

REVOLUTION AND REPRIEVE

Deep as it was, Jew hatred didn't look like being quite enough to save the Czar. Nicholas II's (1868–1918) regime was rocked by unrest in 1905. After Bloody Sunday, when a hunger march was

LEFT:
E = MC² FORMULA
The formula is as famous as its theoretical underpinnings are obscure, and its implications for modern physics – and modern life – have been far-reaching. With his Theory of Relativity, Albert Einstein made quantum mechanics possible – and opened the door to the destructive power of the atomic bomb.

OPPOSITE:
PANAMA CANAL
Over 25,000 workers died during the Panama Canal's construction. Malaria and yellow fever were both rife. It must have saved a few lives since, given the notorious treachery of the waters around Cape Horn. And it has certainly saved time and energy and expense, reducing the sea voyage from North America's east to west coasts by 12,500 km (7,800 miles).

fired on by troops and over 200 people killed, strikes broke out and demonstrations held, and the state came close to collapsing.

Nicholas survived but Puyi (1906–1967), the Xuantong Emperor, wasn't so lucky when China was gripped by revolution in 1911. The Qing dynasty was overthrown and longstanding campaigner Sun Yat-sen was elected provisional President of the Republic of China. Democratic hopes were quickly dashed. His elected successor, General Yuan Shikai, had dictatorial ambitions which provoked a short-lived 'Second Revolution' against him in southern China. Confirmed as president, he promptly suspended the Constitution and expelled Kuomintang nationalists from the Assembly. The news from Korea was no better. More than 30,000 had died fighting the Japanese invasion which had led to the country's annexation in 1910.

In 1908, the Young Turks had mounted a revolution against the Ottoman authorities, calling for a Western-style democracy. They did indeed succeed in establishing constitution rule of a sort and their influence was felt across the Islamic world. Also felt was the realization that Ottoman rule was crumbling. In 1909, Muhammad ibn Ali al-Idrisi (1876–1924) led a revolt in Asir, southwestern Arabia, still not effectively suppressed two years later, by the time Imam Yahya (1869–1948) negotiated autonomy for Yemen.

In Mexico, meanwhile, Porfirio Díaz (1830–1915) had been dictator since 1876. He'd brought a degree of stability, but at

DISAPPOINTED HOPES
Almost half a century after the gold rushes in California and Australia, in 1896–9, prospectors flocked in their thousands to Klondike, in northwestern Canada's Yukon Territory. Of the 100,000 who set out from Seattle and San Francisco, only 40,000 even made it there; only a handful made meaningful finds; most were ruined and many died.

AGE OF EMPIRE

RIGHT:
MANHANDLED
Two policemen tower above the suffragette they are arresting. Though often alienated by the unladylike nature of their protests, the public sometimes felt unease at the rough treatment they received. Over 1,300 suffragettes (and some male supporters) had been arrested by August 1914, when an amnesty was declared at the start of World War I.

OPPOSITE ABOVE:
AIRBORNE!
Orville pilots, his brother Wilbur trots along the sand as wingman, as the Wright Flyer makes the first mechanically powered flight at Kitty Hawk on 17 December, 1903. Aviation design would develop with astonishing speed from this point on.

OPPOSITE BELOW:
BLOODY SUNDAY
Nicholas II wasn't even in St Petersburg when his troops opened fire for his 'protection' outside the Winter Palace. The hunger marchers they aimed at had been hoping to hand in a petition asking the czar to intervene to ease food shortages. The official response did nothing to ease the situation in a Russia that was coming close to social breakdown.

the cost of democratic freedom. He'd also brought a measure of prosperity, but at the expense of economic autonomy because he'd done it by opening up the country – and its important oil industry – to US investors. And he'd done it only for the very wealthy few in a society in which the vast majority were poor.

In 1910, he rigged his re-election but it seemed he'd outstayed his welcome. The whole country appeared to rise up against him. Francisco Madero led the official, liberal opposition, but the real makers of the Mexican Revolution were the popular leaders Emiliano Zapata and Francisco 'Pancho' Villa. Madero took power for a time in 1911, but was quickly toppled in his turn by Victoriano Huerta (1854–1916), a military strongman backed by the USA.

Meanwhile, t's were being crossed and i's dotted in world exploration. Humans had been almost everywhere by now. The first reliable claim to have reached the North Pole wasn't to come until 1968–9, when a British Trans-Arctic Expedition recorded it precisely. But the American Robert Peary most likely reached the Pole in April 1909. The race to the South Pole was won by a party led by Norwegian explorer Roald Amundsen (1872–1928) in 1911–12. But their achievement was overshadowed by the loss of a rival British expedition led by Captain Scott (1868–1912).

AGE OF EMPIRE

311

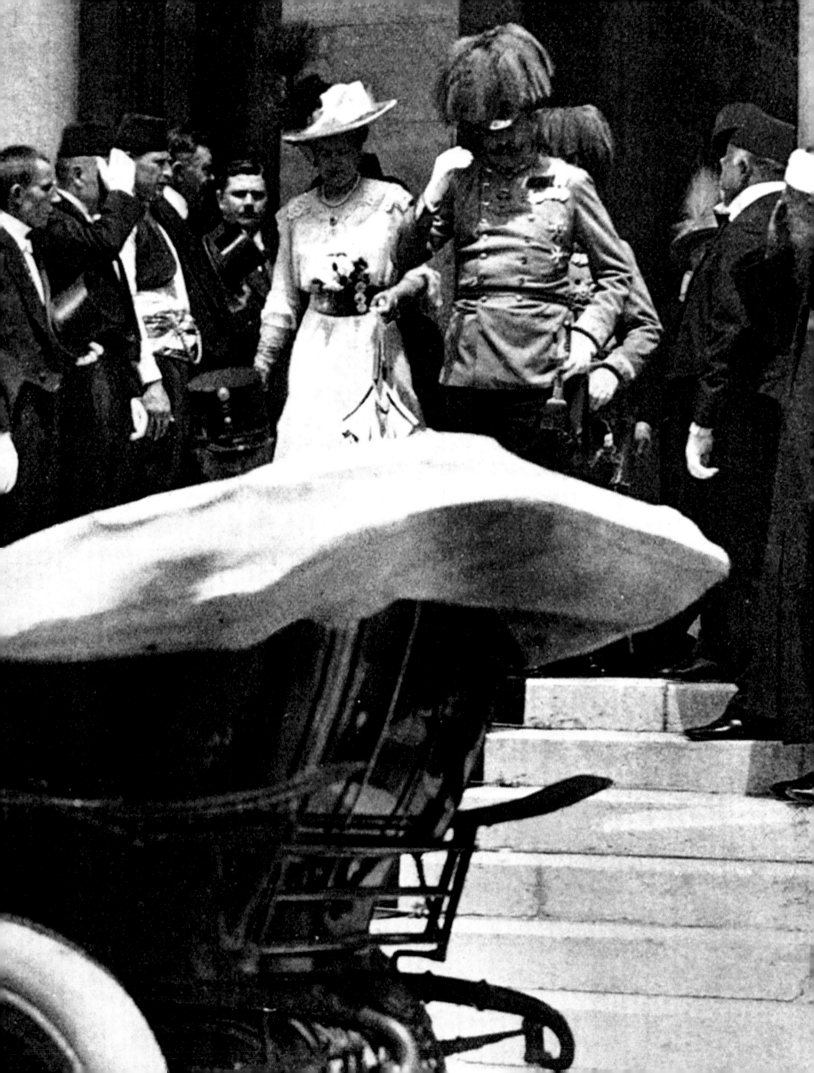

WORLD ON FIRE
1914 – 1945

German unification had been joyous, a people separated by centuries of history reunited, a family again. Many Germans had certainly felt this way. For Bismarck, though, the new *Reich* wasn't about fellowship or freedom but 'Blood and Iron'.

As for Kaiser Wilhelm II (1859–1941), he promised 'glorious times' and a 'place in the sun'. This figuratively suggested a desire to see Germany at the forefront among the European states, though it hinted more literally at his colonial ambitions. He gave his people an enduring if unpleasant nickname when, sending his troops to China to help put down the Boxer Rebellion, he told them to be as ruthless as the ancient Huns. In 1896, he'd asked his senior admiral, Alfred von Tirpitz (1849–1930), to go all out to build the German fleet.

DARKENING SKIES

In 1902, an uneasy Britain had allied with Imperial Japan, so its Royal Navy could concentrate on its home waters. In 1904, it agreed an unprecedented *Entente Cordiale* ('Friendly Agreement') with France, its enemy of centuries. Since Russia already had its own treaty with France, 1907's Anglo-Russian Treaty produced a 'Triple Alliance' between these three powers.

OPPOSITE:
FLASHPOINT
Within minutes of this photo being taken on 28 June 1914, Archduke Franz Ferdinand would be dead; within weeks, the continent of Europe – and the world – would be at war. Within four years, some 20 million people, combatants and civilians, would have been killed.

RIGHT:
FEMINIST MARTYR
A quiet, studious woman, Emily Wilding Davison became a firebrand in the fight for women's suffrage. After serving several prison sentences, going on hunger-strikes and suffering force-feeding, she threw herself beneath the hoofs of the king's horse, Anmer, in the 1913 Derby.

WORLD ON FIRE

ABOVE:
READY TO ROLL
Model Ts stand arrayed at the Ford factory, Detroit. Mass-production transformed workplaces – and lives. You could, notoriously, have any colour you wanted as long as it was black. Standardization seemed a small price to pay for the freedom a car brought.

OPPOSITE:
ROYAL RESEMBLANCES
Europe's ruling houses did not just share enormous privilege: they were closely connected by kinship ties. Here, Queen Victoria, the future Edward VII, Czar Nicholas II, Czarina Alexandra, Kaiser Wilhelm II and Empress Augusta attend a wedding in Coburg, Germany, 1894.

Germany formed its own alliance. Already partnered with Austria-Hungary, it now linked with the Ottoman Empire. Despite its historical fear of the Turks, Bulgaria dreaded Russia even more, so it too allied with the 'Central Powers'.

The commissioning of Britain's HMS *Dreadnought* in 1906 was one response to Germany's naval build-up. Driven by steam turbines, it was far faster than preceding ships. Its big guns allowed it to engage its enemies from beyond torpedo-range. So radically did it transform naval warfare, a whole generation of warships was named after it. By 1908, though, Germany, had its equivalent, the *Nassau*. Press and public enthusiasm fuelled an arms race that extended into other areas of the military – and soon involved other states as well. None felt safe. Especially when news of the Schlieffen Plan leaked. Prepared on the Kaiser's orders by Count Alfred von Schlieffen in 1904, this envisaged simultaneous invasions of Russia and France.

There had been some straws in the colonial wind as well. In March 1905, the Kaiser had visited Tangiers amidst great fanfare, promising the Moroccan king his support against French domination. France and Britain had both reacted angrily to this 'First Morocco Crisis'. A second came when, in 1911, the German gunboat *Panther* was deployed off Agadir but the threat of war in Europe was averted when a face-saving deal was agreed. Germany withdrew its claims in Morocco in return for territory in Equatorial Africa to add to its existing protectorate in Cameroon.

The world of the arts had seen its share of ructions, the Catalan painter Pablo Picasso (1881–1973) having burst upon the scene. Shocking itself for its subject matter, *Les Démoiselles d'Avignon* (1907) – supposedly representing a group of young prostitutes – was still more scandalous in introducing the idea

of Cubism in art. Picasso seemed to collapse conventional perspective, as formalized in the Renaissance, to show the girls from different standpoints simultaneously.

OIL AT ISSUE

On the plus side, from a British perspective, was the signing-over of oil-exploration rights to Britain by Kuwait, and the creation of an Anglo-Persian Oil Company in Iran. It was clear by now that the motor car was here to stay and petroleum supplies were starting to influence geopolitics.

Iran was in any case a cockpit for great-power rivalries. After a brief period of constitutional rule in the country, Shah Muhammad Ali (1872–1925) had suspended the constitution and re-established absolute rule with the backing of a Persian Cossack Brigade from Russia. But the British were still competing as part of the ongoing 'Great Game'. Muhammad Ali was to be deposed again in 1909.

LEFT:
KINGS, COUSINS, ALLIES
George V (left) and Czar Nicholas II were on the same side in World War I, though the British king would be prevented by Parliament from granting his Russian relatives asylum after the Revolution a few years later.

BELOW:
RIOTOUS RITE
Stravinsky's ballet, *The Rite of Spring*, caused a sensation on its premiere in 1913. The new century had brought a transformation in the arts.

At the centre of the news agenda, though, was the crescendoing drumbeat of war. A conflict was coming: the central question was exactly when.

A SPARK AT SARAJEVO

Subsidiary ones were how and why. The broader an alliance, the more potential flashpoints. As it turned out, the fateful spark came in Sarajevo, Bosnia. The assassination of the Archduke of Austria, on 28 June 1914, by the anarchist Gavrilo Princip, precipitated war between the Central Powers and Serbia, a Russian ally. As the czar's forces readied for war, so did France. Britain demanded that Germany promise to respect Belgian

BELOW:
A YOUNG TURK COMES OF AGE
The year 1912 brought the First Balkan War, pitting Bulgaria, Greece, Serbia and Montenegro against Ottoman Turkey. But this ended in 1913 without dragging in the rest of Europe. The Balkan states secured their independence, as did a new one, Albania. A few months later, a Second Balkan War saw Bulgaria seek to relitigate the outcome of the First. The victorious Ottoman general, Enver Pasha, a 'Young Turk', rode the adulation to seize power as dictator.

WORLD ON FIRE

WORLD ON FIRE

ABOVE:
PROSPECTING IN PERSIA
If the nineteenth century had been coal-fired, the twentieth would run on petroleum. Oil wasn't yet driving the geopolitical engine globally, but in certain places it was already shaping events. Iran was emphatically one of these.

LEFT:
MARCHING TO VICTORY?
The mood is upbeat on the streets of Croydon, southern England, as the town's Territorials mobilize for France, 5 August 1914. Most Britons expected the war to be relatively painless and quickly won ('over by Christmas'). But then so did civilians on all sides.

neutrality. Instead, on 4 August, Berlin put its Schlieffen Plan into action, its troops invading Belgium en route for France. Britain couldn't do otherwise than declare war. A few days later, on the Eastern Front, Austria-Hungary invaded Russia.

It was already clear that this would be a global war. Arrayed against the Central Powers were Britain and its imperial possessions like Australia, New Zealand, South Africa, Rhodesia, India and Canada, as well as Russia, Romania, Belgium, Greece, Montenegro, Portugal and Poland. Italy, Japan and the United States would join in later.

BY LAND AND SEA

In September, their French invasion held up by Allied forces at the First Battle of the Marne, the Germans dug in for trench warfare. This would be the defining feature of the conflict. Things weren't yet completely static: the 'Race to the Sea' was just beginning. Naval combat was to be important in the war, and the

WORLD ON FIRE

North Sea coast would eventually be fought over as an important base for German U-boats (submarines). For now, though, the 'race' was about each side trying to avoid being outflanked to the north by the other's armies.

The sea became a theatre in February 1915, when Germany's U-boats began their blockade of Britain. Much 'British' strength – in men, munitions, raw materials and food supplies – actually came from the wider Empire. It was vital to the Germans that this source of strength should be cut off. Britain wasn't to be long in mounting its own blockade on Germany. Logistics were more important than they'd ever been.

A few months later, the war began in earnest for the Ottoman Empire with the landing of Allied forces at Gallipoli, a peninsula on the Dardanelles, between the Aegean and the Black Sea. As was becoming a pattern, the dash and verve of the Allies' initial amphibious operation was quickly mired in mud and stalled in static trench warfare.

Russian, French and 'British' troops were involved, though many of this last group represented ANZAC (the Australian and New Zealand Army Corps). After almost 11 months of fighting, the Ottomans would win, exacting terrible casualties–a disaster for the Allies and a humiliation for Britain's First Lord of the Admiralty, Winston Churchill (1874–1965), who had proposed the plan.

GAS ATTACK

The Second Battle of Ypres (April–May 1915) is best known now as the first major military engagement in which poison gas was deployed. As we've seen, the fighting had very quickly settled down into static stalemate: both sides had been searching for ways to make a breakthrough.

German hopes were high for chlorine gas, and indeed in the first ten minutes, 5,000 Allied soldiers died. As they breathed in, their lungs and throats burst out in blisters and, basically, they drowned. The Germans were able to walk through the gaps opening up in the British line – only to find they couldn't advance further because the air was still filled with clouds of choking, smothering gas.

THE 'MEAT GRINDER'

In February 1916, following the biggest bombardment in history (a million shells in a single day), Germany advanced on the city of Verdun. This battle was to be the longest (at 302 days) and among the cruellest of the war. Such was the carnage that it seemed a force all of its own. Combatants didn't feel they were fighting so much as being fed through a machine. French soldiers called the battle the 'meat grinder'.

RIGHT:
INTO ACTION
A film-still arrests the instant in which an infantry company goes 'over the top' to start its terrifying charge across 'No Man's Land'. The pointed Pickelhaube helmet marks these men out as Germans, but trench warfare was traumatic on both sides.

WORLD ON FIRE

ABOVE:
ATROCITY AT SEA
Among the 1,199 killed when a U-boat torpedoed the Liverpool-bound liner *Lusitania* were 128 Americans. The act very nearly brought the USA into the war. But most Americans were loath to be involved in what seemed someone else's quarrel.

LEFT:
THE WONDER-WEAPON
Submarine warfare was in its infancy. But then so were defences against it, material and tactical. Germany's U-boats wrought havoc among Allied shipping in the first years of the war.

The French were very nearly vanquished in this first assault. They hung on, though, and were gradually able to consolidate their position. They brought up supplies and reinforcements along what they (only half-jokingly) referred to as their *Voie Sacrée* ('Sacred Way'), along which 600 lorries a day plied back and forth.

When the Germans sent observers up in balloons and planes to help their gunners sight, the French deployed Nieuport 16 Bébé ('Baby') fighter planes to shoot them down or see them off. In response, the Germans sent up Fokker Eindecker fighters. 'If we're chased from the skies,' said France's General Philippe Pétain (1856–1951), 'then it's simple. Verdun is lost.' Flying together in disciplined *escadrilles* – little squadrons – the French won this aspect of the fight. A small triumph, but with major implications for the battle as a whole.

Meanwhile, the armies slugged it out in a cycle of attack and counter-attack. In the end, the Germans were exhausted first. Taking over from a discredited Erich Georg Von Falkenhayn (1861–1922), Paul von Hindenburg (1847–1934) admitted that, despite his predecessor's promise to bleed the French white, it had been for his side that Verdun had proven an 'open wound'.

INDECISIVE ENCOUNTERS

On 1 July, the Allies launched a major offensive along the River Somme. This was to be one of the biggest, bloodiest battles of the war. Three million men were involved in total, of whom about a third were killed, with no great gains made by either side. It would come to emblematize the futility of much of the fighting in World War I.

But it was probably beaten for sheer pointlessness by the Battle of Passchendaele (July–November 1917), fought for a railhead in the strategically important Ypres Salient (a 'salient' is a wedge of land sticking out into enemy-held territory). Driving rain – of an intensity and persistence unseasonal even for the West European summer – made the battlefield a morass of deep, thick mud, churned up by vehicles and pitted by shell-craters that filled with

BELOW:
POSTCARD PERFECT
This postcard from 1914 shows French troops marching to the front dressed in their traditional blue coats and red trousers, a style that was quickly discarded once the realities of trench warfare became obvious. Soon, the entire army moved to the light grey and more practical 'horizon blue' colour scheme for the remainder of the war. Between 1914 and 1918, 7.9 million French citizens were called to serve in the armed forces, compared to 11 million Germans.

water. Though 220,000 Germans died and 275,000 on the British side, the outcome was inconclusive once again.

GLOBAL CONFLICT

World War I is generally remembered for the trenches of the Western Front, but it was fought in several theatres and over a variety of terrains. Even within Europe. Between June 1915 and November 1917, the Italians fought 11 battles along the Isonzo River, in the mountains of Slovenia. Not until the last couple would they make any real headway against the Austrians. There was fighting too among the crags and passes of the Alps and Dolomites. A world away from the mud and misery of the Western Front, but just as harsh.

In West Africa, the German colonies of Togo, Cameroon and Southwest Africa (Namibia) were quickly taken by the Allies, though Paul von Lettow-Vorbeck led determined resistance in East Africa. Across the world, Australian and New Zealand forces took German possessions in New Guinea and Samoa; Japan the Mariana, Caroline and Marshall Islands.

Troops from British India fought the Ottoman Turks in Mesopotamia, defeating them at Basra before fighting their way through to Baghdad. The hold they gained in what is now Iraq prevented the Germans from completing the railway they'd been building from Hamburg to Baghdad – and from gaining access to the oilfields of Iran. Likewise, later in the mountains of the Caucasus, Russian armies would engage Ottoman troops to secure the vital oilfields of Baku, Azerbaijan.

World War I was all-encompassing, a global conflict but also a local one in which the most parochial feuds might be continued or scores settled. Just because they were local didn't mean that they were small or insignificant. Up to 1.5 million Armenians were killed by Ottoman forces in the genocide of 1915–17 on what seem to have been a blend of religious (they were Christian) and racist grounds.

OPPOSITE:
PATRIOTISM BY PROXY?
It wasn't just its geographical reach that made it a 'world war': it brought in colonial troops from far and wide. Fighting, as here in Palestine, seems simultaneously to have cemented Indians' sense of Britishness and started to stir the desire for self-rule.

BELOW:
ACCLIMATIZED
The first gas attacks were experienced as assault by an advancing front of evil, overwhelmingly insidious, though the Allies fairly quickly developed tactics and equipment to protect themselves. Even the horses are masked-up in this German artillery train.

WORLD ON FIRE

RETREATS AND RISINGS

By summer 1915, things were going badly enough for an ill-equipped and poorly provisioned Russian army that its commanders had to order a 'Great Retreat'. This was billed as a tactical withdrawal, but it didn't suggest success; any more than the Serbian retreat before the advancing armies of Austria-Hungary and Bulgaria.

Another writer, Thomas Edward ('T.E.') Lawrence (1888–1935), was embedded with the desert Arabs who, that June, under the leadership of Sharif Hussein, rose in revolt against their Ottoman oppressors. They captured Aqaba, Baghdad and Damascus. 'Lawrence of Arabia' acquired mythic status in the West, to some extent unjustly overshadowing his hosts.

LEARNING CURVES

Broad as it was in geographical range, the war went on for long enough to see developments – in technology; in tactics; in equipment. The tank made an early appearance at the Somme, but improved models deployed at Cambrai, France in 1917 made much more impact. Even now, it was cumbersome and slow, used as a moving bulwark for advancing infantry, crushing barbed wire and providing protection against enemy fire.

ABOVE:
DREADNOUGHT ON DISPLAY
May 1916 brought an encounter between big battleships at the Battle of Jutland, fought just off the Danish coast. Over 150 British fighting vessels (including 28 dreadnoughts) faced 99 German ships (including 16 dreadnoughts, like the SMS *Schleswig-Holstein* we see here). Almost 180,000 tonnes (198,420 tons) of shipping were sunk and over 8,000 men lost in total. The Germans, though outgunned, got off more lightly than the Royal Navy, but neither side could claim a convincing victory.

RIGHT:
LANDSCAPE OF THE DAMNED
'I died in hell … they called it Passchendaele,' recalled the speaker in Siegfried Sassoon's famous poem. The battle bequeathed posterity this picture, iconic in its awfulness, which has helped shape the way the war has been remembered ever since.

RIGHT:
DEATH FROM ABOVE
Aerial bombardment was another innovation of the war. On some occasions it was actually decisive. A daylight raid on Istanbul in October 1918, intended to kill civilians and destroy morale, succeeded in both objectives – 50 died and the Ottomans quickly folded.

Though the aerial dogfights of 'Red Baron' Manfred von Richthofen (1892–1918) and other 'aces' stole the show, aviation was in some ways as important in assisting in reconnaissance and in the sighting of artillery. Either directly, in guiding gun crews, or in the preparation of superior maps that allowed gunners to sight their weapons with unprecedented accuracy.

'YOUR COUNTRY NEEDS YOU'

The war had a huge impact on its home fronts too, starting with the near-euphoria of the early enlistment drives. Young men flocked to enlist, though enthusiasm palled over time as the death toll rose and stories came back of terrible conditions in the trenches. From January 1916, the British introduced conscription. Britain's was famously headed by Baron Kitchener of Khartoum (1850–1916), a figure taken to exemplify the qualities of courage and duty the country was calling on.

This was well-established in the Russian Empire – which didn't mean that it was accepted. Conscription riots broke out in several cities. The deterioration of the situation in Russia underlined the extent to which the war could create difficulties far from the battle-front. The precarious social balance of the Czarist state and the myriad inadequacies of the country's infrastructure left it ill-equipped to meet the demands of a major modern conflict.

The effects of naval blockades were quickly felt in food shortages and faltering industrial production on all sides. The lack of equipment and munitions hampered armies in the field. The employment of women in armaments factories was not only a boon to the war effort but also an important social shift.

RUSSIA IN TURMOIL

By early 1917, food shortages were hitting people hard and strikes crippling Russia's factories. Mass protests started against the Czarist government. Steeled by his experiences in 1905, Nicholas II was unperturbed – until, that is, the city garrison in Petrograd mutinied. The czar had no alternative but to stand down. A provisional government took charge under a partnership of Prince Georgy Lvov (1861–1925) and the Petrograd Soviet. This 'worker's council' was more a group of middle-class intellectuals.

It certainly seemed tokenistic to the Communists. Vladimir Ulyanov ('Lenin') (1870–1924), leader of the Bolsheviks, the Party's most extreme faction, had been in Switzerland, in exile, when the trouble started. With the co-operation of the Germans,

RIGHT:
AN UPHILL STRUGGLE
Some of the war's most ferocious fighting took place over the high passes and mountainsides of the Alps, as Italian and Austro-Hungarian forces slugged it out at high altitude in dreadful conditions in bitter cold.

BELOW:
ASKARIS IN ACTION
The Germans had been recruiting Askaris (East African soldiers) like these signallers since the 1890s, but so had other European countries with colonies in the region, like Italy and Britain. They played an important part in the fighting in East Africa.

WORLD ON FIRE

ABOVE:
TRUNDLING TRIUMPH
The tank made its debut in World War I, and technology and tactics advanced considerably, even over its four-year course. Here an American soldier walks before a British-built Mark IV.

LEFT:
EASTER RISING
British soldiers stand behind a makeshift barricade in Dublin, 1916. The war was big and grand enough to carry an array of smaller conflicts in its slipstream – often dramatic and important in themselves. Like the Easter Rising of 1916, in which a group of rebels led by the poet Padraic Pearse and the socialist James Connolly took over Dublin's General Post Office and proclaimed an Irish Republic. The British responded furiously, bringing up a gunboat and artillery, and several days' fighting left the centre of the city a smoking ruin. Pearse, Connolly and their chief supporters were brought before a firing squad. Connolly, badly wounded, had to be tied up in a chair to face his executioners.

happy to make whatever trouble they could for their enemy, he'd made his way to the Baltic coast by train. Travelling through Sweden and Finland by train and ferry, he'd arrived at Petrograd's Finland Station on 16 April, to a hero's welcome. The crowd listened raptly as he excoriated Lvov's 'bourgeois revolution'.

KERENSKY IN CRISIS

As autumn approached, Russians found themselves in a society adrift. Kerensky's government had tackled all sorts of injustices in theory. In practice, though, their problems remained the same. Chronic food shortages, strikes and social chaos – just as under the czar. They might have a voice on their factory committee or in their city soviet but their material circumstances hadn't changed.

The Bolsheviks were extremists – and elitists. Lenin made no apologies for arguing that it was for him and his comrades to shape the 'workers' revolution' on their behalf. Liberal democracy was a fraud, infinitely manipulable by the rich and powerful. It was up to the Communists to tell the people what they really thought. Provocative views, which might in normal times have alienated ordinary Russians. But these, only too clearly, weren't normal times.

Kerensky soon fled into exile. Under covering fire from the cruiser *Aurora*, Lenin led his Bolsheviks against Petrograd's Winter Palace, where the remainder of the Provisional Government had taken refuge. Soviet tradition says they 'stormed' the palace – the event was endlessly and epically

ABOVE:
REVOLUTIONARY RHETORIC
Lenin electrifies the waiting crowd on his arrival back from exile in April 1917. In the months that followed, he and his Bolsheviks would ride a tide of support to political power – and, ultimately, dictatorship.

reproduced in the revolutionary propaganda – though in reality Lenin and his troops simply sauntered into the unguarded building.

In March 1918, the Soviet government signed the Treaty of Brest-Litovsk. Russia was out of the war, but it was forced to concede huge swathes of territory to the Central Powers: the Baltic states, Ukraine and much of the Caucasus.

PUNCHING A HOLE

The war had been continuing, the balance altered by the addition of the Americans on the Allied side. Tiring of the toll taken of their merchant shipping by the German U-boats, Congress had voted to declare war in April 1917. Even so, it had taken their armed forces months to mobilize and get themselves to Europe. Not till early 1918 was there a significant US presence on the Western Front.

Germany was under real pressure in the West, weakened by the cumulative effects of the blockade, its soldiers battle-weary. Yet commander Erich Ludendorff (1865–1937), though sombre in his mood, hadn't quite concluded that his situation was completely hopeless. Whilst Allied numbers were swollen by the arrival of the Americans, he had fresh forces freed up by the withdrawal of the Russians. Extended in its eastward advance, asked to send units south to support the French – and to the Italian Front – the British line felt precariously thin. Ludendorff's plan for his Spring Offensive was simply to 'punch a hole' in it and see what happened.

The lack of any further plan came back to bite him when, launched in late March, Operation Michael quickly succeeded and then slowly failed. While the Germans' massive infantry attack opened up an 80-km (50-mile) gap in the British line – and threw it back some 64 km (40 miles), this didn't gain the Germans any special prize. The town of Amiens, ahead of them, remained stoutly defended, while further attacks (Operations Georgette, Blücher-Yorck, Gneisenau …) secured diminishing returns. On 7 September, Ludendorff had to withdraw his armies

ABOVE:
STORMING THE WINTER PALACE
Demonstrators gather before the Winter Palace in Petrograd (St Petersburg) in January 1917, prior to the revolution of the following month.

LEFT:
COMPIÈGNE CARRIAGE
The welcome was respectful, the surroundings grand, but the knowledge that this was the private train of France's Marshal Foch would have reminded German negotiators that any armistice was going to be very much on the Allies' terms.

BACK IN BUSINESS?
If Europe had been yearning for peace, many of its people had been hungering even more immediately for food. Here, scant stalls are set out as something like normal life resumes amidst the ruins of a street in Tannenberg, East Prussia (now Polish Olsztyn).

LEFT:
WOMEN AT WAR
Female munitions workers make bullets at the Royal Arsenal, Woolwich, in March 1918. The war would soon be over, and these women returning to their homes, but they would never be quite so self-effacing – socially or politically – again.

to the Hindenburg Line (a defensive fortification running down through the northeast of France); by the end of the month, that line had been breached and the way to Germany lay open.

WINDING UP THE WAR

Exploratory communications were sent to US President Woodrow Wilson, calling for a peace plan. Germany's generals seem to have been hoping simply to buy some time to rest and rebuild their forces, ready to resume the war some time in 1919. Only if all territories taken were restored, came the reply. And if the Kaiser abdicated. That the Germans bridled at these conditions only underlined their importance for the Allies: Germany had to be completely decommissioned as a threat.

On 9 November, the Kaiser stepped down and German representatives met those of the Allies on a private train parked discreetly in the Forest of Compiègne, northeast of Paris. It was agreed that at 11 o'clock on the morning of 11 November – the eleventh month, of course – that the fighting was to cease. That was still six hours away and in the meantime, oddly, the war went on. Almost 3,000 lives are believed to have been lost in this brief interim. Overall, including civilians, the war had cost almost 20 million lives. An appalling figure, though interestingly, to provide perspective, the so-called 'Spanish flu' (actually first identified in the United States) epidemic of 1918–20 would cause 50 million deaths worldwide.

CONTINUING CONFLICT

Among the Versailles Treaty's other elements was the creation of a League of Nations to referee relations and promote world peace. But the reality was that, the world war over, normal conflict could be resumed. Ireland's independence struggle took up where it had left off in 1916. In 1921 the British conceded all but the northeasternmost six counties as a 'Free State', and the conflict promptly became a civil war. Free Staters who accepted the offer feeling that the loss of Northern Ireland was a price worth paying, fought a bitter war with Republicans, who disagreed. In 1923, the Pro-Treaty side prevailed. (Northern Ireland remained a proudly Protestant-dominated outpost of the UK, its Catholic minority left more or less marooned.)

The Russian Civil War (1917–23) continued too. The Allies initially helped the Soviets, hoping they would continue to hold up German expansion in the east, but after the Treaty of Brest-Litovsk in 1918 this seemed pointless. Now, reverting to capitalist type, and Churchill's view that the 'Bolshevik baby' should be 'strangled in its cradle', they openly started supporting the 'Whites'. Despite this, the Reds would eventually win.

In April 1919, Russia went to war with the recently established Second Polish Republic (the first had been the 'Commonwealth'). Its troops had invaded Ukraine in April 1919 and, with local anti-Soviet fighters, come close to taking Kyiv. Russia's counter-attack looked like bringing Poland under Soviet rule until it was held and then turned back at Warsaw. The Peace of Riga (1921) divided Belarus and Ukraine between Poland and Soviet Russia. Not until June 1923 would Russia's own civil war come to an end. By the time the dust had settled, the Union of Soviet Socialist Republics (founded in 1922) had 15 constituent states, supposedly a federation though in reality governed by the Communists from Moscow. It extended from Belarus and Moldova in the west through Russia and Ukraine to Central Asia (Kazakhstan, Tajikistan, Turkmenistan …) all the way to Siberia's Pacific coast.

BELOW:
VERSAILLES CONFERENCE
Peace negotiators gather at the Palace of Versailles, 1918. The treaty they agreed did much to repair France's damaged pride. But its conditions were so stringent as arguably to prevent post-war Germany from making a go of things economically or politically.

MUDDLING UP THE MIDDLE EAST

In their eagerness to drum up support at the outbreak of the war, the Allies had made many promises – not all of them consistent. In his 'Balfour Declaration' of 1917, Britain's Foreign Secretary Arthur Balfour had declared his country's support for the establishment of a 'national home for the Jewish people in Palestine'. Unfortunately, he had given similar reassurances to the local Arabs, creating a conflict which has yet to be resolved.

Likewise, in the confusion immediately following the war, when the Allies asked Greece to play a policing role in Smyrna, in western Turkey, Greek patriots saw it as endorsing their ambition to build an expansionist Greater Greece. Much of Smyrna's population was ethnically Greek (just as much of western Thrace and Macedonia's was Turkish). The Greeks had established colonies in Anatolia in pre-classical times, and the region had later belonged to the Greek-speaking Byzantine Empire. Unpersuaded by this reasoning, the Turks mounted a 'Great Offensive' and in 1922 won the Battle of Dumlupinar and recaptured Smyrna. The compromise agreed was a large-scale population-exchange, conceptually neat but a fearful trauma

WORLD ON FIRE

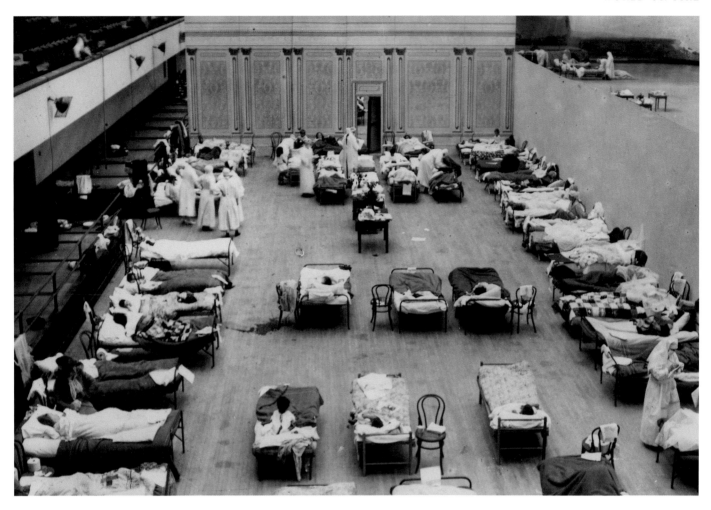

ABOVE:
TRAGIC DRAMA
As Oakland, California, was ravaged by the flu, the city's civic auditorium was turned into a makeshift hospital. Stage scenery partitions off the men's ward in the background here. More than 500 people died in less than 60 days in Oakland alone.

LEFT:
MASKING THE PROBLEM
The fear of 'Spanish flu' couldn't quite quell the desire for a return to post-war normality, so official strictures were widely resisted. Or, as here at a baseball game in the United States, at what we would now see as the classic 'superspreader event', complied with in the letter but sidestepped in spirit.

WORLD ON FIRE

LEFT:
IN THE SHADOW OF CONFLICT
The war might have been over, but the fighting was by no means done. This child is one of many hundreds of thousands orphaned by the Russian Civil War, in which more than 10 million (mostly civilians) may have been killed.

OPPOSITE:
BERATING BALFOUR
Arab protestors make their way towards Amman (now Jordan) to demonstrate against the Balfour Declaration, 1917. 'Palestine for the Arabs', and 'Our Homeland is Our Faith and Complete Freedom is Our Life', their banners read.

BELOW:
HURRAH!
Cossacks canter across the snow in a dramatic scene from Russia's Civil War. This was an endlessly confusing conflict, in which the 'Reds' and 'Whites' were just the start. Innumerable smaller groups were involved at local level, advancing their own agendas and settling their own scores.

for those involved. Up to 400,000 Muslims were expelled from Greece and some 1.2 million Greek Christians from what was now definitively Turkish territory.

The disintegration of the Ottoman Empire had far-reaching implications. Imam Yahya became the autocratic ruler of an independent Yemen. Many Iranians were outraged at the handing-over of their oil-rich country to Britain as a 'protectorate'. In Afghanistan, a bitter succession struggle followed the assassination of Emir Habibullah. His third son, Amanullah, eventually won backing as Emir.

FROM BANANAS TO BOOZE

The Americas had felt far removed from World War I. Canada had been in the thick of the fighting from the first, on the British side of course, but the United States had lent its support to the Allies only at a comparatively late stage. The Latin American nations had remained neutral. The important dynamic for them throughout this period (as it would be later) was the growing bullishness of the United States in its 'Backyard'. America had promoted Victoriano Huerta (1854–1916) to power in Mexico, then brought him down in 1914 when he'd stood out against them, Woodrow Wilson sending the Marines in to Veracruz. Venustiano Carranza (1859–1920) seized power with US support. The following year, the Marines were sent in to Haiti to end the dominance of German capital investors there.

In 1919, the Americans invaded Honduras, in support of an uprising by General Rafael López Gutiérrez (1855–1924). He became president and established a right-wing dictatorship, only to be toppled five years later. That same year Costa Rica too had a visit from the US Marines. They were reinforced in August 1921, when war with neighbouring Panama seemed imminent. A longstanding border dispute had suddenly flared up, but the Panamanians thought better of the fight when America took Costa Rica's side.

The biggest news in the United States itself, perhaps, was the outlawing of alcohol by the 1919 Volstead Act. Coming into force in 1920, it was repealed in 1933. Notoriously, it brought about a boom in organized crime. And, maybe worse, gave gangsters an apparently beneficent role as providers of 'bootleg' liquor and proprietors of illicit clubs or 'speakeasies'.

ABOVE:
ALCOHOL OUTLAWED
Men at a Brooklyn army base drain 10,000 barrels of beer into New York Harbor for the sake of America's moral health. The immediate consequence was an explosion in organized crime. After the 1919 Volstead Act, Prohibition came into force on 17 January 1920.

ROARING RACISM?

It's hard to know whether the 'Roaring Twenties' would have been so raucous without Prohibition. The new jazz music certainly flourished in these illegal venues. There was, however, a general mood of optimism in the aftermath of the war. The relative prosperity of the time, and the availability of radio, the phonograph, car transport and other key attributes of a conspicuously 'modern' lifestyle brought a buzz to social life in big cities from Berlin to Buenos Aires.

The rise of jazz, from New Orleans, reflected the changing situation of African Americans and the way they saw themselves. The excitement it held for white consumers (and the racist condescension that could underlie this) is illustrated by the success of Hollywood's first ever 'talkie', Al Jolson's *The Jazz Singer* (1927). Of Lithuanian-Jewish antecedents, Jolson performed in blackface, but this was also a time in which Black artists began to find recognition for themselves. Not necessarily in America, at first. St Louis-born Josephine Baker became a star in Paris, in the musical *La Revue Nègre* (1925).

SHOWTIME

A star of a very different sort had now been born in Italy with the rise of the first Fascist dictator, Benito Mussolini (1883–1945). Neither Jolson nor Baker would have been able to teach him much about performance. Though late in enlisting, Italy had been on the winning side in the war but hadn't seen the rewards it had been expecting. Specifically, territories in its far northeast, around the Adriatic, annexed years before by Austria-Hungary.

Benito Mussolini had seen his chance. A sometime socialist, in 1919 he had founded the Fascist Party. It took its name from the *fasces* (the bundle of rods tied together with the axe that could be used to cut them) carried as an emblem of authority by the *aediles* who had kept order in ancient Rome. It was of course no coincidence that he took his emblem from an empire built in Italy but extending over most of the then-known world. Mussolini was frank in his imperial ambitions. In 1935, hoping to build on the possessions it had secured in the Horn of Africa in the 1880s, he would order the invasion of Abyssinia (Ethiopia).

Fascism was frank in its authoritarianism, Mussolini's personal dominance as *Il Duce* ('The Leader') central to its message. It was central to its aesthetic too – hence the macho look of its black-shirted young supporters. On the evening of 27 October 1922, these *Camicie Nere* ('Blackshirts') converged on the country's capital in their tens of thousands. When the elected government appealed to Victor Emmanuel III (1869–1947) to call a state of emergency, the (highly conservative) king flatly refused. It seemed like a special stage-effect – no one had been overthrown; no actual violence had been used – but suddenly Mussolini was Italy's dictator.

MUSSOLINI MARK II

Watching closely from Munich, the young Adolf Hitler (1889–1945) was much impressed. A failure as an artist but successful as an antisemitic rabble-rouser, he had already copied the paramilitary 'look' Mussolini had given his Blackshirts for his *Sturmabteilung*. These 'stormtroopers' wore brown shirts instead of black for their work in beating up Jews and defending meetings of Hitler's National Socialist ('Nazi') Party, but otherwise they were pretty much the same. That Hitler *had* supporters is testimony to the hold taken on many Germans by the 'stab-in-the-back' myth – the idea that certain victory in the recent war had been snatched from Germany by the underhand attacks of Jews and socialists from within.

This view didn't just exist among the lower-middle classes who were stereotypically to be Nazism's main constituency but among people in a position to have known better. Of course, the military elite (Hitler's early admirers included Erich Ludendorff) had an interest in seeing the blame for their failings placed elsewhere.

MAN OF STEEL

Stalin's ideological background was very different. A committed revolutionary from youth, the name Josef Vissarionovich (1878–1953) was known by (it means 'Man of Steel') had been his clandestine codename in former days. He did, however, share tyrannical tendencies with the Fascist leaders and, in the 'totalitarian' direction he'd take it in, the Soviet Union would have key things in common with their countries. First, a subordination of the individual to the all-powerful and all-encompassing one-party state, then the construction of a 'cult of personality' around himself as leader.

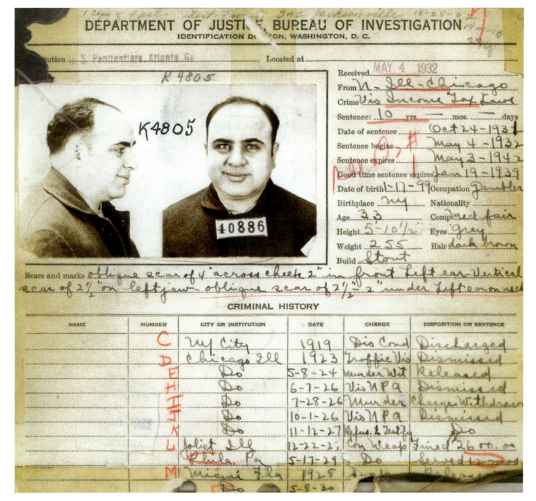

LEFT:
MOBSTER CHARGE SHEET
One of America's most notorious gangsters, Chicago crime boss Al Capone was successfully prosecuted for tax evasion and Volstead Act violations (Prohibition laws) in 1931. Pictured is Capone's FBI criminal record in 1932, showing that most of his previous criminal charges were discharged or dismissed.

LEFT:
THE BOLSHEVIK BOYS
Between them, Lenin (left) and Stalin (right) would be responsible for millions of deaths. The exact numbers have of course been contested in an ideologically charged debate. As indeed have the Bolshevik leaders' lasting reputations: were they liberators, or enslavers, of the working class?

OPPOSITE:
CASTING HER VOTE
A woman goes to the polls at the British General Election of December 1918, the first at which any form of female suffrage had been granted. The victory was as yet only partial, the franchise restricted to women over the age of 30 and with certain property qualifications.

For the moment, though, he was still finding his feet as General Secretary of the Soviet Communist Party (he'd been appointed in 1922); Mussolini was just setting out his Fascist stall, while Hitler, in prison for organizing the Munich Putsch, was writing a self-serving memoir/manifesto named *Mein Kampf* ('*My Struggle*'). Not until 1928 would Stalin start to implement the first of several Five-Year Plans: it tried to turn a backward country into a modern industrial nation. Starting with heavy industry, because Stalin believed that this would provide a foundation on which further development could build.

CHINA'S LONG MARCH

Meanwhile, Mao Zedong (1893–1976) had set in motion his bid to bring Communist rule to China. The year 1927 had seen the start of the country's civil war as Mao's supporters attacked the Kuomintang forces of Chiang Kai-shek (1887–1975). The Nationalist leader had won the succession struggle following the death of Sun Yat-Sen (1866–1925) and built himself a powerbase in the north around Nanjing. The Communists had co-operated with the Kuomintang till now but could see no way of working with Chiang. Things weren't going Mao's way, though. By 1934, he was all but beaten, cornered in southern China's Jiangxi province with a respectable-sounding 69,000 supporters but facing a Nationalist army 360,000-strong. In a bold – or desperate – move, Mao led his Red Army on a 'Long March' of 9,000 km (5,600 miles) under frequent enemy attack all the way up to Shaanxi, in northeast China, where they were able to link up with another Communist force. Their journey had taken them just over a year and cost over 60,000 lives.

CRASH AND CONSEQUENCES

The Roaring Twenties sputtered to a startling stop in September 1929, when the Wall Street Crash sent share prices tumbling. A decade-long and global Great Depression followed, creating chronic uncertainty for the previously comfortable middle class and downright destitution for many. 'Hoovervilles' – shanty-towns named in honour of President Herbert Hoover – sprang up around American cities. Agricultural regions of the Midwest

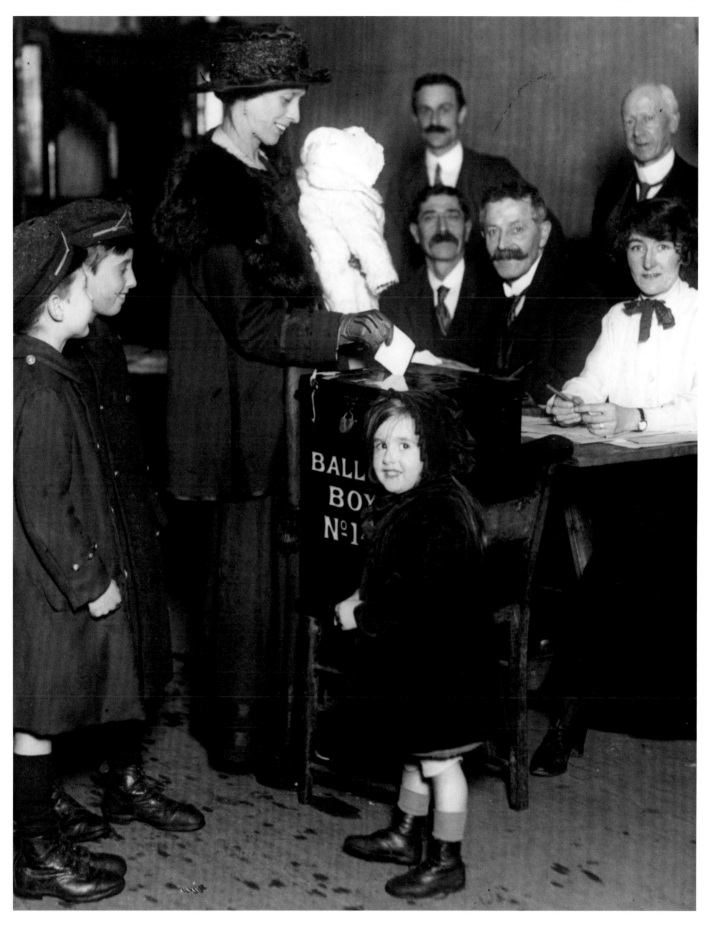

OPPOSITE:
MARCHING FOR MAO
The 'Long March' of 1934–6 almost broke China's Communist Party but ultimately made it, taking on the status of a 'founding myth'. It also confirmed Mao's assumption that he could exact any sacrifice from his supporters and still command their unswerving loyalty.

RIGHT:
JAZZING IT UP
US musician Louis Armstrong (centre, dark-suited) poses with the band at the WMSB Radio Station, New Orleans. A sensibility as much as a musical style, jazz gave the 1920s an effervescent, upbeat feel, with the music's syncopated rhythms and audacious harmonies.

BELOW:
BANISHING THE BLUES
Cab Calloway leads the band at the Cotton Club's New Year's celebrations, New York 1937. The Great Depression wasn't depressing for everyone – and even when it was, that only intensified an almost desperate desire for entertainment and fun.

WORLD ON FIRE

ABOVE:
PENICILLIN PIONEER
Sir Alexander Fleming works in his lab at London University's St Mary's Medical School. It was here that, in 1928, he identified a mould which, as it grew, destroyed bacteria around it. He named it penicillin and it marked a major breakthrough.

LEFT:
OUT IN FORCE
Leading Nazi Julius Streicher addresses supporters outside the New Town Hall on Munich's Marienplatz, November 1923. Though quickly suppressed, the 'Beer Hall Putsch' was not quite as bathetic as its name perhaps suggests. Hitler was entitled to feel encouraged.

were ravaged by the 'Dust Bowl' – droughts and crop failures leading to exposed topsoil being carried off by winds. Thousands of families were displaced.

Elected in 1932, US President Franklin D. Roosevelt (1882–1945) tried to tackle the problem with a 'New Deal', deploying government funds to organize major projects of public works, in hopes that this would stimulate the economy at large. The depth of the slowdown puts an ironic gloss on the stunning frescos commissioned in 1932 from the famous Mexican muralist (and communist – another irony) Diego Rivera (1886–1957). Endowing everyday factory work with epic excitement and monumental stature, the *Detroit Industry Murals* give a sense of modern labour as something heroically worthwhile.

Too few would get the chance, however. The despair the Depression brought produced political extremism and a search for scapegoats. Hitler reaped the benefits in Germany. Elected Chancellor in 1933, the following year he was able to make himself *Führer* ('Leader'), with more or less unlimited powers as dictator. The 'Third Reich' his reign was inaugurating wasn't just bringing Germany to the height of its greatness: it was bringing racially pure Germanic humanhood to its height as well. (This was to be the message of the 1936 Berlin Olympics, till Hitler's Aryans were upstaged by the Black American athlete, Jesse Owens.)

Mostly, though, Hitler built loyalty and cohesion by intensifying his rhetoric against socialists and Jews. And not just the rhetoric. Passed in 1935, the Nuremberg Laws

ABOVE:
MUSSOLINI IN THE COLOSSEUM
Benito Mussolini is backed by Blackshirts during his March on Rome, 1922. Some 30,000 supporters turned out, but the show of strength was sufficient to convince King Victor Emmanuel III to step down and hand power to the Fascists without a fight.

RIGHT:
RURAL REVOLUTION
'Immediately exterminate the Kulaks as a class,' reads the banner carried by loyal Communists come to work a new collective farm. The collectivization of agriculture formed part of Stalin's First Five-Year Plan (1928–32), pushed through amidst savage repression and famines in which millions died.

made antisemitism official policy. Over 90 Jews were killed on the night of 9–10 November 1938. This became known as *Kristallnacht* ('Night of Broken Glass') for the attacks the Nazis mounted against Jewish businesses, homes and synagogues.

SAVAGERY IN SPAIN

Spain's First Republic had been fairly quickly overthrown. A Second began with the deposition of Alfonso XIII (1886–1941) in 1931. Prime Minister Manuel Azaña's position was precarious: even so the threat of Fascism was kept at bay. But his government's drive to reduce the Church's power and reform the military brought it into conflict with two of the country's strongest and most conservative institutions. Unrest on a Left impatient with what it saw as the slow pace of social and economic reform allowed the Right to suggest that Spain had become ungovernable. Which allowed General Francisco Franco (1892–1975) – who in July 1936 led a military revolt in Morocco – to present himself as saviour of his country.

ABOVE:
FROM FREEDOM TO FREE-FALL
'Black Thursday', 1929, and as the New York Stock Market plummets, people gather on the steps of Wall Street's Federal Hall National Memorial, round the Washington statue.

RIGHT:
FOOTBALL GOES GLOBAL?
The first World Cup for soccer was played in Uruguay in 1930. Teams came from as far away as France and Yugoslavia, but countries from the Americas predominated. The final, indeed, was something of a local derby, the hosts playing Argentina, and winning 4–2.

OPPOSITE:
'MIGRANT MOTHER'
A study in hopelessness, Dorothea Lange's classic photo was taken at a migrant pea-pickers' camp at Nipomo, California. Its subject was subsequently identified as Oklahoma-born Florence Owens Thompson, at the time 32 and a mother of seven.

Up to 450,000 people were killed in the civil war that followed. Only about half were soldiers (including foreign volunteers) killed in action. Prisoners were routinely shot and suspect civilians rounded up and executed in vast numbers in both the Republican and Nationalist zones. Notoriously, Nazi Germany and Stalin's USSR viewed Spain as a dress-rehearsal for the bigger conflict they saw as coming and sent in aid and arms. (The Western powers found reasons to refuse to help the Republic.)

By 1936, Franco was in a position to call himself *Caudillo* or 'Dictator'. Always authoritarian, his 39-year reign began with a nine-year programme of repression in which many thousands more would lose their lives.

China's Civil War was shelved in 1937 to allow both sides to co-operate against a Japanese invasion. This Second Sino-

RIGHT:
IN COMMAND
By 1933, Hitler was his country's Chancellor, powerful in the most conventional terms, but his paramilitary persona was still key to who he was. We see him here flanked by brown-shirted supporters with swastika armbands, the embodiment of the Nazis' street-fighting spirit.

BELOW:
UP IN FLAMES
A crowd collects in Mosbach's city square to see the furnishings and ritual objects of the local synagogue burned in the aftermath of *Kristallnacht*, November 1938. Hundreds of synagogues – and over 7,500 businesses – had been attacked and scores of people killed.

ABOVE:
NEW DEAL
US President from 1933, Franklin Delano Roosevelt tried to jump-start a US economy mired in the Great Depression, jolting it out of its lethargy with massive programmes of state investment and public projects. Economists disagree on the success of his 'New Deal'.

RIGHT:
BAIRD'S BOX
Scottish-born inventor John Logie Baird was arguably to open a Pandora's box when he invented 'wireless vision' (television) in 1926. This version is hardly lounge-ready, but the essential technology is all in place. Baird looks in where the picture will appear.

Japanese War (1937–45) is best remembered now for the Nanjing Massacre (1937), during which the Japanese attackers killed over 300,000 of the city's inhabitants and raped more than 80,000 of its girls and women.

PAVING THE WAY TO WAR

A second world war seemed inevitable now and the powers were positioning themselves for when it started. In 1936, Hitler and Mussolini entered into an alliance they called the 'Axis', Japan

WORLD ON FIRE

joining them in an Anti-Comintern Pact. (The Comintern was the international grouping of Communist countries.) In 1940, this three-way alliance would be formalized as the Tripartite Pact. Still at war in China, Japan invaded Indochina in 1940, maintaining that the Chinese were being supplied through the French colony.

By 1937, Mussolini's Italy had successfully (if with illegal cruelty) pacified Abyssinia. Closer to home, meanwhile, in 1938 Austrians voted to support the *Anschluss* (literally, 'connection'), their country officially joining the German Reich. Many outsiders were appalled by what seemed like imperialism by stealth. Winston Churchill was one of these. Though subsequently seen as shameful, the Munich Agreement reached by Prime Minister Neville Chamberlain (30 September 1938), accepting Germany's right to annex the Sudetenland, a historically German-speaking part of Czechoslovakia, was viewed as a great achievement by much of Britain.

BELOW:
BACK-SEAT DRIVER
In 1928, Amelia Earhart became the first woman to fly across the Atlantic Ocean, but only as the passenger of Wilmer Stultz (left). But she became a pioneer aviator in her own right, before being lost in the Pacific while trying to fly around the world.

In 1939, the foreign ministers of the USSR and Germany signed the Molotov–Ribbentrop Pact, agreeing not to go to war – and to allow each other free rein in 'their' halves of Eastern Europe. Stalin may have felt impelled to sign in part because he'd been unable to get Britain and France to agree an anti-Nazi deal with him. So, he signed the treaty and was to take the fullest advantage of his terms. Then, on 1 September, Germany invaded Poland from the west.

THE FIGHTING BEGINS

This was unambiguously a hostile act. Britain gave Germany an ultimatum to withdraw and, when it ignored this, made a declaration of war in which it was accompanied by France. Several months of 'Phoney War' followed in the west, neither side doing much more than making preparations, though the British did send an expeditionary force to help in the defence of France. In Poland, however, while Germany consolidated its hold on the west, Stalin swallowed up the east, in keeping with the Nazi–Soviet Pact, before attacking Finland in what became the Winter War. (Finland managed to maintain its independence while ceding some border territories to Russia.) The following summer, Soviet troops would occupy the Baltic states (Latvia, Lithuania, Estonia).

LEFT:
THE FUTURE IN FLAMES
Colliding with its mooring mast on arrival in New Jersey, the hydrogen-filled German airship *Hindenburg* caught fire. Thirty-five people were killed in thbe ensuing inferno, a terrifying emblem of technology's limitations and the curtailment of what had seemed an exciting future of airship travel.

BELOW:
¡VIVA LA REPÚBLICA!
Left-wing volunteers flocked to the defence of the Spanish Republic, from Spain itself and from the world beyond. On the other hand, conservative feeling crystallized into support for General Franco, despite his authoritarianism, in what already seemed to be a showdown between rival worldviews.

WORLD ON FIRE

By that time, Germany had conquered Denmark and Norway with bewildering speed and the Western Allies were in confusion. Neville Chamberlain (1869–1940) had been replaced as Britain's prime minister by Winston Churchill. The Battle of France had begun, Germany sweeping in across the Low Countries on 10 May. Such swift progress had it made with its high-speed, highly mechanized approach of *Blitzkrieg* or 'lightning war' that the British Expeditionary Force had found itself encircled. Its evacuation from Dunkirk (26 May–4 June) by a hastily assembled fleet of 'little ships' was a marvellous story of pluck and resourcefulness but ominous in its indications about the way the war was going.

By the end of June, Germany and France had signed an Armistice (again at Compiègne – indeed in the same railway carriage): Germany would continue to occupy the north of the country while an ostensibly neutral France would be run by World War I-hero Marshal Philippe Pétain from the town of Vichy. A French government-in-exile was set up in London under General Charles de Gaulle (1890–1970). The German occupation had left France itself in a state of shock, but a Resistance movement gradually grew.

INVASION AVOIDED

Hitler's next move was intended to be an invasion of Britain, but this would require control of the English Channel. And, for that to be possible, control of the skies above England's southern coasts. The 'Battle of Britain' began in July 1940, but

RIGHT:
RACING AGAINST RACISM
Jesse breasts the tape – again. The star of the 1936 Olympics, Oakville, Alabama-born Owens won not only the all-important 100 m race but also the 200 m race, the 4 x 100 m relay and the long jump. African American rights campaigners had advised him to boycott Hitler's Nazi games.

BELOW:
A TRAIL OF DESTRUCTION
Japanese forces pull out of a ruined town under Chinese fire in the Second Sino-Japanese War. More than a million Japanese combatants died to 3.2 million Chinese soldiers. But anything up to 18 million Chinese civilians appear to have been killed.

WORLD ON FIRE

RIGHT:
DEATH FROM THE SKY
The Junkers Ju-87 or 'Stuka' dive-bomber was the pride of the Luftwaffe in the opening phases of the war. Hitler saw his airborne Blitz on Britain's cities as the key to that country's conquest, but the RAF (Royal Air Force) managed at least to hold the threat at bay.

the Luftwaffe failed to defeat the fighters of the RAF. Germany's bombers could still mount night-time raids on Britain's cities, and did so in the months of the 'Blitz'. U-boat bases were built on the Atlantic coast of France, from which Germany's submarines went out to harass Allied shipping. Causing widespread loss of life, destroying ships and disrupting supplies, these attacks undoubtedly made it harder for Britain to wage its war. They did nothing to advance Hitler's invasion plans, however. These had by now had to be put on hold.

The United States remained aloof for now, despite the Allies' efforts to involve them and President Roosevelt's evident sympathy. The war on the ground was widening. A new theatre opened in North Africa – where the Italians were trying to force their way through from their colony in Libya to the Suez Canal (and whence, ultimately, any future attack on the Axis from the south was going to have to come). In the event, the British pushed the Italians back deep into their own territory. The arrival of Field Marshal Erwin Rommel's (1891–1944) Afrika Korps would make the struggle less one-sided. The open sands of the Sahara became the arena for a new kind of tank warfare.

In April 1941, Germany attacked Yugoslavia and Greece, in preparation for the invasion of Soviet Russia. In June 1941, Hitler tore up his pact with Stalin, and launched the largest land invasions the world had ever seen: Operation Barbarossa. More than 4 million troops poured into the Soviet Union. The Eastern Front had the character of a race-war for the Germans, Nazi theory seeing the Slavs as subhuman in a way that the Dutch, French and British weren't, making this campaign particularly cruel. Prisoners-of-war and civilians were massacred and women raped on a horrific scale. Leningrad (as St Petersburg/Petrograd) was now called, was besieged in 1941 and was to hold out successfully against a siege lasting more than two years; Moscow was saved by the ferocious courage of its defenders, with a little help from 'General Winter'.

On 7 December, Japan entered the war with a surprise attack on the US fleet in Pearl Harbor, Honolulu, Hawaii. America and Japan were now self-evidently at war. Almost as surprising as the attack, however, was Germany and Italy's declaration of war with the United States. They hadn't had to do this, and it meant Britain and France having a powerful ally in Europe.

Another powerful ally, that is, given that the Soviet Union was now de facto on their side, though for the moment it was very much on the back foot. As Napoleon had found, however, the Russians were unwilling to admit defeat however badly beaten.

RIGHT:
SPIRIT OF THE BLITZ
The city may be under aerial bombardment, the library itself a smoking ruin, but the Great British Browser is unperturbed. This scene at London's Holland House was almost certainly staged, of course, but it embodied qualities the British liked to feel they showed.

BELOW:
GERMANS IN PARIS
July 1940: German artillery march down the Champs-Élysées from the Arc de Triomphe, following the surrender of France the previous month.

Entire steelworks and factories were dismantled and moved by rail to new sites east of the Urals so the country's industrial productivity could go on. The Germans still had the initiative. They were pushing their way southward into the Caucasus and in the summer of 1942 laid siege to Stalingrad, an important industrial centre on the Volga.

The attack on Pearl Harbor had caught America off-balance. The Japanese had the freedom of the Pacific and quickly conquered much of Southeast Asia and the Dutch East Indies. British-occupied Singapore followed, after which the Japanese invaded Burma – taking them to the doorstep of the British Raj. They even menaced Australia, carrying out air raids against towns and cities in the tropic north.

As the US Navy rallied, though, its carriers started gaining ground, bringing Allied victories at the Battle of Midway (1942) and in the Guadalcanal campaign (1942–3). These were not just naval engagements but full-scale battles fought ferociously by land, sea and air, and they slowly started tipping the advantage the Allies' way.

A 'FINAL SOLUTION'

In January 1942, meanwhile, important German officials had gathered at Wannsee House, a suburban villa in Berlin, where they had agreed to pursue a 'Final Solution' to the 'Jewish Problem'. Jews had always been targets of Nazi aggression and had been informally persecuted throughout the war so far. After this Wannsee Conference, though, the concentration camps, like Auschwitz and Bergen-Belsen, began to be built. Jews (and other outcasts, including Roma, Jehovah's Witnesses, homosexuals and some criminals) were rounded up wholesale and transported here to be held in squalor before being taken to purpose-built gas chambers. Six million Jews were to be killed.

BELOW:
A WAVE OF FIRE
Operation Barbarossa sent 4 million German soldiers into Soviet territory, backed by 5,000 aircraft and 3,500 tanks. The Red Army numbered just under 3 million. It had more tanks and aircraft, but could not resist the onslaught. Within a week, the Germans had advanced 320 km (200 miles).

OPPOSITE:
THE ADVANTAGE OF SURPRISE
In all, 353 Japanese planes took part in the Pearl Harbor raid. They killed 2,403 people, sank nine ships, damaged many more and destroyed 180 aircraft. More important, they shocked Americans to the core. and got a head-start in their race to build an empire in the Pacific region.

WORLD ON FIRE

363

ABOVE:
CLOSE QUARTERS
Soviet troops at Stalingrad 'hug the enemy', so close to the Germans they can't be fired on from the air. The spirit of self-sacrifice (reinforced by fear of the Communist authorities) was the Soviets' secret weapon here and key to their eventual victory in the 'Great Patriotic War'.

OUTFOXED

Rommel, the dashing 'Desert Fox', was by now winning in the desert. Not only had he driven the British out of Libya, but he was poised to drive on into Egypt to the Suez Canal. In July 1942, however, he was held at El Alamein. In a Second Battle of El Alamein a few months later, under its new commander General Bernard Law Montgomery (1887–1976), Britain's Eighth Army won a major victory.

Montgomery made discreet use of information secured by Allied intelligence project ULTRA. Thanks to innovations in computing made by Alan Turing (1912–54) and others (including what was arguably the world's first programmable digital computer, the Colossus), staff at Bletchley Park in Buckinghamshire were routinely reading top-secret German communications. These were supposedly locked down in a constantly changing code by the ingenious ENIGMA machine, but the British could now crack this with ease and speed.

Another important breakthrough came at Stalingrad, in February 1943, when the Germans were forced to surrender after five months' fierce fighting. They were defeated again that summer at Kursk in history's greatest-ever tank battle. Germany's invasion of the Soviet Union was unravelling.

WAITING FOR A SECOND FRONT

Good news, but Soviet forces were exhausted now. They weren't doing it alone but it must have felt that way. The Western Allies were close to winning the 'Battle of the Atlantic' now: thanks in large part to the availability of ULTRA intelligence, the U-boat threat was being nullified. The British and Americans had also kept up the pressure on Germany with saturation-bombing of its cities. The first 'thousand-bomber raid', on Cologne, had been mounted that summer, followed a few weeks later by the

RIGHT:
THE CODEBREAKER
Alan Turing's visionary work in computer science opened up the possibility of breaking the ever-changing ENIGMA codes the Germans used. Long necessarily secret, Turing's role was then played down for years because his homosexuality was regarded as a disgrace. He committed suicide in 1954.

BELOW:
CAPTURING TARAWA, NOVEMBER 1943
Smoke darkens the sky as Marines clamber over a wall of coconut logs and advance toward the airstrip on the islet of Betio. The assault on Betio laid bare numerous shortcomings in American amphibious doctrine, and the lessons learned were applied to future such operations in the Pacific.

WORLD ON FIRE

RIGHT:
VICTIMS ON PARADE
Child survivors line up behind the wire at Auschwitz-Birkenau after its liberation by the Red Army in January 1945. The Russians dressed these children in adult uniforms for the photo: the facts of the war were already being improved upon, reinterpreted and reframed.

BELOW:
'THE JAWS OF DEATH'
US troops leave a landing-craft under heavy fire at Omaha Beach on D-Day, 6 June 1944. As at Auschwitz, a picture is never just a picture. 'Taxis to Hell – and Back – Into the Jaws of Death' was the half-laconic, half-heroic title given to this dramatic shot by American photographer Robert F. Sargent.

destruction of Hamburg in a firestorm. That summer had also seen the Allied invasion of Sicily. Moving swiftly up through Italy, they had deposed Mussolini (who'd been executed by Italian partisans). Germany had been forced to take over the defence of Italy in the north. Another responsibility for the increasingly beleaguered Nazi state.

Despite this, the Allies seemed no nearer to opening up the full-scale 'second front' that Stalin had been demanding since 1941. This, apart from a photo opportunity for the Allied 'Big Three' (Roosevelt, Churchill, Stalin) was the main item on the agenda at their summit in Tehran (28 November–1 December). It was agreed that Britain and America would lead an attack on France with the intention of advancing upon Germany from the west.

D-DAY AND AFTER

It took six months for Operation Overlord to be planned and prepared-for; then an airborne assault by 1,200 aircraft on the coast of Normandy on 'D-Day' (6 June 1944) was followed by a fleet of 5,000 vessels, bringing 160,000 troops ashore. Reinforcements followed in the days that followed: soon the Allies had 2 million troops on French soil.

But the establishment of a beachhead here was only a beginning. It took till late August for the Allied armies to break out of Normandy, where for several weeks they'd been kept contained. Now, though, they were pressing eastward, their progress mirroring that of Soviet forces pushing westward out of Russia via the Baltic States and Poland and heading in the general direction of Berlin.

RIGHT:
PEENEMÜNDE, V2 ROCKET
Too late to save the Nazis, the V2 rocket was one for the future, the ancestor of the cruise missiles of the Cold War (p. 397). The US and USSR alike brought German scientists in discreetly to help them with their developing weapons programmes.

In January 1945, Soviet forces liberated Auschwitz. Soldiers and reporters were deeply shocked at what they saw. That April, British troops entered Bergen-Belsen, finding 60,000 emaciated inmates, many dying from sickness or starvation, crammed into a camp designed to hold 2,000.

Meanwhile, Stalin had scores to settle – and an eye on postwar arrangements in Eastern Europe. In anticipation of their deliverance, the Polish Resistance rose up in Warsaw. Rather than relieving them, though, the Soviet Army waited outside the city for the Germans to finish putting down the insurrection – which they did with the utmost savagery – before resuming their westward advance. Notoriously, as they reached the German homeland, the Soviet troops were given the green light to rape women as they went in a collective act of sexualized revenge.

ATTRITION IN THE EAST

British forces had meanwhile been beating the Japanese back in Burma. American forces were fighting for the Marianas and the Philippines. Over 100,000 civilians would be killed – mostly massacred by Japanese soldiers – in the Battle of Manila, February–March 1945. At much the same time, US Marines were battling for the island of Iwo Jima, whose Japanese defenders were dug in to bunkers and a warren (11 km, 8 miles) of tunnels.

After this, in April–June, the fight was on for Okinawa in the Ryukyu group, south of Japan. Some 110,000 Japanese troops, 12,500 Americans and anything up to 80,000 indigenous Okinawans died in what was remembered as 'the cruellest battle'. With desperation creeping in, the Japanese turned to suicide attacks in explosives-laden aircraft: *kamikaze* flights; the name meant 'divine wind'.

An end to the war at last in sight, the Allies met again at Yalta, in the Crimea, to decide on the shape Europe would take when the fighting stopped. Uneasy as Churchill in particular felt, the Soviet contribution to the Allied victory had to be recognized. It was acknowledged that the Soviet sphere of influence would extend over Eastern Europe.

LEFT:
FRIENDS … FOR NOW
From left to right: The Big Three – British Prime Minister Winston Churchill, US President Harry S. Truman and Soviet leader Josef Stalin – sit in the garden of Cecilienhof Palace before meeting for the Potsdam Conference to negotiate terms for the end of the war in Europe (25 July 1945). As vice president, Truman had assumed the presidency with the death of Roosevelt on 12 April 1945.

BELOW:
THE MOMENT OF VICTORY
The Red Flag goes up over the Reichstag, marking the end of the Third Reich in Germany – and the start of the Soviet presence in Central Europe. The West could neither ignore the Communists' contribution nor accept them as political partners. A lengthy period of 'Cold War' lay in store.

DEVASTATING TECHNOLOGY

Given continuing losses, the Allies were eager to take the war to the German and Japanese home fronts in hopes that people would put pressure on their rulers to sue for peace. Controversial, because it was frankly an attack on a civilian population rather than a strategic target, the carpet-bombing of Dresden in February 1945 killed up to 25,000 people and destroyed much of the city.

And, while Operation Starvation targeted Japanese shipping to cut off food and other supplies, waves of bombing made life hell for people in their homes. On the night of 9–10 March, incendiaries were strewn from over 300 US B-29s, starting what would be known as the 'Tokyo Firestorm'. Even so, the Japanese military fought on.

War had concentrated scientific minds. Not only had the Germans been developing jet aviation engines (just too late to be of use in the present conflict): they had, in the V1, created a 'flying bomb' and, in its successor the V2, the first supersonic ballistic missile. Meanwhile, in the 'Manhattan Project', exiled European scientists working at labs in Los Alamos, New Mexico, had, with American assistance, built the world's first atomic bomb.

WRAPPING THINGS UP

By now, it was clear, Germany had been defeated. Despite a desperate rearguard action, its forces were being pushed back remorselessly. Already aware that, in any post-war settlement, the possession of territory might prove crucial, Western and

LEFT:
ATOM BOMB
The blasts at Hiroshima and (here) Nagasaki may have brought the war to a welcome end but they had also ushered in a new and frightening era. Humankind's destructiveness had always been alarming. Now its capacity to destroy and kill was astronomically multiplied.

OPPOSITE TOP:
IN THE DOCK
Nazi officials face the judges at the Nuremberg trials of 1945–6. Though selective in their scope and condemned then and since as 'victors' justice', they held the Nazi leadership to some sort of account. And allowed a line to be drawn and a divided Germany to be accepted by the world. Pictured here in the front row are Hermann Göring, chief of the Luftwaffe; Rudolph Hess, former deputy to Hitler; foreign minister Joachim von Ribbentrop; and Field Marshall Wilhelm Keitel, commander of the armed forces.

OPPOSITE BOTTOM:
A CONTROVERSIAL KISS
The sailor spontaneously grabbing a nurse and kissing her in Times Square seemed to sum up America's jubilation on VJ Day. Posterity has looked less kindly on what some have seen as a sexual assault, just as it has looked more critically on other aspects of America's war.

Soviet forces were in an informal 'Race for the Rhine'. By the end of April, Soviet troops were in the suburbs of Berlin. Hitler, facing certain defeat, committed suicide. On the morning of 2 May, the Soviets raised their flag over the German parliament building, the Reichstag.

VE ('Victory in Europe') Day prompted rejoicing across the Allied countries but the war in the Pacific still went on. On 6 August, though, a US B-29 dropped an atomic bomb, 'Little Boy', on the city, razing its constructions and claiming 70,000 lives. On 9 August, the Americans followed up with an attack on Nagasaki, believed to have killed over 40,000 people. Longer-term casualties would be higher still: the effects of radioactivity were still scarcely understood but would take their toll of those exposed in the decades that followed. The agreement of the Emperor Hirohito (1901–89) to surrender, on 14 August, was celebrated as VJ ('Victory over Japan') Day, though the surrender wouldn't actually be signed till some time later.

In Britain, a General Election was held in July – so less than two months after VE Day. Whatever gratitude may have been felt for Churchill, it wasn't transferred to his Conservative Party. Instead, Clement Attlee's Labour won by a landslide. People wanted change in the country they'd fought and suffered for.

TIME FOR CHANGE
1945 – 2000

World War II passed imperceptibly into the Cold War as the United States and its Western allies confronted the Soviet Union and its bloc. This, in accordance with the Yalta Agreement, included much of eastern Europe, behind what Winston Churchill had memorably called the 'Iron Curtain'. (Germany itself had been divided into two, a Communist East and a capitalist West, with a new capital in Bonn. Former capital Berlin – itself divided into Western and Eastern sides – formed an exclave within the East.)

In some of these countries, voters had actually chosen leftist governments, but in most they hadn't. Even where they had, moreover, they got more than they bargained for, their Communist leaders outlawing opposition. Poland, Czechoslovakia, Hungary, Romania, Bulgaria and Albania were all firmly in the Soviet sphere, though Marshal Josip Broz (1892–1980) or 'Tito' managed to secure a degree of autonomy for Yugoslavia, within the Eastern Bloc.

INDIAN INDEPENDENCE

Not surprisingly, the same applied in other countries of the Empire. India had lost over 87,000 soldiers in what many had felt like someone else's war. Up to 3 million civilians had died in the Bengal Famine of 1943, blame for which was lain at Britain's door. Under wartime conditions it had undoubtedly been difficult for relief supplies to

OPPOSITE:
BERLIN WALL
The most visible symbol of the 'Iron Curtain' was actually a wall. This eyesore went up abruptly in Berlin in 1961. By then the city had been divided for 15 years, but the stream of escapees from the East was embarrassing the Communist authorities.

RIGHT:
FULTON FUSILLADE
Winston Churchill thought of it as his 'Sinews of Peace' speech; for everyone else it was a rhetorical attack on the evils of a Communist system that, 'from Stettin in the Baltic to Trieste in the Adriatic', had brought down an 'Iron Curtain' across Europe.

TIME FOR CHANGE

ABOVE:
DRESSED BY THE WEST
The British berets and American jackets, trimmed with fur, these Greek commandos wear leaves little doubt of their ideological loyalties. Greece's civil war was the first of a series of proxy conflicts between the two great power blocs, the Soviets supporting left-wing partisans.

be brought in, but the feeling that this hadn't been enough of a priority was difficult to shift. An independence movement which had been growing for several decades now gained unstoppable strength. Indeed, in March 1946, Clement Attlee announced that India was going to be granted its independence.

CONTESTED HOMELANDS

It was complicated, though, by the desires of different religious communities to see their interests safeguarded. Muslims – concentrated in India's northwestern Punjab province and its northeastern province of Bengal – wanted their own homeland of Pakistan. In August 1946, a 'Direct Action Day' in Kolkata, West Bengal, occasioned widespread violence between Hindus and Muslims. Several thousand people lost their lives. Even so, Indian self-government went ahead a few weeks later, with nationalist leader Jawaharlal Nehru (1889–1964) as interim prime minister.

The inter-communal violence continued, though, so when in August 1947 the country won full independence, it was as a (broadly) Hindu India and (mostly) Muslim Pakistan – a West Pakistan in Punjab and East Pakistan in Bengal. Millions found themselves on the 'wrong' side of these new boundaries, leading to further violence, and major population movements. As important as religious allegiances had been, they weren't the only loyalties people had: many East Pakistani Muslims felt a strong sense of Bengali identity as well. They became involved in a second independence struggle, this time against Pakistan, winning their freedom as Bangladesh in 1971.

The year 1948 saw the State of Israel created, with the blessing of both the USA and the USSR, though it immediately had to fight off determined attacks by its Arab neighbours. In consolidating its position, Israel violently expelled over half a million local Palestinian Arabs, razing villages and laying waste fields and olive groves. This action came to be called the Nakba ('Catastrophe') by the Palestinians, most of whom were to spend the decades that followed in refugee camps in adjacent Arab states.

OPPOSITE:
A PAINFUL EXCHANGE
Hindu refugees wait anxiously at Amritsar for the train that will take them to safer areas deeper into India. Hundreds of thousands of displaced people passed through the city in both directions, at what was a terrifying time for Hindus and Muslims alike.

TIME FOR CHANGE

THE BIG CHILL

In Greece, civil war had broken out between leftist partisans and conservative monarchists. The USSR had helped the former; the USA the latter. By 1949, the Western side had won. This 'proxy' war set a paradigm for the entire Cold War period, though the outcome wasn't necessarily the same each time. In the First Indochina War, from 1946, the Americans discreetly supported the French as they defended their colony against the Soviet-backed Viet Minh. The fighting went on for eight years before the Communists beat the French at Dien Bien Phu, March–May 1954.

Elsewhere in the East as well, the abrupt withdrawal of the defeated Japanese had created a power vacuum in what had been colonial possessions of the European powers a few years before. Soviet Communism provided both ideological structure and material support for liberation movements from Burma (Myanmar) to Indonesia.

THE COMMONWEALTH QUESTIONED

The brutality of Britain's attempts to deal with its 'Malayan Emergency' (1948–60) only increased the desire of local people for their freedom. Likewise in Africa: the cruelty with which its so-called 'Mau Mau' Rebellion was put down underlined the justice of the Kenya Land and Freedom Party's cause. But Britain could read the writing on the wall. In 1949, it created a 'Commonwealth' to maintain positive relations between Britain and those 'free and equal' former-imperial possessions who still held King George VI (or, from 1952, Queen Elizabeth II) as their head of state.

In South Africa, it was the Dutch-descended Afrikaners who were now asserting themselves against Anglo-Saxon domination. The National Party's victory in the (whites only) election of 1948 allowed them to introduce a system of apartheid: literally 'apart-hood', the enforced allocation of different geographical zones and political and economic freedoms to the country's white, Black and 'coloured' (Asian and mixed-race) populations. In rural areas, Black Africans were restricted to 'tribal homelands' or 'Bantustans'; around the cities to peripheral 'townships', poor and overcrowded. In 1960, (white) South Africans would vote to withdraw from the British Commonwealth and make their country a republic in its own right.

PARITY AND PARANOIA

The Cold War gained in intensity in August 1949 when the Soviets successfully tested an atomic bomb of their own, placing them on parity with the USA. It gained in complexity a few months later, with the victory of Mao's Communists in China and the establishment of the People's Republic of China (PRC). (And of a Western-orientated Republic of China run by Chiang Kai-shek and his surviving Kuomintang, though this was confined to the

RIGHT:
RACIST RULE
South Africans protest the formal implementation of apartheid in Soweto, outside Johannesburg, in the early 1950s. Daniel Malan's white minority government had been ratcheting up segregation and discrimination measures since 1948, stripping away the rights of Black and 'coloured' citizens.

TIME FOR CHANGE

island of Taiwan.) Whilst in theory the USSR gained an important ally in the PRC, their relationship wasn't always to be easy.

The Cold War created suspicion at home. Called for by the right-wing senator Joseph McCarthy (1908–57), the hearings of the House Un-American Activities Committee inaugurated a witch hunt for Communists and 'fellow-travellers' in US politics, media and the arts. (On the other hand, the trial and execution of Julius and Ethel Rosenberg as spies, long adduced as an example of McCarthyite paranoia outstripping truth and justice, would finally turn out to have been well-founded.)

CONFRONTATION IN KOREA

Minds were further concentrated by the outbreak of the Korean War in June 1950. In the confusion following Japanese withdrawal, the North had become a Communist state (the Democratic People's Republic of Korea) under Kim Il-Sung (1912–94) and a Western-orientated South, which was also nominally democratic but really ruled by the strongman Syngman Rhee (1875–1965).

The border between the two ran along the 38th Parallel (the line of 38° latitude). America's lack of enthusiasm for its corrupt

RIGHT:
BLOOD RED
China's revolutionary leader was undoubtedly a visionary. But between Chairman Mao's war on the country's landowning class, the famine fallout from his Great Leap Forward, his Cultural Revolution and his various other purges, he may have been responsible for as many as 80 million deaths in China.

ABOVE:
FRAUGHT FRONTIER
The Korean War had a faintly farcical aspect, armies chasing each other back and forth across the border, but it was nevertheless a devastating conflict. Hundreds of thousands of troops were killed, though these military casualties were overshadowed by the deaths of 2–3 million civilians.

Korean ally was so well-known it may have encouraged Kim to launch his invasion of the South. The South was taken by surprise. Within three days, the Communists had taken Seoul.

By then, though, US forces were being brought in from Japan. General Douglas MacArthur (1880–1964), in charge of the occupation there, landed with 400,000 troops. The Americans received support from others, detachments arriving from Britain and its Commonwealth and some West European states. The numbers were small (the UK sent 14,000 troops; Luxembourg only 44), but their arrival signified a degree of international support. An anti-Communist Western Bloc was taking shape.

This force quickly put the Communists to flight, chasing them back to their border – and, indeed, beyond. This was MacArthur's own initiative – and a clear breach of his orders. The Chinese had made clear that they'd regard any attack on North Korea as an attack on them. MacArthur led his troops all the way to the border with Chinese Manchuria, prompting a furious counter-attack – which in turn prompted him to recommend a nuclear attack on China. MacArthur was recalled to Washington in disgrace (amid suspicions that he'd been making a pitch for a presidential run). His replacement managed to push the Communists back to the 28th Parallel so the North–South boundary ended up back where it had begun.

China's foreign policy remained unassertive for the most part, though it continued in its claims on the island of Taiwan. Its annexation of Tibet in 1951 didn't create too many ripples in the world, though the nationalist uprising of 1959 – and the repression that followed – did. China could point to genuine improvements (modern infrastructure, food- and health-provision, rocketing life expectancy …) in Tibet in the years that followed but it also did its best to obliterate the country's traditional Buddhist culture.

RIGHT:
DOUBLE HELIX DUO
With the paper they wrote in 1953, Francis Crick (pictured right) and James Watson (left) laid the foundation for all subsequent research into the structure and functions of deoxyribonucleic acid (DNA). Research which would bring a new and completely unprecedented understanding of the molecular basis of all life.

OPPOSITE:
FIRST ELECTIONS
As European powers withdrew from their former colonial possessions, democratic elections were held for the first time across Asia, Africa and the Caribbean. Here, an elderly woman waits for the result of the Citizens' Committee elections in Johore, Malaya, 1955. The new country of Malaysia became independent in 1957.

OF DOMINOES AND DICTATORS

The superpowers' enmity was shaping the way the whole world worked. In 1954, US President Eisenhower (1890–1969) introduced the 'Domino Theory'. If one state in a region turned Communist, the argument went, the precedent it set and the practical assistance it gave its neighbours would set them falling, like toppled dominoes.

With this concern in mind, the Americans intervened to overthrow democratically elected governments in Iran and Guatemala. Jacobo Árbenz (1913–71) had wanted Guatemala to have the political and economic freedoms of the USA itself, but this was enough to brand him a Communist now. For similar reasons, the USA supported Britain's efforts to overthrow Mohammad Mosaddegh (1882–1967), Iran's elected leader, and make the country's sitting monarch, the Reza Shah, a dictator.

Effectively dictator in Argentina since 1946, Juan Perón (1895–1974) (with his charismatic wife Evita) did succeed in carving out a 'third way' between capitalism and communism. With its high-profile trades unions and welfare programmes, his populist regime struck certain leftist notes whilst steering clear of the Soviet camp – and, indeed, cracking down on more radically left-wing activism of any kind.

Soviet Communists, for their part, were doing some serious soul-searching. Stalin had died in 1953. At the Party's annual congress in February 1956, Nikita Khrushchev (1894–1971) denounced his predecessor's 'intolerance … brutality … abuse of power'. Ironically, his reformist rhetoric raised the hackles of diehards in the Party and the military, and Khrushchev quickly found himself boxed in. Later that year, he was forced to intervene more aggressively than he might have liked in Hungary, where workers and students had risen up to try and bring about a more democratically responsive socialism.

Fortunately for Khrushchev, the world was distracted from the bloodshed by the spectacle of France and (especially) Britain making colonial fools of themselves in Suez. Egypt's President Gamal Abdel Nasser's (1918–70) move to nationalize the Canal prompted armed intervention by the Western powers (against US advice), who tried to topple him with Israeli help. US pressure forced them to withdraw, leaving Nasser looking triumphant and Britain very much a former-power.

FORWARD INTO FAMINE

While Khrushchev was reconsidering, Mao was doubling down in the 'Great Leap Forward' of January 1958. The Stalin-style five-year plans China had already embarked on weren't ambitious enough for the Chairman. He wanted to accelerate his country's industrialization and agrarian collectivism but to do it in a cheap and low-tech way by harnessing its vast reserves of labour. The result was economic catastrophe and a famine that killed over 50 million people.

World Communism had better news in 1957, when the Soviet Union successfully launched the first artificial satellite, the Sputnik. The flight of the first 'cosmonaut', Yuri Gagarin, in 1961, showed the USSR leading the exploration of space. This would become the 'Space Race' when, in 1962, President John F. Kennedy (1917–63) announced America's intention of landing a man on the Moon by 1970.

In 1959, so six years after starting his Cuban Revolution, Fidel Castro (1926–2016) and his fighters took Havana. With them was the Argentinian firebrand Ernesto 'Che' Guevara, who was to become an iconic leftist figure, till his death at the hands of Bolivia's armed forces as he tried to bring about a revolution in that country in 1967. Castro's position was only to be strengthened by the failure of the 'Bay of Pigs' attack in 1961. A band of Cuban emigres, with indecisive support from the newly elected President Kennedy, attempted an invasion but was badly beaten.

In Vietnam, the North Vietnamese Army had started opening up the 'Ho Chi Minh Trail' to the south, where the Viet Cong (VC) guerrillas were battling Ngo Dinh Diem's (1901–63) US-backed government. Much of the trail ran through neighbouring Laos, which would draw that country into the conflict later. The year 1961 saw the 'Berlin Wall' go up, an admission of failure by the government of Communist East Germany (the German

TIME FOR CHANGE

ABOVE:
MOURNING A MONSTER
Stalin's hold on the USSR had been steel-strong, his cult of personality pervasive. His loss was always going to leave a gap. Nikita Khrushchev's administration was altogether more humane but struggled to maintain the stability Soviet citizens had come to crave.

LEFT:
'IN THE NAME OF THE WORKING CLASS'
Soviet tanks move in to Budapest to crush the 'bourgeois' and 'reactionary' rising of 1956. Thousands of rebels were killed in 12 days of fighting. 'Help Hungary', the message went out from Hungary's state radio station, but Western attention was elsewhere, on Suez.

Democratic Republic), since it was clearly designed to keep disgruntled citizens in.

FROM DOMINOES TO POKER

As Árbenz had found in Guatemala, it didn't take much reformist talk to see a democratic leader put down as a 'Communist' in US eyes. One such was Patrice Lumumba who, for a few short weeks, was prime minister of the Republic of the Congo (now the DRC) before being overthrown by his Chief of Staff of the Army Mobutu Sese Seko (1930–97), with Western backing. Mobutu had Lumumba executed in January 1961. In 1965, US troops were sent in to occupy the Dominican Republic after it elected the moderately reform-minded Juan Bosch (1909–2001).

Historians still debate whether Cuba's Castro was a Soviet sympathizer from the start or just a democrat forced into the Communist corner by American hostility. In the aftermath of the Bay of Pigs, he certainly became much closer to the Soviets, in early 1963 agreeing to host their missile site. In the geopolitical poker game that followed, it was generally agreed that 'Khrushchev blinked' – the missiles were removed; a much-needed fillip for Kennedy's presidency.

Not that he'd enjoy it long. On 22 November, he was assassinated during a motorcade in Dallas, Texas. The memory of his administration was promptly mythologized as a modern 'Camelot' (the medieval court of the legendary King Arthur, famous for the courage and chivalry of its knights).

TIME FOR CHANGE

RIGHT:
INTO ORBIT
The Soviets were out of the starting blocks before the Americans realized the 'Space Race' had started. The launching of the first satellite, Sputnik 1, on 4 October 1957, was an enormous coup. Here a technician makes some last-minute adjustments.

BELOW:
LEADING THE WAY
On 12 April 1961, Yuri Gagarin became the first human being ever to travel in outer space when he orbited the Earth in his flight Vostok 1. His achievement was excruciating for the United States: Communism was the future, it seemed to show.

A SOUTHEAST ASIAN NIGHTMARE

Ho Chi Minh (1890–1969) had made no secret of his Communist allegiances since the 1940s. By 1964, he and the Viet Cong were gaining ground in the South, despite the Kennedy administration's background support for Diem's Saigon regime. Kennedy's successor Lyndon Johnson (1908–73) sent in US armed forces in response to a claimed 'attack' (by his own subsequent admission bogus) by North Vietnamese patrol boats on US vessels in the Gulf of Tonkin.

This commitment grew until the Americans had half a million troops in the country – over 58,000 of their men would ultimately be killed. Military casualties among their South Vietnamese allies were many times that number, as were those on the Communist side, while civilians across the country died in their millions. That the VC came from the general population of the South was arguably evidence of the popularity of their cause. It certainly made every peasant a potential 'hostile' in South Vietnamese and US eyes. Leaving aside notorious atrocities like the My Lai massacre of 1968, the destruction of villages and paddy fields was routine. As was the use of defoliants like Agent Orange over vast areas of virgin rainforest, causing catastrophic environmental damage – and, for the human population, health problems that are still being felt.

ABOVE:
CHINESE CULTURAL REVOLUTION
Mao believed in divide-and-rule. Far from striving for stability and purpose, he delivered his people a succession of jolting shocks. Just as things seemed to be getting back to normal after the Great Leap Forward, in 1966, he threw China into violent turmoil with his Cultural Revolution.

BELOW:
CANAL CATASTROPHE
The British commando carrier HMS *Theseus* was moved to carry troops ashore during the Suez Crisis. A show of strength that only ended up advertising Britain's weakness, the conflict was a turning point in the country's post-war history, curtailing British influence in region.

TIME FOR CHANGE

With the inauguration of Operation Rolling Thunder (April 1965), aerial bombing of the North began – a way of turning up the pressure on the Hanoi regime without committing US troops in a ground invasion. Though in theory not even a combatant, Laos became the most heavily bombed land in history as US planes tried to knock out the Ho Chi Minh Trail. All they succeeded in doing was increasing support for the country's own Communist insurgents, the Pathet Lao.

By 1968, unrest was mounting on the American home front as casualties rose and reports filtered back of atrocities and oppressive conduct in Vietnam. The 'Tet Offensive' in January 1968, a major push by Communist forces there, was comprehensively defeated. But, given the reassurances they'd received from the Johnson administration that the war was all but won, the American public were taken unpleasantly by surprise by its having taken place at all. Opposition to the war grew deeper still.

LEFT:
ROMANTIC REBEL
'Che' Guevara played an important part in Cuba's Revolution, but this was nothing to his importance as an icon. That said, the hothead had a cold and calculating side; he was severely puritanical, and ruthless in his dedication to the 'struggle'.

BELOW:
PRESIDENTIAL MOTORCADE
Young and virile, John F. Kennedy had seemed a counter to the glamour of the Cuban Revolutionaries, promising to lead Americans to a 'New Frontier' of space travel, scientific innovation, economic enterprise and social reform. But within moments of this picture being taken he would be dead.

OPPOSITE:
CUBAN CHARISMA
'El Comandante' electrifies another crowd. Beside the boring Western leaders in their suits or the drab gerontocrats of the USSR, Fidel Castro and 'Che' Guevara seemed a breath of fresh air, bringing a touch of star quality to the geopolitical scene.

ABOVE:
YOUNG SACRIFICE
Almost 60,000 American soldiers were to be killed in Vietnam. Their average age was 23, the youngest just 16. America's military strength was overwhelming, but increasingly it struggled to cope with the conflict's human cost and a determined, motivated enemy in the North Vietnamese and Viet Cong insurgents.

RIGHT:
LETHAL FORCE
The war in Vietnam produced a shadow second front at home as young people protested what they saw as an oppressive intervention. On 4 May 1970, at Kent State University, Ohio, National Guardsmen opened fire on demonstrators, killing four and wounding nine.

'RADICAL CHIC'

The 1960s had in any case seen the norms of Western life widely questioned by the young. America had 'had a good war', having entered as, still, a 'junior' power and emerged as the most powerful country in the world. Industrially it had grown, thanks to war production, yet its infrastructure hadn't been damaged by bombing as others' had. Europeans had looked enviously across the Atlantic to where Americans lived in abundance, in comfortable homes, with fridges, TVs and cars.

In this post-war prosperity, America had raised a relatively affluent generation of teenagers, newly recognized as a demographic of their own. Music had been crucial: the popularity of Elvis Presley and of 'Rock and Roll' had prepared the way for groups like the (British) Beatles. A parallel vogue for 'folk'-derived music and the 'protest' songs of artists like America's Bob Dylan

TIME FOR CHANGE

TIME FOR CHANGE

THIS PAGE, CLOCKWISE FROM TOP LEFT:
ROCK AND SOUL
Black performers pioneered many of the newest and freshest sounds of the 1960s: talents like Chuck Berry (left above) and Aretha Franklin (above). The appeal of Elvis 'the Pelvis' Presley, his thrilling singing voice and his racy 'rubber legs' dance style was seen – quite seriously – as a threat to social order. The background story of America's 1960s was a boring one of young people's increasing purchasing power but the headline narrative was more sensational and much more exciting.

reflected the generation's interest in the need for social change. 'Black music' was reaching wider audiences through Motown Records. Berry Gordy's Detroit-based outfit was consciously mass-producing hits like cars. America's Civil Rights Movement had gained what seemed unstoppable momentum with Martin Luther King Jr's 'I have a dream …' speech from the steps of the Lincoln Memorial, Washington, in 1963. His assassination in April 1968 gave the idealism an edge of bitterness. Formed in 1966, the Black Panther Party maintained that King's strategy of peaceful protest wasn't going to be adequate to bring 'Black Power' and that sometimes-violent direct action would be needed. This rising consciousness meshed with opposition to the war: Black youth were seen as disproportionately impacted by the call-up. As boxer Muhammad Ali put it at the time of his trial for refusing to obey the draft: 'No Viet Cong ever called me Nigger.'

Unrest was growing elsewhere too. As with other fashions, France led the way. In May 1968, the country came close to revolution with weeks of rioting in Paris and other cities. Along with the 'mainstreaming' of Marxism, the so-called 'Counterculture' brought new styles in everything from art to fashion and new subcultures revolving around hallucinogenic drugs and eastern spiritual beliefs. The Iron Curtain had its own equivalent, though the 'Prague Spring' – the attempt of Alexander Dubček (1921–92) and his Czechoslovak people to build 'socialism with a human face' – brought a repressive summer when the Soviet tanks rolled in.

It was about now too that Catholics in Northern Ireland suffering discrimination in electoral rights and social housing started organizing civil rights marches for equal treatment. The excessive violence employed by representatives of the 'Orange State' in putting down these protests led to the dispatching of British troops to keep order in 1969. The reaction by Republicans in the Catholic community to what they saw as a reassertion of British colonialist authority prompted a paramilitary campaign by the Provisional IRA (Irish Republican Army).

BELOW:
THE BEATLES
'Four Mop-Tops from Liverpool' (John Lennon, Paul McCartney, George Harrison and Ringo Starr) took America by storm in 1964. As they grew older and more artistically enterprising, the Beatles would bring their fans with them, taking 'pop' music off in new directions.

LEFT:
'THE GREATEST'
Muhammad Ali beats Ernie Terrell to become WBA heavyweight champion, 6 February 1967. 'I want to torture him', Ali had said of Terrell, who had insisted on using Ali's 'slave name', Cassius Clay. Ali would soon be stripped of the title for refusing the draft to Vietnam.

The situation was only exacerbated when, on 'Bloody Sunday', 1972, paratroopers fired into a crowd of civil rights protesters, killing 14 people. Over the next quarter-century, 3,500 people would be killed. By the IRA (who nominally targeted soldiers, police and prison officers and other representatives of the British Crown, but killed hundreds of civilians too), in sectarian killings by the Protestant paramilitary groups which sprang up as the 'Troubles' escalated; and, of course, by the Army, the Royal Ulster Constabulary and other agents of the British state.

In the China of Mao, even 'popular' unrest was ordered by the state, which started its own 'Cultural Revolution' in 1966. Armies of students formed bands of 'Red Guards' who roamed the streets of the main cities and took to the railways to visit outlying towns and villages, killing 'class enemies' and attacking monuments and museums – anything they associated with elitism and with reactionary former times. Many thousands, maybe millions, of people – mainly those considered to be intellectuals and authority figures – were killed in six years of violent turmoil.

UNDESIRABLE ALLIES

As, under pressure from Washington, America's Southern states dropped their more openly segregationist policies, South African apartheid looked increasingly aberrant. But Cold War considerations caused the Western powers to support the whites-only government in its campaign against the African National Congress (ANC). ANC leader Nelson Mandela (1918–2013) remained in prison, where he'd been since 1963. At the Rivonia Trial, named for the farmhouse in which the defendants had been arrested, he'd been convicted of 'terrorism' (a campaign of sabotage against military camps, electric substations, telephone and power lines …). The former German colony of South West Africa was effectively governed by South Africa, again with US blessing: the rebels of SWAPO (South West Africa People's Organisation) were viewed as Communists.

Despite misgivings, the West also supported the regime of Ian Smith (1919–2007) in Rhodesia. In response to British demands that he give the country's Black majority more of a democratic

OPPOSITE:
'I'VE SEEN THE PROMISED LAND …'
'I may not get there with you. But … we, as a people, will get to the Promised Land.' Within a day of delivering this speech in Memphis, Martin Luther King was dead, his dream of racial justice at the very least delayed.

TIME FOR CHANGE

TIME FOR CHANGE

ABOVE:
PRAGUE SPRING
The bid to build 'Socialism with a Human Face' in Prague is put down, crushed by the tanks of the Soviet Union and its allies from the Warsaw Pact, Czechoslovakia's supposed friends, in the spring of 1968.

LEFT:
LE '68
Riot police take to the streets of Paris to put down angry demonstrators, 15 May 1968. Unusually, students and workers formed a common front in protest against poverty, unemployment and the conservative government of Charles de Gaulle. (Who actually fled France in secret for some days.)

voice, he made a 'Unilateral Declaration of Independence' (UDI). But rebel leaders like Joshua Nkomo (1917–99) and Robert Mugabe (1924–2019) were seen as 'natural' allies of the Soviets in Southern Africa. 'Northern Rhodesia' had gained its independence as Zambia in 1964, as had Kenya. (Though independent since 1962, Uganda had quickly been subjected to the dictatorship of Milton Obote [1925–2005], followed by that of the dementedly tyrannical Idi Amin [1928–2003].)

Likewise in Latin America, America maintained its long-term strategy of support for 'sonofabitch' dictators, like the generals who took charge in Brazil in 1964 and Juan Carlos Onganía (1914–95), who seized power in Argentina two years later. The drift to dictatorship would continue with a military takeover in Uruguay in 1973. That same year saw the democratically elected leftist government of Salvador Allende (1908–73), in Chile, being overthrown by Augusto Pinochet (1915–2006) with open US backing. A campaign of ferocious repression followed here and elsewhere in Latin America. In 1976, a generals' junta in Argentina cracked down savagely on all left-liberal dissent. Many thousands were imprisoned and executed – or simply 'disappeared'.

In 1968, the USA supported Indonesia's military commander General Suharto (1921–2008) when he overthrew the country's elected President Sukarno (1901–70). Suharto immediately embarked on a repressive campaign against any possible opposition. In Europe, the USA interfered less (or less directly). Even so, it backed the group of colonels who in 1967 imposed a military dictatorship on Greece.

ARAB–ISRAELI ISSUES

Israel, increasingly beleaguered, in June 1967 launched a preemptive attack against Egypt, Syria, Jordan and Iraq, scoring a

speedy victory in what became known as the 'Six-Day War'. Its position in the region was now much stronger, not least because it had taken the West Bank from Jordan. It has held on to it, despite international condemnation, ever since.

When Egypt and Syria attacked in 1973 on the Jewish holy day of Yom Kippur, Israel had no difficulty defeating Syria, conquering the strategic Golan Heights, though its victory over Egypt was less conclusive. The plight of the Palestinians remained a running sore in the region, their overcrowded 'camps' in Jordan, Lebanon, Syria, the West Bank and Gaza places of unhappiness and mounting anger. In the West Bank and Gaza, this boiled over in a sustained period of rioting in the Intifada (literally 'stone uprising') of 1987–93.

GOOD NEWS, BAD NEWS

On 20 July 1969, Neil Armstrong fulfilled John F. Kennedy's earlier promise by becoming the first human being to walk upon the Moon. America's commitments to Vietnam were proving harder to deliver on. There were, indeed, signs that it was thinking of giving up. Since the end of 1969, Johnson's successor, Richard Nixon (1913–94), had been pursuing a policy of 'Vietnamization', scaling down the active involvement of US forces in the war and leaving South Vietnamese forces to bear the brunt of combat duties.

On the other hand, in April 1970, the Americans widened the war by attacking targets in Cambodia, where the Communist Khmer Rouge had toppled Sihanouk, the country's king. As the confusion mounted, so did discontent in the USA, which led in turn to disillusion and disengagement. At the Paris Peace Talks of 1973, the USA effectively abandoned the Republic of Vietnam. Despite everyone's signatures on a supposed 'peace', the war went on without America. In 1975, South Vietnam collapsed and Saigon was taken.

Not that the proxy wars were done. In 1976, the Soviet- (and Cuban-) backed MPLA took power in Angola. The ensuing civil war with US-supported UNITA would continue till 2002. Mozambique was torn by similar strife, a leftist FRELIMO government beset by Western-backed RENAMO rebels from 1977–92. In both countries it was the civilians who suffered most. As it was in the island of East Timor, whose people had declared independence from Indonesia in November 1975. Suharto's importance to the Americans as a supporter in the region led them to overlook the cruelty of a response in which 180,000 Timorese were killed.

Widely welcomed was the news (in March 1979) that Israel's President Menachem Begin (1913–92) and Egypt's Anwar Sadat (1918–81) had signed a peace treaty. The deal had been brokered by US President Jimmy Carter (1924–) at Camp David – a presidential retreat in rural Maryland – the year before. Heartening for some was the news from Nicaragua that Anastasio Somoza – last of a family line of US-friendly dictators – had been overthrown by the leftists of the Sandinista Front. American intelligence promptly set about giving covert support to the right-wing 'Contra' rebels.

Mao's passing (in 1976) was always going to have a major impact on China but no one could have foreseen how far-reaching the reforms of his successor, Deng Xiaoping (1904–97), would be. Deng didn't do anything to liberalize his country

TIME FOR CHANGE

OPPOSITE:
FREEDOM FIGHTERS
Volunteers are drilled in Chuadanga Barracks in readiness for war after East Pakistan's declaration of independence as Bangladesh (1971). Up to 3 million civilians were killed in the fighting, the vast majority civilians, when Pakistani troops conducted an ethnic cleansing of Bengali Hindus.

RIGHT:
NO QUARTER
A mural in Derry's Bogside district commemorates the Bloody Sunday shootings of 1971. A group carries the body of one of the victims, while local priest Father Edward Daly (later Bishop of Derry) goes ahead waving a white handkerchief as a flag of truce.

BELOW:
SIX-DAY WAR
Egyptian MiG-21 warplanes lie destroyed on the tarmac after an Israeli Air Force pre-emptive strike on 5 June 1967 against Egyptian airfields at the start of the Six-Day War. Thirty-eight years after Israel captured the Gaza Strip from the Egyptians during the campaign, the Jewish state looks poised to leave the populous Palestinian territory as Prime Minister Ariel Sharon's disengagement plan approaches its 15 August 2005 implementation.

TIME FOR CHANGE

RIGHT:
NEW CENTURY, NEW ART
'It seems to me that the modern painter cannot express his age – the airplane, the atom bomb, the radio – in the old forms.' Even by the standards of America's abstract expressionists, Paul Jackson Pollock became notorious for the works he dripped, poured and spattered on to canvases.

BELOW:
POWER COUPLE
Feminist philosopher Simone de Beauvoir and her long-time companion, the existentialist philosopher Jean-Paul Sartre, sit studying together in the latter's flat in the Rue Bonaparte. The famous couple would for years be at the very heart of intellectual life in Paris' Left Bank.

ABOVE:
POLITICAL PAWNS
The US–Soviet rivalry extended far beyond tanks and ICBMs, encompassing everything from science to literature – even chess. Hence the high stakes attached to this 1970 match between Bobby Fischer (right) and Russia's Boris Spassky. The latter won, but the American triumphed two years later.

culturally or politically – his was still a one-party, Communist state. He did, however, allow quasi-capitalist market freedoms in large areas of the economy and open up certain ports and their hinterlands to foreign trade as Special Economic Zones.

COMMUNIST QUAGMIRE

The 1970s ended with the USSR marching – eyes wide open – into what Western analysts gleefully predicted would be 'their Vietnam'. A Soviet-backed government installed some years before in what Moscow feared was becoming an unstable state on their southern border had been coming under pressure from Islamic fighters (mujahideen) and rebel tribesmen. America lent discreet support to the resistance – with gratifying results. The war proved a costly and demoralizing drain on the Soviet Union. Insult was added to injury by the Western boycott of the 1980 Moscow Olympics. The Eastern Bloc would get its chance to retaliate over Los Angeles 1984. Generally, though, the Soviets were having a torrid time. The Afghan War's economic and human costs were hard to bear by a beleaguered USSR now struggling to hold on to its superpower status.

Inspired by a visit from their compatriot Pope John Paul II in 1979, Poles experienced an access of nationalistic self-confidence. A strike by workers in Gdansk's Lenin Shipyard in 1980 led to the birth of the Solidarność ('Solidarity') movement and to leader Lech Wałęsa (1943–) becoming an international celebrity. Polish Communist leader General Wojciech Jaruzelski (1923–2014) introduced martial law in December 1981 but was unable to quell the unrest completely or stop its spread to other Iron Curtain countries.

TIGER TIME

Japan's extraordinary rise out of the ashes of Tokyo, Hiroshima and Nagasaki already seemed one of the economic wonders of the world. Brands like Honda, Toyota, Sony and Mitsubishi

TIME FOR CHANGE

ABOVE:
'ENGLAND SWINGS'
British fashion was all the rage in the 1960s. Geopolitically it might be a fading force but, on the back of 'Beatlemania', the UK wielded disproportionate cultural influence, the kind of clout that later came to be characterized as 'soft power'.

weren't just bywords for value: their products – and those of other Japanese manufacturers – were coming to be seen as objectively among the best in the world. The rest of the world is only now catching up with the achievements of the country's engineers in designing the Shinkansen 'bullet trains' since the 1960s. (The 2015 version reached a speed of 603 km/h [375 mph].) While China was finding its own idiosyncratic way to capitalistic success, others in the region were beginning to catch up. In the 1980s, the 'Four Asian Tigers' – South Korea, Taiwan, Hong Kong and Singapore – emerged to become rich and successful industrial countries. Others, including Vietnam, Indonesia, Malaysia and the Philippines would follow. All, including Japan, would struggle to recover from the Asian Financial Crisis of 1997, but they've remained important manufacturing nations.

FROM ISLAM TO IBM

In 1979, the Shah of Iran was overthrown by an Islamic Revolution, his ideological tyranny replaced by a different sort. His state, though repressive, had been freely secular in

RIGHT:
HIPPY HEAVEN
In August 1969, over 450,000 young people flocked to upstate New York for the Woodstock festival to see performers from Janis Joplin to Joan Baez and from Jimi Hendrix to Jefferson Airplane. The event marked a milestone for the 1960s' 'counterculture'.

TIME FOR CHANGE

its attitudes. The Ayatollah Khomeini enforced strict codes of religious observance and modesty of conduct. For women in particular: hijab head-coverings, banned by the Shah, were now made mandatory; women were no longer allowed to divorce their husbands and adultery was severely criminalized.

A revolution of a very different sort took place in 1981 when IBM released their 'Personal Computer'. Computers had been steadily shrinking in size and increasing in speed since the time of Colossus but the idea that people might be able to work on one at their office desks – or even in their homes – was wholly new. So much so that few could even imagine the need for a device like this. (A still earlier personal computer, the Kenbak-1, had actually appeared a decade earlier only to disappear again virtually without trace.) The appearance of the 'user-friendly' Apple Macintosh in 1984 made the new 'Information Technology' that much more accessible.

The year 1981 had also seen the inauguration of Ronald Reagan (1911–2004) as US president, promising a programme of tax- and regulation-cutting 'Reaganomics'. In theory, the benefits of this, though most immediately helping the already-affluent, would 'trickle down' so all in society would gain. Welfare support for the poor was slashed but this was justified by the new employment opportunities a recovering economy would create. The former film star's upbeat manner made him the perfect person to administer what was going to be unpalatable medicine for most, convincing them that it was 'Morning in America'.

There was mourning, meanwhile, for those now coming down with a scary new sickness: AIDS (acquired immune deficiency syndrome). The HIV virus attacked sufferers' immune defences, so they succumbed to what would otherwise be trivial infections. Not as much mourning as there should have been, some felt. That the brunt was borne by male homosexuals, who contracted it during unprotected sex, made it easy for the problem to be dismissed as a 'gay plague'. Over 15 million had died by 2021.

Cheery as he was, Reagan could speak seriously when he needed to. Early in 1983, he denounced the USSR as an 'Evil Empire'. Mere rhetoric, perhaps, but when a fortnight later he announced his Strategic Defense Initiative (SDI) – the development of a system which would identify and knock out intercontinental ballistic missiles (ICBMs) as they headed towards the USA – he sent a shudder through his hearers in the Soviet sphere. In so far as the peace had been maintained till now it had been by the balancing strength of the enemies' nuclear forces and the prospect of mutually assured destruction (MAD) if either side decided to attack.

The first-ever Live Aid concert occurred in 1985, held simultaneously in London and Philadelphia, where more than 160,000 watched, with spin-off concerts in several other countries. Altogether, 1.9 billion viewed the proceedings on TV worldwide. Musicians Bob Geldof and Midge Ure had dreamed the event up as a response to TV footage of famine-hit Ethiopia. How much Africa was ever helped by Live Aid or the many

OPPOSITE:
MAN ON THE MOON
Buzz Aldrin became the second man to walk on the Moon after the Apollo 11's mission commander Neil Armstrong in 1969. An extraordinary achievement for humanity, but for America as important in marking victory in the decade-long 'Space Race'.

RIGHT:
THE BEST OF ENEMIES
Richard Nixon meets Mao on his 1972 state visit to Beijing. No Democrat would have dared to cozy up to the Communists this way, but Nixon's credentials were impeccably right-wing. He hoped to exploit divisions between the PRC and the Soviet Union.

TIME FOR CHANGE

RIGHT:
HOSTAGE TAKERS
At the Munich Olympics in 1972, Palestinians from the 'Black September' held Israeli athletes hostage and killed eleven. High-profile hiijackings by Palestinian terrorists were already a feature of the news-cycle. In 1985, the cruise ship the *Achille Lauro* would also be taken.

BELOW:
WATERLOO REVISITED
'The history book on the shelf,/is always repeating itself.' So it was to many more times when Sweden's ABBA (Anni-Frid Lyngstad, Benny Andersson, Björn Ulvaeus and Agnetha Fältskog) won Eurovision in 1974 before returning to the top with a seemingly endless string of number ones.

TIME FOR CHANGE

RIGHT:
HAND ON HEART
A pledge of peace. US President Jimmy Carter stands for 'The Star Spangled Banner' between Egypt's Anwar Sadat (left) and Israel's Menachem Begin after their agreement on the Camp David Accords, 1979.

BELOW:
IN ALLAH'S NAME
The Ayatollah Khomeini addresses supporters in Tehran. His return from a 14-year exile was the culmination of a year-long revolution. Under his leadership, the Shah's repressive secularism was to be replaced by a hard-line Islamic theocracy in Iran.

ABOVE:
ILL-FATED ALUMNI
A Cambodian visitor looks at pictures of his compatriots tortured and executed at Tuol Sleng high school between 1975 and 1979. By this time a museum, the school had been taken over by the Khmer Rouge as a prison and interrogation centre.

OPPOSITE:
SPEAKING FOR THE PEOPLE
Outside the Lenin Shipyard, Lech Wałęsa announces the Gdansk Agreement in which the Polish government recognized the striking workers' union, Solidarity. The strike was over, but Solidarity was to play a crucial part in Polish politics – and the overthrow of Communist oppression in Eastern Europe.

similar events it subsequently inspired is hotly debated, but it certainly helped give more affluent societies some inkling of what others suffered.

MARXIST MELTDOWN

Running just to stand still in an arms race which had now been going on for three decades, the Soviet Union was heading for bankruptcy. When Mikhail Gorbachev (1931–2022) became premier in March 1985, he faced the challenge of rebuilding a failing state. An April 1986 explosion at the Chernobyl nuclear power station in Ukraine wasn't just a major disaster (it sent a cloud of radioactive dust across much of central and northern Europe): it summed up the economic weakness and infrastructural decrepitude of the USSR.

Apart from imposing a moratorium on nuclear weapons' testing, Gorbachev introduced far-reaching policies of perestroika ('restructuring') and glasnost ('openness'). The second of these in particular seemed to open the USSR up to political freedom and cultural liberalization of a sort that unsettled the old guard in the Communist Party.

It was still too little, too late. After securing at least a show of success in Afghanistan (installing a National Reconciliation government under Mohammad Najibullah), Soviet forces began withdrawing from the country in May 1988. That December, scaling back further on the USSR's commitments, Gorbachev announced that it would no longer intervene militarily in Eastern Europe. Popular democratic movements in the Iron Curtain countries could hardly miss the hint. Campaigns for change began in Hungary, Poland, the Czech Republic, Bulgaria and Romania in the months that followed. As the 1980s ended, the clamour for freedom crescendoed. When German demonstrators marched on the Berlin Wall in

TIME FOR CHANGE

RIGHT:
AFGHAN FIGHTERS
Mujahideen in Afghanistan's Kunar province stand ready to resist their country's Soviet invaders. Their courage and commitment made them formidable fighters. But they were inherently anarchic and primarily loyal to their warlords – whom the West would find less biddable than they might have liked.

BELOW:
NEW HOPE FROM THE 'HOOD
African American hip hop music and dance styles travelled around the world in the 1980s with spin-offs from rap and record 'scratching' to MC-ing and graffiti-art. An affirmation for groups long marginalized in mainstream culture. These breakdancers, the 'Eastwood Rockers', are in Liverpool, England (1984).

TIME FOR CHANGE

LEFT:
BILL BOOTS UP
It wasn't yet completely clear that the Nerds were going to inherit the earth, but a bespectacled Bill Gates was already on the rise. He had registered the trade name Microsoft as early as 1976, would launch Windows in 1985, and would be a billionaire just two years later.

ABOVE:
AIDS
Gay activists in San Francisco march to draw attention to the AIDS epidemic, which by this time (1984) had claimed over 3,000 lives in the USA. There would be almost twice that number the following year alone, and little faith that the authorities really cared.

November 1990, guards stood by while they first vandalized and then systematically demolished it.

The authorities in Beijing had been nothing like so tolerant when pro-democracy protesters had occupied the city's central Tiananmen Square in summer 1989 – though they'd let them gather for several weeks before they intervened. Finally, though, they'd sent in troops with tanks to retake the area by force: anything from 300 to 1,000 demonstrators had been killed.

A NEW ERA

In Europe, the Communist system came apart. Gorbachev remained in place at the top of the Soviet Party but the initiative lay with Boris Yeltsin's (1931–2007) reformist government. The people of Georgia and the Baltic States voted to leave the Union early in 1991, with other nationalities following, before Russia was rocked by that year's 'August Coup'. This attempt by hard-line Communists to put the clock back failed, but also underlined the inadequacy of Gorbachev's reforms. By the end of the year, he'd resigned, leaving Yeltsin at the

TIME FOR CHANGE

RIGHT:
LIVE AID
No good deed goes unpunished. The critics weren't entirely wrong: the blood-rush of benevolence, however gratifying, was no solution to the problems of structural inequality. Live Aid's most important achievement was perhaps to spark a deeper – and still-continuing – debate.

BELOW:
APOCALYPSE AVERTED?
The Chernobyl explosion and the radiation leak that followed sent a cloud of consternation spreading across Europe and beyond. In the event, the number of deaths directly caused was limited to about 60; several thousand more may have been brought forward as an indirect result.

head of Russia and of a smaller and freer – but economically anarchic and chronically corrupt – 'Commonwealth of Independent States'. The 'Shock Therapy' he prescribed for the economy was every bit as traumatic as might have been expected without producing obvious dividends, except for a few 'oligarchs'. Even so, Yeltsin managed to see off a hard-line Communists' coup attempt in 1993.

Russia was determined to make it clear that it remained the leader of the Commonwealth and rejected the Chechen Republic's bid to break away. In the First Chechen War (1994–6), Russian forces failed to prevent this – despite the loss of 5,000 lives (and those of over 27,000 Chechen civilians). In a Second Chechen War (1999–2009), the Russians would prevail, though at the cost of many more thousands of lives. Russia's commitment to this conflict is now widely seen as Prime Minister Vladimir Putin's (1952–) attempt to stamp his authority on the country. In 2000, he'd succeed Boris Yeltsin as president.

The collapse of Communism in Yugoslavia left that country – brought together under the authoritarian rule of Marshal Tito until his death in 1980 – without a unifying ideology. It began to break down into component republics (Bosnia-Herzegovina, Croatia, Macedonia, Montenegro, Serbia and Slovenia). At the same time, though, a tide of Serbian nationalism rose, giving that state expansionist ideas, leading to – often savage – civil war. Serbian soldiers slaughtered 8,000 Bosnian Muslims in the Srebrenica massacre of 1995 in pursuit of their wider policy of 'ethnic cleansing'.

In China, Communism continued, its power unchecked, though neither Marx nor Mao would have recognized their influence in a system that brought together buccaneering market freedom with iron authoritarianism in the political sphere. Even so, there was a sense that the world had changed and it didn't seem so extravagant that US President George H.W. Bush (1924–2018) should have announced the commencement of a 'New World Order'.

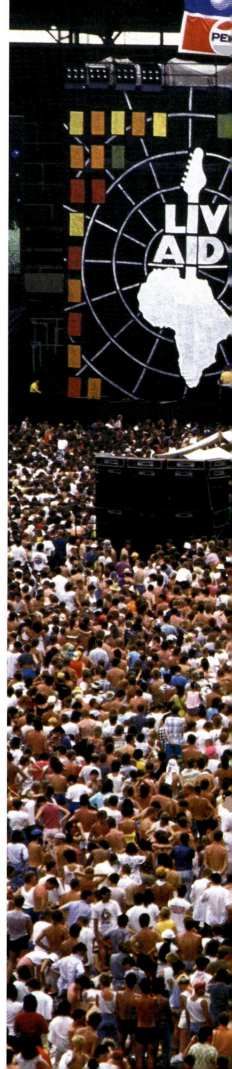

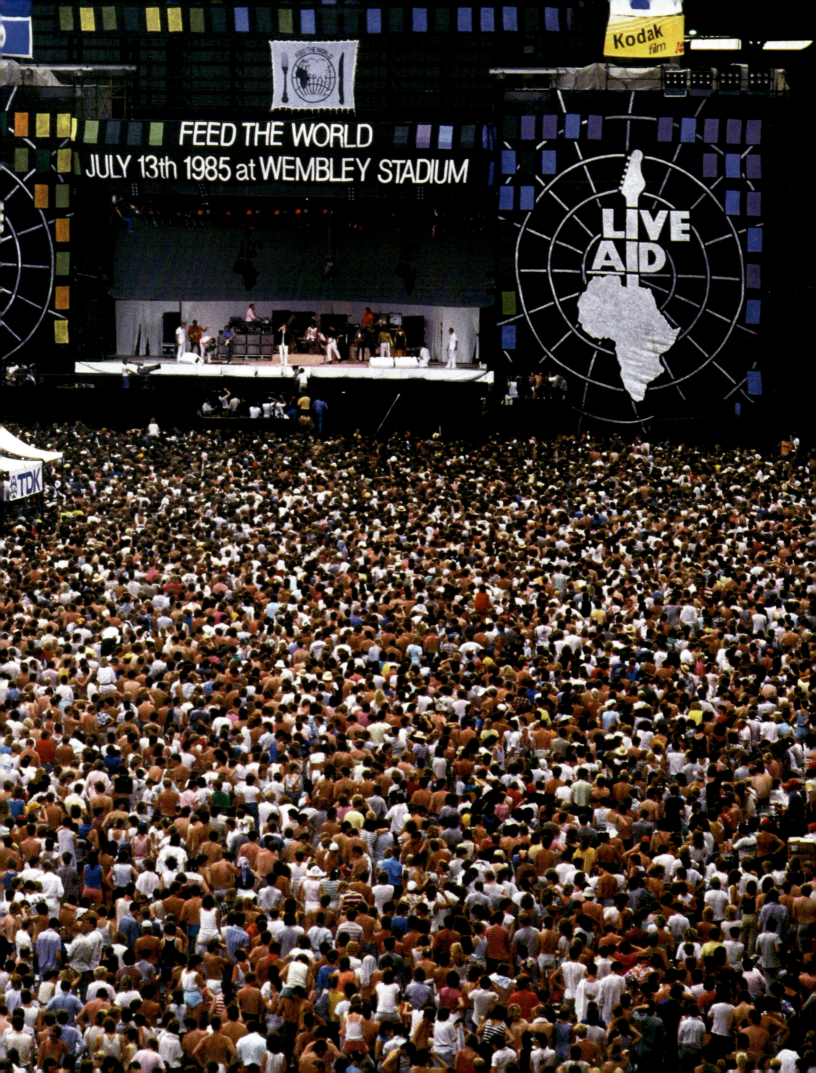

ABOVE:
BERLIN WALL
Dramatically framed by the Brandenburg Gate, a jubilant crowd collects atop the Berlin Wall. Within a few hours they will start systematically demolishing it. The days of Communist rule, and of Europe's division, are clearly numbered.

RIGHT:
DEFIANCE
A lone protester faces down a column of tanks after days of demonstrations in Tiananmen Square. A stirring sight, but normal Beijing business was very soon to be resumed with the massacre of hundreds of people and an official crackdown.

Not just in geopolitics. The application of IT to banking and the buying and selling of shares was making money more fluid – less locally attached – than it had ever been. Finance had always been international. Now national borders were coming to seem meaningless as economic 'globalization' gained seemingly irresistible force. As geographical and political demarcations became less crucial, so did those of past and present: rampant capitalism lived very much in the now. Even so, reports of the 'End of History' proved premature. People's sense that cherished ideas, identities and traditions were threatened seemed to be getting stronger in response. History was always ready with an unexpected turn-up here, a violent ambush there.

NEW WORLD DISORDER

Organized crime had always existed, but the rise of Pablo Escobar was something new. A local gang leader in Medellín, Colombia, he had in 1976 founded the 'Medellín Cartel', bringing together drugs gangs from that city; he'd then expanded till his operations covered not only the rest of Colombia but the world. In the 1980s, he took his trade to a new level entirely, monopolizing the North American market in cocaine. This drug had become an addictive style accessory for the new breed of super-rich, flamboyantly Wall Street trader the globalizing market was now creating.

The financial clout of the narcotics gangs matched that of whole countries. The daily grind of murder, extortion, kidnapping and everything else apart, the traffic had a distorting effect on the international trading and banking systems more widely. The inadequacy of Western policy in coming up with an answer to the problem posed by drugs is exemplified in the US First Lady Nancy Reagan's slogan 'Just say no!'

South America had what now seemed an old-fashioned scourge in Abimael Guzmán's 'Shining Path' guerrillas, avowed Maoists who

TIME FOR CHANGE

TIME FOR CHANGE

ABOVE:
TOXIC LEGACY
Pablo Escobar revelled in his status as an international celebrity, 'Prince of Cocaine'. He died, shot by the authorities, in 1993. Thirty years later it was reported that the hippos he imported to his country estate as exotic pets had multiplied and become a public danger.

nevertheless – along with members of the Peruvian security forces – killed rival communists and trade unionists and massacred whole communities in the countryside. Operative since the 1980s, it had resisted all attempts by the authorities to put it down but ebbed in importance after Guzmán's capture in 1992.

THE ISLAMIC IMPERATIVE

Iraqi dictator Saddam Hussein (1937–2006) fought a lengthy war (1980–8) with Iran because he'd feared the spread of Islamic radicalism. He had the leftist's disdain for religious 'superstition' (and the autocrat's suspicion of any belief system that didn't centre him). This conflict had finally petered out in an exhausted stalemate. When, in 1990, he sent his forces into Kuwait, it was in an old-fashioned attempt to extend his territories. After his defeat by an international coalition in the Gulf War, however, he started sprinkling his speeches and letters with Islamic pieties.

LEFT:
FAILED COUP
Demonstrators gather on the steps of the Russian White House during a 1991 coup attempt in Moscow. The State Committee for the State of Emergency, a group led by USSR Vice President Gennady Yanayev and other officials, attempts to overthrow President Mikhail Gorbachev and the Soviet government in August 1991.

LEFT:
HIGHWAY OF DEATH
Coalition forces carried out a 'turkey shoot' against Iraqis fleeing Kuwait City, 26–27 February 1991. Up to a thousand were killed and twice that number captured. The scorched shells of some 2,000 military vehicles were left abandoned.

OPPOSITE TOP:
BOSNIAN WAR
A Bosnian woman mourns over coffins of a newly identified victim of the 1995 Srebrenica massacre during preparation for mass burial at the Potocari memorial cemetery near Srebrenica on 10 July 2010. More than 775 bodies found in mass grave sites in eastern Bosnia were reburied on the 15th anniversary of the Srebrenica massacre. Nearly 8,000 men and boys from the enclave were captured and systematically killed by Bosnian Serb forces in the days after the fall of Srebrenica on 11 July 1995.

OPPOSITE BOTTOM:
RWANDA GENOCIDE
Youths gather behind the fence of a refugee camp in May 1994 at the border of Rwanda and Tanzania. Hutu refugees fled to Tanzania across the Akagera River in order to escape reprisals by Tutsi rebels.

Not that anyone believed in his conversion. The US-led coalition had chosen to leave him in place after the success of Operation Desert Storm because they saw him as an important bulwark against Islamist expansion in the Middle East. It was, however, a straw in the wind. For a few years now, what had been 'Arab nationalist' causes had been becoming 'Islamist' ones. The Islamic resistance movement Hamas was already marginalizing the secular Fatah organization till now in charge in the Palestinian West Bank and Gaza Strip.

Islamism was the radicalizing force that drove a group of terrorists to place a bomb in a van at New York's World Trade Center in 1993, killing five and injuring over a thousand. In Somalia, it united a collection of rebel groups against the dictatorship of Siad Barre (c. 1919–95). So disruptive were they that Somalia was classed as a 'failed state' by the international community and US troops were sent to the aid of a self-styled 'socialist' regime. At the Battle of Mogadishu (1993), 18 US Marines were killed and over 70 wounded, the highest casualties they'd sustained since Vietnam.

Islam had of course also inspired the mujahideen in Afghanistan (with, as we've seen, the quiet assistance of the USA). Islamism continued to be a factor in that country's politics. The departure of the Soviets might have meant a victory for Afghans

but it had left the violent chaos of another 'failed state' behind. It was up to another avowedly Islamist force, the Taliban (literally 'Scholars'), to impose some sort of order on the country. It was, however, a deeply repressive, puritanical order, harsh in its treatment of women, and of dissent of any kind.

There was better news from South Africa where, in 1990, Nelson Mandela had been freed. In the elections of 1994 all races could vote and Mandela and his ANC were swept to power. Namibia had won its freedom with Black South Africa. (Ian Smith's Rhodesia had been replaced by Zimbabwe in 1980 after the final triumph of the rebels there.) All these countries have had their problems with corruption and crime in the decades since, but few have ever mourned the passing of white rule.

The Rwanda genocide also took place in 1994, when members of the Tutsi ethnic group were slaughtered by members of the Hutu people. Up to 800,000 were killed and half a million women raped in the violence, whose motivation hasn't been satisfactorily explained.

INDIA EMERGENT

India's problems had been measuring themselves out in presidential assassinations. Indira Gandhi's killing in 1984 by two of her Sikh bodyguards, angered at her government's

TIME FOR CHANGE

TIME FOR CHANGE

treatment of their community, was followed in 1991 by her son Rajiv's by a member of the 'Tamil Tigers'. This group blamed India for supporting Sri Lanka's Sinhalese majority in its oppression of the Tamil minority in that island state.

Intercommunal violence continued. An outbreak in 1992, following the destruction of the Babri Mosque by a Hindu nationalist mob, ended with over 10,000 people being killed. Kashmir continued to be a problem. This was business left unfinished at the time of Partition when the wishes of the Hindu ruler had prevailed over those of his (mostly Muslim) people. The Kargil War of 1999 was fought by Pakistan and India over part of this territory but it ended inconclusively with no change. The wider rivalry between these countries entered a new and potentially disturbing phase when Pakistan became a nuclear power in 1998 (India had been one since the 1970s).

AN UNHAPPY AMERICA

The deaths of 168 people and the wounding of over 600 more in the Oklahoma City bombing in 1995 highlighted the threat to the USA by domestic terrorism. The attack, on a Federal Government Complex, using a truck laden with explosives, was similar to the World Trade Center bombing a couple of years before. This time, though, the culprits, Timothy McVeigh and Terry Nichols, were white supremacist adherents of the 'militia' movement. Fired by paranoia about the controlling tendencies of the US government and its supposed favouring of non-white and immigrant groups, right-wing radicals were mobilizing to defend the interests (as they saw them) of their race.

If the militias' motives sound perverse, this was nothing to that of Aum Shinrikyo, a doomsday cult which had grown up in Japan in the 1990s. A curious hybrid of Hindu and Buddhist belief and Christian millenarianism (the belief that the world as we know it is ending to make way for an entirely new order), its members in 1995 carried out an attack on the Tokyo metro. Releasing sarin, a highly toxic organophosphate gas, on trains in the morning rush hour, they killed 13 people and injured thousands more.

More happily, the Americans helped to broker a long-overdue resolution to the Northern Ireland Troubles. In the Good Friday Agreement of 1998, Britain accepted that the province could be reunited with the rest of Ireland if its people could be shown to want it (reassuring to Irish Nationalists) while the Republic allayed Unionist fears by renouncing its longstanding claim to the North. Since the European Union (of which at this time both Britain and Ireland were members) was to some extent making old national borders redundant anyway, it seemed Ireland would in some ways be effectively united by default.

LEFT:
THE UNIVERSE REVEALED
The year 1990 saw the launch of the Hubble Space Telescope into low-Earth orbit. Since then the pictures it has streamed back have transformed our understanding of the universe. Here we see the Pinwheel Galaxy, a spiral galaxy in the constellation Ursa Major.

HISTORY OF THE WORLD

LONG WALK
Nelson Mandela (centre, with wife Winnie) was released from prison in South Africa, 11 February 1990. By May 1994, the ANC leader would be the president of a free South Africa. His autobiography, *Long Walk to Freedom*, was published in 1994.

THE DIGITAL AGE

21st CENTURY

The start of a new century is typically anticipated with a blend of excitement and apprehension. The year 2000 was going to bring a new millennium. Appropriately enough in the new era, fears became concentrated on the computers of the world and whether they'd be able to cope with the transition from one century to the next. Since the 'year' component in their programming was recorded only by the last two digits (1999 went down as '99'), the concern arose that they wouldn't be able to distinguish between years belonging to the twentieth (1900) and twenty-first (2000) centuries. Industrial machinery would seize up; medical equipment would fail and aircraft navigational systems would cut out simultaneously around the world with apocalyptic results.

In the event, software workarounds were mostly sufficient to smooth the whole thing over. The 'Y2K Bug' barely caused a flicker as the new century began. The lessons to be drawn from this were clear – if contradictory. First, that, despite the hype, the Digital Age was going to be pretty much a continuation of what had gone before. Second, though, that the new information technology had over just a few short years genuinely changed the way we saw and experienced our world.

OPPOSITE:
RETROMANIA?
Apple CEO Steve Jobs shows reporters how his new iPhone downloads music (2007). The digital media moguls made great play of prizing creativity, but critics claim the continuing success of Jobs' beloved Beatles suggests that real innovation has been scarce.

RIGHT:
SELLING SCIENCE
Since 6 February 2018, 'Starman' – a crash-dummy mannequin – has been orbiting the Sun in his Tesla Roadster. He was lifted into space by a Falcon Heavy rocket, built by SpaceX, another company owned by Tesla-founder Elon Musk.

THE DIGITAL AGE

AMERICA ATTACKED

For much of the world, in memory at least, the real opening of the new era came a couple of years into the century with the attacks of 11 September 2001. Hijackers associated with the Islamic Al-Qaeda group crashed planes into both towers of New York's World Trade Center and the Pentagon. A fourth plane crashed in rural Pennsylvania after passengers overpowered their hijackers.

The death toll in the attacks was 2,977 – not counting the 19 hijackers. The shockwave was felt around the world – though not always negatively. The Twin Towers were seen as having been emblematic both of America's geopolitical dominance and of the globalized economy it presided over.

Al-Qaeda leader Osama bin Laden (1957–2011) became an international bogeyman and America inaugurated a far-reaching 'War on Terror'. A new 'Department of Homeland Security' was created to protect the USA; a 'Patriot Act' passed to allow ever-greater investigative powers to the authorities. Critics claimed that these responses licensed the harassment of Muslim immigrants and – more generally – an unwarranted upsurge in state surveillance.

International cynicism was heightened by US actions abroad. It made sense to attack Afghanistan, whose Taliban regime had

OPPOSITE:
UP IN FLAMES
The '9/11' attack was unambiguously a shock, but harder to read in the fullness of its meaning. A grim gamechanger? Or a licence for the USA to double down on its global dominance? Only with time would the real implications become clearer.

ABOVE RIGHT:
BATTLE READY
ISIS fighters in Iraq put on a show of strength from the back of a glorified pickup truck. Ragtag militias like these have proven difficult for conventional forces to operate against effectively and have had a remarkable influence on recent conflicts.

RIGHT:
BOMBING RUN
An Afghan fighter watches as American aircraft bomb Al-Qaeda targets in the Tora Bora mountains of Afghanistan, December 2001. Osama bin Laden and his supporters were believed to have hidden in cave complexes in the Tora Bora mountains, and were targeted by US special forces on the ground with air support.

THE DIGITAL AGE

ABOVE:
LONG REACH
President Obama (second from left) and Secretary of State Hillary Clinton (second from right) watch Osama bin Laden's assassination in real time. Modern communications and weapons technology had much extended America's military 'reach' – but arguably left it dangerously risk-averse with regard to US lives.

OPPOSITE:
AFTER ARAFAT
2004 saw the death of the PLO (Palestine Liberation Organization) leader Yasser Arafat but Israel's bugbear had been becoming an irrelevance for some years. His brand of Arab Nationalism had increasingly been marginalized as Islamic radicalism swept the Middle East and the Muslim world.

harboured Al-Qaeda leaders and the madrasa training camps in which, along with scripture, terrorist methods had been taught. But President George W. Bush's (1946–) decision to go to war with Saddam Hussein's Iraq seemed inspired only by a wish to 'finish the job' his father George H.W. had started and by America's habitual desire to shape the world to suit its interests. Supporting Bush, the British Prime Minister Tony Blair's (1953–) administration lost credibility with its claims – backed by a 'dodgy dossier' of 'evidence' – that Iraq had weapons of mass destruction with which it was capable of attacking Western Europe at 45 minutes' notice.

The Iraq War (2003–11) went ahead and Saddam was toppled (2003) but the country wasn't really pacified. Quite the contrary, indeed. The earlier American view that he'd been keeping a lid on Islamism was ironically confirmed as the Western-supported government struggled to contain the threat from Islamic militias.

ISIS ON THE RISE
And, in 2014, the occupation of Iraq's northwestern corner, as well as part of Syria, by the forces of Islamic State, or 'ISIS'. An ongoing threat to the security of both these countries, the Islamic State also oppressed the local Yazidi (a Kurdish religious group), whose women and girls it forced into sex-slavery. They were joined by 'Jihadi Brides', as they were to be known in the UK media: British Muslim girls who made their own way willingly to join ISIS as wives and mothers.

Syria's secular ruler, Bashar al-Assad (1965–; son of Hafez al-Assad, who'd been dictator in the country from 1970 to 2000) went to war with the Islamists with the support of Russia. Allies of the Assad regime since the Soviet era, Russia remained loyal under President Vladimir Putin, despite Assad's horrendous human rights record.

TOPPLING THE TALIBAN
The war in Afghanistan was easier to justify than the Iraq War. The Taliban had clearly given comfort to Al-Qaeda. Its trajectory turned out to be similar, though. It started well, from the Western perspective, the Islamic Emirate being relatively quickly overthrown and an Islamic Republic founded. Taliban supporters fled into the mountains of the east, and across the

THE DIGITAL AGE

THE DIGITAL AGE

ABOVE:
THE WAVE
The morning of 26 December 2004, and it dawns on bathers at Krabi, Thailand, that the approaching wave is something out of the ordinary. Only as it made its way up the shelving beach would the tsunami reveal itself in its full ferocity and scale.

RIGHT:
JAPANESE TSUNAMI
Another year, another tsunami, this one following the Japanese Tohoku earthquake of 2011. Amidst the wreckage of Iwate, the 109-tonne *Hamayuri* sits atop a ruined inn some 396 m (1,300 ft) inland. The Fukushima nuclear power station was dangerously damaged by the wave.

Pakistani border. In the years that followed, though, after the Western coalition partners ended their involvement, the Taliban mounted an insurgency which gradually gained ground and led to their taking over the country again in 2021.

Cynicism about America's motives seemed to some extent to be justified by its establishment of a super-secret camp at its base in Guantánamo, Cuba, to which suspects were brought from around the world, under conditions of 'extraordinary rendition', held for years (and allegedly tortured) without trial. Minority Muslim populations felt that 'anti-terrorist' measures were really licensing racism and religious persecution while in Western-orientated Muslim states the suspicion was that they were a way of suppressing all sorts of dissent.

It would, however, be hard to argue that Islamist terrorism wasn't 'real'. Over 200 tourists were killed in a bombing on the Indonesian island of Bali (2002); 192 in the bombing of commuter trains in Madrid (2004); and a further 52 died in associated attacks on tube trains and a bus in London (2005). Trains were the target too when that same year Islamists bombed commuter services around Mumbai, India. Western tourists in resorts in Muslim countries were attacked, as were presumptively exploitative shoppers in high-end malls. Inevitably, though, as in the attack on the Westgate Mall in Nairobi, Kenya, shop staff and

OVERLEAF:
'WE THE PEOPLE …'
Barack Obama (1961–) was inaugurated on 20 January 2009, before a crowd of almost 2 million people. America's first Black president was concerned as much to reassure as to inspire, his speech harking back to overarching historical continuities and to small-c conservative values.

THE DIGITAL AGE

RIGHT:
ARAB SPRING
Tunisians take to the streets to protest misgovernment and corruption. Their action triggered unrest across the Maghreb and beyond. Some leaders were overthrown, but the optimistically entitled 'Arab Spring' became a brutal autumn as governments across the region began cracking down.

BELOW:
BUILDING BOOM
A frenzy of construction accompanied China's rise to superpower status, a previously poor country becoming a cornerstone of the world economy. In the longer term, however, the boom proved unsustainable, whole 'ghost cities' slowly crumbling as buildings failed to find buyers.

OPPOSITE BELOW:
PERIL ON THE SEA
Barely afloat, spilling over with its human cargo, a boat limps its way across the Mediterranean for European shores. By its very nature a clandestine traffic, people-smuggling doesn't produce statistics, but it's believed that more than 3,000 migrants were lost in the Mediterranean in 2023.

432

THE DIGITAL AGE

maintenance workers were also killed. In 2015, French Islamists murdered 12 people in a gun attack at the offices of the satirical newspaper *Charlie Hebdo*.

The killing of Osama bin Laden by US Navy Seals where he'd been hiding out in Abbottabad, Pakistan, in 2011, drew a line of sorts under the 9/11 story. Militant Islam would remain an issue, but some of the heat was taken out of the situation, even as conflicts in Iraq and Afghanistan – and Islamist terrorism – went on.

In some ways, 9/11, like the Y2K bug, seemed unprecedented; in others, spectacular as the attack on America had been, it showed things going on much as they had before. The nothing-changed view was evidenced by the continuation of the civil war in the Democratic Republic of the Congo. Having started in 1998, this would end in 2003 having cost 5.4 million lives – mostly through malnutrition and disease, but still a higher number than any other conflict since World War II.

By this time, war had already begun in the Darfur region of western Sudan, whose government's Arabized fighters were ethnically cleansing non-Arab populations. By 2005, 200,000 had been killed. The opposition was represented militarily by the Sudan Liberation Movement (SLM) and Justice and Equality Movement (JEM) but the conflict ended inconclusively in 2020.

ON THE MOVE

One remarkable feature of the end of the twentieth century and – still more – the start of the twenty-first was the number of migrants on the move. As in the nineteenth century, they were both 'pushed' and 'pulled'. Pushed by the fear, disruption and environmental damage caused by the various conflicts of the time; pulled by the growing affluence of the 'Global North'.

Rightly or wrongly, this has been seen as a 'problem' by many in the richer economies, their fears whipped up (it's alleged) by right-wing politicians and media. Conservatives generally claim to respect the right of the refugee – fleeing war or other danger – to claim asylum, but not that of the 'economic migrant' to come simply in search of a 'better life'. Completed in 1994, the Channel Tunnel, between France and England, represented a major engineering achievement, but for many in Britain it was seen mainly as a conduit for illegal immigration. At the same time, America was beefing up border security to create what many Mexicans called the 'Wall of Shame' along its southern border. (Though Donald Trump was later to call for the construction of a literal wall.)

The migrants were easily scapegoated. In 2000, in El Ejido, southern Spain, three murders by Moroccan immigrants triggered several days of rioting by Spanish citizens (and Black African immigrants). Moroccans in the town were held collectively responsible for two men's crimes.

ABOVE:
MORTGAGE MELTDOWN
The 2000s were buoyant times for the US housing market. But the rush to sell 'subprime' mortgages to poorer customers made the boom a bubble. In 2008 it burst, the failure of New York's Lehman Brothers prompting a near-collapse in the global financial system and the loss of many millions of jobs worldwide.

There's little doubt, though, that many in affluent Europe and North America were only too ready to see immigrants 'othered'. In Britain, the issue became central in the months leading up to the referendum over continued membership of the European Union (EU) in 2016. Right-wing pro-'Brexit' campaigner Nigel Farage called the news from Cologne a 'nuclear bomb' in the debate. Even more orthodox Conservative politicians hinted at the likelihood of a wave of millions of Turkish immigrants arriving if Britain remained in the EU.

As it turned out, by ending co-operation with France, Brexit only seemed to make Britain's refugee 'problem' worse, thousands camping out on France's Channel coast, waiting for a chance to be brought across by people-traffickers. But this problem in its turn was to be harnessed by the Right: 'Stop the Boats' became a key Conservative slogan.

EMERGING GIANTS

That things were changing in the world was illustrated by the growing economic influence of India, transformed beyond recognition since the 1990s. The growth of a large and affluent middle class banished the old stereotypes of the country as a sink of unspeakable poverty. The new India is massively unequal in a way it wasn't previously, but the conditions of the poorest aren't quite as bad as they once were.

China too, of course, was well on the way to superpower status, though questions continued over how far economic freedom and Communist politics could coexist. More disconcertingly, it was starting to carry itself in the wider world as a superpower, starting its own brand of colonial expansionism, especially in Africa. In 2005 alone, it invested almost US$200 million there. Western worries may in truth have centred on anxiety about competition in the continent. It was nevertheless true that China showed little interest in the idea of human rights.

This was also evident in China's handling of the threat of Islamism in its own western Xinjiang province and the separatist tendencies this was fostering among the Uighur population. From about 2014, it undertook an offensive against rebels which critics claimed was genocidal in its scope, and built a network of internment camps in which thousands of Uighurs were confined to be 're-educated' into loyalty by a range of methods, including torture. Additionally, China was using ever more sophisticated facial-recognition technology to monitor the population for suspected activists.

The West's own commitment to human rights was to be tested by these policies, given the reliance of its consumers and companies on Chinese products. Not to mention the

LEFT:
PATIENCE
Boris Yeltsin (1931–2007), right, stands with his protégé, and caretaker-successor Vladimir Putin, in 2000, soon after Putin's re-election as President of Russia in his own right. The years that followed would see Putin slowly strengthening his grip on the country.

involvement of Western IT companies in the development of the surveillance software used.

Britain was particularly challenged by the situation in Hong Kong. Its lease on Kowloon had expired in 1997, making Hong Kong's continuing status as a British colony untenable. The handover had been less traumatic than might have been expected given China's clear commitment to (and interest in) Hong Kong's longstanding role as an autonomous community and as an economic engine for the region as a whole. In the era of 'market communism', Hong Kong seemed the most special special economic zone of all. As the new century went on, China's assurances were to be tested by pro-democracy demonstrations which were eventually – sometimes violently – suppressed.

AN INTERACTIVE AGE

This was at once an exciting and a problematic time for democracy. On the one hand, people had a voice – and access to information – in a way they'd never had before. The Los Angeles Police Department's violent arrest of Rodney King in 1992, filmed on amateur video, had produced rioting. Ross Perot's presidential campaigns in 1992 and 1996 didn't get anywhere – but his call for 'electronic town hall' meetings would prove prophetic.

ABOVE:
AFRICAN FOOTBALL WORLD CUP
Vuvuzelas rang out as, in 2010, South Africa became the first African nation to host the World Cup. Ghana made it to the quarter-finals. Spain won the trophy but the tournament left no doubt that Africa was now a force in world football.

OPPOSITE:
XI JINPING
The most powerful man in China since Mao Zedong, Xi Jinping (1953–) has built a personality cult around himself. He abolished the limits on presidential terms before his re-election for his third term in 2023 and has promoted a more assertive military and foreign policy.

The World Wide Web, as inaugurated in 1990, was accessible only to a few, but the advent of high-speed broadband brought it to much of the world. However, even now, it should be remembered, millions around the world lacked telephone access, let alone the internet, but the cultural force was increasingly with those who could be 'online'. A new interactive culture informed everything from politics to talent contests. 'You' were *Time* magazine's 'person of the year' for 2006. People who had contentedly trotted along to vote every four to five years before expected immediate responses from their representatives on social media. Individuals expected to be 'consulted' on issues of all sorts.

And to be able to do what they wanted; fulfil their deeper desires if they weren't harming others. People took a more 'live and let live' attitude than perhaps they'd done before. Hence the 2001 decision of the Dutch parliament to legalize same-sex marriage. The UK followed in 2004 (except Northern Ireland, which would have to wait till 2020); Spain in 2005; Iceland in 2010; France in 2013 and Germany in 2014.

In the advanced industrialized countries, meanwhile, the limits of the new freedom were becoming clear. Media mega-corporations were rapidly buying up what had been an arena for free expression and packaging it in ways that suited them. Faced with such a superabundance of information, individuals ended up accepting what the corporate providers served them with – or took themselves off into online communities.

One paradoxical aspect of the new tolerance was the space it gave to intolerance. Right-wing conspiracy theory; left-wing 'wokeness'; Islamic radicalism; the misogynistic rantings of 'incels' – 'involuntary celibates' who blamed women for their lack of sexual success – all had their forums on the internet. The absence of any wider perspective or corrective context encouraged the adoption of extremist views, and, as members vied with one another for the radical high ground, 'purity spirals'.

A notable beneficiary of this culture was to be Donald Trump (1946–), a pantomime-businessman known to millions of Americans from *The Apprentice* TV show. His command of media and his populist pronouncements allowed him to bypass the political system almost completely to become America's Republican President in 2017. The first president of the 'post-truth' era, Trump was recorded by the *Washington Post* as having uttered over 30,000 falsehoods in the course of his four-year term.

OPPOSITE:
CRACKDOWN
Police deploy tear gas against demonstrators in Hong Kong's Sheung Wan district, July 2019. An apparently technical change to extradition rules, placing citizens of Hong Kong and Mainland China on the same jurisdictional footing, had confirmed fears that Hong Kong's prized autonomy was threatened. The protesters found a unique way of defending against tear-gas attacks, by deploying umbrellas as protection.

WEATHER WARNING

In August 2005, Hurricane Katrina hit New Orleans and the Mississippi Delta, killing 1,836 and causing US$125 billion damage. The disaster's disproportionate impact on African American communities highlighted how badly placed they were in US societies, despite decades of supposed reform.

A clear mismatch was evident between official equality and actual disadvantage. If the election of America's first African American President in 2008 was a sign of seeming progress, the angry and often abusive reaction of white Republicans to President Barack and First Lady, Michelle, Obama augured less well.

The murder of George Floyd by a police officer in Minneapolis in 2020 prompted a wave of protests which quickly spread worldwide. Bystanders had filmed the officer kneeling on Floyd's neck for nine minutes while he complained he couldn't breathe. For many, the moment emblematized African Americans' position vis-à-vis the law.

But of course Katrina had come as a shock simply as a storm. Existing flood defences in the city had proven woefully inadequate. America had been slow to accept the growing consensus on the idea of 'global warming', which had gradually gained acceptance in other countries. A programme of reforms had indeed been rolled out at Earth Summits in Rio de Janeiro (1992) and Kyoto (1997).

Alongside this there had been many statistical straws in the wind. In 1997, malaria – formerly confined to the lowlands of Irian Jaya – had been found over 2,000 m (6,560 ft) up in the country's highlands. Between 15 and 17 August 1998, a rainstorm had dumped over 30 cm (almost 12 in) of rain on Sydney – 8 cm (just over 3 in) more than in a normal month. In 1998, 2 million hectares (7,700 square miles) of Indonesian rainforest had been burned. In 1999, it had been discovered that the glaciers of New Zealand's South Island had retreated by more than 90 m (98 yards).

Till now, most Americans had seen the idea of human-produced climate change as an eccentric theory. Now many were prepared to think again. In 2015, the USA would even sign up to the Paris Agreement on climate change, committing to a significant lowering in carbon emissions. Even then, it was ambivalent, withdrawing from the agreement in 2020 under the Republican President Donald Trump only to renew its commitment a year later under Democrat Joe Biden (1942–).

BELOW:
STOCK MARKET MELTDOWN
The New York Stock Exchange index fell over 500 points on 15 September 2008, and further in the days that followed, as the subprime scandal chickens came home to roost. A great global depression was narrowly averted, but serious after-effects were felt for several years.

THE DIGITAL AGE

BEAR RAMPANT

In Russia, fears that Vladimir Putin had dictatorial ambitions had only partly been allayed by his stepping back from the presidency in 2008 to be succeeded by his prime minister, Dmitry Medvedev (1965–). By 2012, it was clear that Medvedev had indeed been keeping the seat warm for his master, with Putin resuming his presidential rule.

A creation of the old Communist system – a former officer with the state security service, the KGB – Putin followed Soviet precedent in siding with Syria's Bashar al-Assad. Exhibitionistically tough, his handling of Chechen terrorism (the Moscow theatre hostage crisis of 2002; the Beslan school siege of 2004) allowed Putin a cloak for the strengthening of his authoritarian rule. In 2014, he sent Russian troops into Ukraine to occupy and annex the Crimea.

He followed up in February 2022 by invading Ukraine in what was evidently supposed to be overwhelming force. It was expected that Kyiv would be taken in the first few days. In the event, though badly rocked, the Ukrainian defences held firm under the leadership of the country's colourfully charismatic President Volodymyr Zelensky (1978–). By the second half of the year, Ukraine had launched what seemed a successful counteroffensive, but this too became bogged down.

As the weeks went by in 2022, the conflict seemed to be settling into a war of attrition. Putin's forces seemed unable to gain any sort of significant strategic victory but, constantly replenished by fresh recruits (albeit of steadily decreasing quality), they couldn't be conclusively defeated by the Ukrainians either. Russia's widely reported war crimes (rapes, beheadings, prisoner-executions, bombing and shelling of civilian targets …) seem to have stemmed partly from the poor quality of their troops but also from a conscious desire to demoralize Ukraine.

PANDEMIC PROBLEMS

The world wasn't well-equipped to deal with the crisis that arose when the virus SARS-CoV-2, first identified in Wuhan China, produced the COVID-19 pandemic. Governments struggled to find a response to what seemed an unprecedented problem. There had of course been precedents, but with the possible exception of the 'Spanish Flu', they'd taken place in the historically distant past under conditions which couldn't meaningfully be compared with those of our own time. Air travel, mass-migration, modern working life with its morning and evening commute – all of these seemed to be facilitating the virus' spread.

LEFT:
FALSE DAWN
Kim Jong Un (1984–) of North Korea (left) and his South Korean counterpart Moon Jae-in (1953–) celebrate the signing of the Panmunjom Declaration for Peace, Prosperity and Unification of the Korean Peninsula, 27 April 2018. A historic treaty, it seemed, but relations continued difficult and in 2023 the pact was formally revoked.

OPPOSITE TOP:
WELCOMING THE FUTURE
Japan's prime minister Yukio Hatoyama (1947–) shakes hands with Honda's humanoid robot, ASIMO, December 2009. Pretty much avowedly a gimmick, ASIMO nevertheless signalled the importance robotics and artificial intelligence were going to have in industrial technology and economic planning going forward.

OPPOSITE BELOW:
FATAL THAW
Sightseers watch an Alaskan glacier 'calving' – creating a new iceberg as it reaches the coast. A thrilling spectacle, but the fact that a new kind of 'eco-tourism' could be established around such experiences was arguably an indication of the accelerating pace of global warming.

THE DIGITAL AGE

As did the average age of the population in the advanced industrial countries. Younger people shook off the infection as little more than a glorified cough but it caused severe respiratory problems in the older and less robust. For children under the age of ten, the infection fatality rate was 0.002 per cent; for 25-year-olds it was 0.01 per cent; but for 65-year-olds it was 1.4 per cent and for 85-year-olds it was 15 per cent. Where the population was relatively elderly, overall death rates were accordingly higher: up to 2 per cent of those infected in Australia and Britain; in Italy, even higher.

Culture had a bearing too – certainly in states' responses to the crisis. Countries near the site of origin were naturally quicker off the mark. But China was a police state, and besides this, it shared with South Korea, Singapore and other Eastern countries what might loosely be characterized as 'Confucian' attitudes. The kind of measures called for – travel restrictions, home confinement, strict limitations to social contact – were much easier to impose against this cultural background than they were in what had traditionally been more individualistic Western societies. These Eastern countries took relatively draconian measures and contained the virus quickly. (Though, for this very reason perhaps, they did experience flare-ups again thereafter.)

In New Zealand, geographical considerations won out over liberal traditions. The island nation placed severe restrictions on visits from outside. That way, it managed more or less to exclude

ABOVE:
COMBATING COVID
In November 2022, almost three years after the outbreak of the COVID-19 epidemic, a control worker crosses a deserted street in Beijing's Central Business District. China's authoritarian approach scored some significant victories, but its overall success remains uncertain.

LEFT:
LEADING FROM THE FRONT
Volodymyr Zelensky came to prominence as Ukraine's fictional president in a satirical TV comedy *Servant of the People*. Name-recognition eased his path to real power. After the Russian invasion of February 2022, however, he was forced to reinvent himself as a real war leader.

OPPOSITE:
INDIAN TAKE-OFF
Chandrayaan-3 launches from the Satish Dhawan Space Centre, India, on 14 July 2023. The space shuttle touched down on the lunar surface in August 2023, making India the fourth country to successfully land on the Moon. The lunar lander was able to gather data about the surface temperature.

the virus for a lengthy period, though the infection caught up to some extent in later waves as the rules relaxed.

More often, Western governments struggled to impose the sort of social discipline needed to crack down on the virus' spread. Britain's lockdown was effective but a reluctant government was arguably both late in imposing it and premature in lifting it, costing – critics have charged – many thousands of lives. (It was, however, swift in developing a workable vaccination programme.)

THE DIGITAL AGE

LIBERTY AND DEATH

In the USA, attitudes quickly became polarized along existing ideological lines. Conservatives saw centrally directed interventions as sinister – a communistic threat to the founding US ideal of liberty. In implicit acknowledgement of this, the Federal Government was quick to hand off the problem to the states, whose performance varied according to local political and social conditions. The imposition of any meaningful lockdown was difficult in these circumstances, and slowed the take-up of vaccination programmes as they became available. In terms of numbers of overall fatalities, states such as Vermont, New Hampshire and Washington fared as well as European nations like Denmark, Germany and Switzerland – the best in the world in handling the virus. By contrast, states like Arizona and Mississippi fared as badly as Bulgaria, Peru and Russia – the world's worst.

Like a second cyber-virus, meanwhile, speculation was spreading rapidly among Americans stuck fast to their computer keyboards and mobile phones. Effective action was rendered even more difficult by the clamour of conspiracy theories suggesting that the whole health scare had been conjured up by an interfering Federal Government in order to increase its control over its citizens. Some conspiracy theorists even claimed that vaccination involved the injection of microchips which would allow the individual's movements to be monitored.

COVID CONCLUSIONS

In fairness, the jury is still out over which governments did well or badly internationally – and this is likely to remain the case for quite some time. The cost of the pandemic can't in any case be measured solely in the numbers of lives lost or (presumptively) saved. The benefits of tougher lockdown policies have to be weighed against the costs in educational opportunities to children while schools were closed (or, later, open but under restrictive conditions) or the knock-on health implications of delayed or cancelled treatment of cancer and other illnesses. There have been effects on mental health as well, many living isolated for weeks and months on end during the crisis. Lockdown also brought a rise in alcoholism and domestic violence (with severely limited recourse for victims).

A clearer view of this complexity will of course only be possible in hindsight. Which is, of course, why in general we read history. On the other hand, it's important to remember that in its own time every event that ever took place was more complicated – the values at stake more subtly varied and morally ambivalent – than the historian's fluent narrative might make it seem.

OPPOSITE:
'LONG LIVE THE WALLS WE CRASHED THROUGH'
American songstress Taylor Swift broke all revenue records with her The Eras Tour of 2023–4, mounting more than 150 shows on five continents. Swift has attracted both admiration and disdain with her ability to make artistic creativity and business acumen work hand-in-hand.

BELOW:
REDUCED TO RUBBLE
The Hamas attacks of 7 October 2023 had been a horrendous spree of rape, killing and hostage-taking in Israel. Even so, the destructiveness of Israel's retaliatory attack on Gaza was to shock the world.

INDEX

9/11 attacks 424–5, 433

Abbasids 82, 84, 96
accountancy 128–9, 130
Achaemenid Empire 37, 40, 43, 44–8
Act of Union (1707) 181, 190, 215
Adena culture 33, 35
Adolphus, Gustavus 174
Aethelstan 87
Afghanistan 74, 191, 262, 264, 264–5, 341
Taliban 416–7, 425–6, 428
and USSR 399, 406, 408
AIDS 403, 409
Al-Qaeda 424–6
Alexander the Great 49
Alexander VI, Pope 138, 142
Ali, Muhammad 390, 393
America 187, 339, 376, 399, 439, 445
ancient era 33, 35
Civil War 273, 278–82
and communism 376, 378–84, 386, 388–9, 396, 399, 403
and Cuba 298, 381, 383, 386–7
first explorers and settlers 121, 123, 125, 165, 166–8, 177, 206, 207, 232, 234
Gold Rush 257, 260
Great Depression 344, 347, 349, 355
Guantánamo Bay 428
immigration 257, 352, 433–4
and Indonesia 395, 396
and Iraq 416, 426
and Israel 396, 405
and Japan 261–2, 274–5
and Korea 378–9
and Latin America 243, 341, 395
and Mexico 310, 341
Monroe Doctrine 249
Napoleonic Wars 237, 240
Native Americans 165, 167, 197, 223, 240, 289, 291, 292–3, 301
Prohibition 341, 342
racial segregation 291, 294, 390, 393
railroads 283–4, 299
slavery 165, 187, 213, 273, 278–82, 289
and Somalia 416
space exploration 381, 396, 402
Spanish–American War 298
terrorism 416, 419, 424–6, 428, 433
and Vietnam 381, 384, 386, 388–9, 396
voting rights 289, 302
War of Independence 209, 210–13, 217
WWI 319, 322, 332, 337, 341
WWII 360, 362, 363, 365, 366, 368, 369, 371
see also individual presidents
anaesthetics 259, 276–7
Anatolia 18, 20, 119
anatomical science 148
Angkor Wat 98, 101–3
Anglo-Saxons 65, 79, 87, 89, 96
Angola 295, 396
Anthony, Susan B. 289
Arab Spring 432
Archimedes 49
Argentina 243, 244, 245, 257, 289, 380, 395
Aristotle 49
Armada 158, 162
Armenia 325
Armstrong, Neil 396
Asante Kingdom 249
Assyria 15, 38
astronomy 144, 148, 166, 168, 205, 418–19
space exploration 7, 381, 384, 396, 402, 443
Athens 43–9
atomic bombs 370, 371, 376
Aum Shinrikyo 419
Australia 166, 205, 212, 215, 223, 250, 257, 362
WWI 319, 320, 325
Austria 135, 157, 162, 272, 356
and France 219, 226–7, 232, 234
revolution 266–7, 266–7
Austria-Hungary 315, 319, 326, 329
aviation 302, 311, 328, 356–7
Aztecs 112, 114, 125, 126, 127

Babylon 15, 36, 38–9, 40
Bach, Johann Sebastian 187, 191, 194
Baird, John Logie 355
Balfour, Arthur 338
ballet 316
Bangladesh 374, 396
banking 112, 139
Banks, Joseph 205, 207
Bantu peoples 75–6
Barcelona 186
Bath 65, 215
Bayeux Tapestry 96
Beethoven, Ludwig van 229, 232
Begin, Menachem 396, 405
Belgium 137, 154, 158, 245, 291, 295, 319
Bell, Alexander Graham 284, 303
Bengal 373–4
Benin 198
Benz, Karl 298, 302
Berlin Wall 372, 381, 406, 409, 412
bicycle 271
bin Laden, Osama 425, 426, 433
Bismarck, Otto von 289, 313
Blair, Tony 426
Blenheim, Battle of (1704) 186
Boers 257, 259, 260, 294, 301, 304
Boleyn, Anne 142
Bolívar, Simón 241, 242, 243–5
Bolivia 128, 244, 381
Bolsheviks 329, 331–2, 337, 344
Bonnie Prince Charlie 191
books 135, 137, 197
Borobudur 88–9, 89, 90–1
Bosnia 410, 417
Boston Massacre (1770) 206, 210
Boston Tea Party (1773) 210
botany 205, 207
Botticelli, Sandro 132, 133
Bougainville, Louis-Antoine 205
Boxer Rebellion (1899) 301
Boyne, Battle of (1690) 180
Brazil 180, 289, 395
Brown, John 278
Bruegel, Pieter (the Elder) 160–1
Brunel, Isambard Kingdom 255
Buddhism 39–40, 41, 49–50, 76, 77, 88–91, 92, 93, 96
Bulgaria 317, 326, 373, 406
Burke, Robert O'Hara 250
Burns, Robert 181
Bush, George W. 426
Byron, Lord 237, 256, 258
Byzantium 30, 65, 69–71, 73–4, 80, 81, 85, 89, 96–7, 119

Calvin, Jean 140–1
Cambodia 76, 92, 98, 101–3, 396, 406
Canada 86, 89, 180, 194, 207, 219, 223, 240, 259
Gold Rush 308–9
WWI 319, 341
Cape Colony 291, 294, 301
cars 298, 302, 315, 316
Carter, President Jimmy 396, 405
Carthage 30, 48, 58
Castro, Fidel 381, 383, 387
Catherine II of Russia 202, 203–4
Chamberlain, Neville 356, 358
Charlemagne 84, 85
Charles I of England 170, 179
Charles IX of France 154
Charles V of Spain 151
Chechen Republic 410
Chernobyl nuclear disaster 406, 410
Chile 125, 243, 395
Chimú empire 93
China
and Africa 434
Age of Reason 166, 168, 171, 191
and America 257, 403
Boxer Rebellion 301
and Britain 223, 261, 262–3, 301, 435
communism 344, 346, 376, 378, 381, 385, 396, 399, 409–10, 413, 434, 437
COVID-19 pandemic 442
Cultural Revolution 385, 393
early history 10, 18, 20, 28, 30, 50–1, 53, 54–5
economic influence 432, 434–5
and France 284
and Hong Kong 400, 435, 438
and Islam 434
and Korea 298–9
Kuomintang 298–9, 305, 307, 344, 376
Medieval period 76, 77, 92–3, 110, 115–17
Opium Wars 261, 262–3
reform and revolution 299, 301, 307
Renaissance 134, 135, 148, 158
and Russia 301
Sino-Japanese Wars 298, 299, 354–5, 358
Sun Tzu 40
Tiananmen Square 409, 413
and USSR 378
Christianity
Age of Reason 168–70, 172–4, 178, 184, 194
Boxer Rebellion (1899) 301
Crusades 97, 98, 99, 100, 104, 106, 112
early 26, 29, 61, 63, 65
indulgences 137, 138
Inquisition 122
Ireland 227–8
Jesuits 145, 145, 148, 149, 194
Medieval period 69, 74–6, 78, 81–7, 96–100, 104, 106, 107, 111–12, 115
Reformation 138, 140–1, 142, 145–8, 150, 154, 162, 168, 172–4, 180, 267
religious art 115, 130, 132–4
Churchill, Winston 320, 337, 356, 358, 366, 368, 369, 371, 373
Cieza de León, Pedro de 127–8
cinema 302, 342
city-states 30
Civil Rights Movement 390, 391
Cleopatra 53, 59
coffee 196
Colombia 243, 245, 412, 415
Columbus, Christopher 121, 122–3
Commerçon, Philibert 205
Commonwealth 376
communism
and America 376, 378–84, 386, 388–9, 396, 399, 403
in China 344, 346, 376, 378, 381, 385, 396, 399, 409–10, 413, 434, 437
collapse of 406–7, 409–10
Domino Theory 380
Joseph McCarthy 378
Korean War 378–9
Marx, Karl 254
in Soviet Union 329, 331–2, 338, 343–4, 350–1, 380, 383
Vietnam War 381, 384, 386, 388–9
computing/technology 258, 364, 365, 403, 409, 412, 422, 423, 436
Confucius 38, 40
Constantinople 65, 69–71, 73, 80, 89, 97, 98, 119
Cook, Captain James 204, 205, 207–8, 212
Copernicus, Nicolas 144, 148
Cornwallis, Lord 212–13
Cortés, Hernán 125, 126
Costa Rica 341
cotton 224, 256
Cotton, Sir Willoughby 262, 264
Council of Trent (1545–63) 145, 146–7
counter-culture 390–1, 400–1
COVID-19 pandemic 440–2, 445
Crimean War (1853–6) 271–2
Cromwell, Oliver 170, 174, 178
Crusades 97, 98, 99, 100, 104, 106, 112
Cuba 283, 298, 381, 383, 386–7, 396
Culloden, Battle of (1745) 191, 197
cuneiform 14, 15
Cyrus II of Persia 38, 40
Czechoslovakia 168, 170, 373, 391, 395, 406

D-Day 366
Daimler, Gottlieb 302
Danton, Georges 221
Darius I of Persia 40, 44, 46–7
Darwin, Charles 259
Davison Wilding, Emily 301–2, 313
de Balboa, Vasco Nunez 123, 125
de Beauvoir, Simone 398
de Coronado, Francisco Vázquez 125
de las Casas, Bartolomé 128, 129
de Lesseps, Ferdinand 284, 288
de Miranda, Francisco 241
de Orellana, Francisco 125
de Soto, Hernando 125
de Sucre, Antonio José 243–4
de Valdivia, Pedro 125
Decembrists 249–50, 252–3
Defenestration of Prague 168, 170
del Sarto, Andrea 136
democracy 43–4
Democratic Republic of the Congo 383, 433
Deng Xiaoping 396, 399
Denmark 89, 358
Descartes, René 165, 166
Dias, Bartolomeu 121
Díaz, Porfirio 307, 310
Diderot, Denis 197, 199, 203
Diesel, Rudolf 302
DNA discovery 380
Dominican Republic 383
Dreyfus Case (1894) 305
drugs 412, 415
Dunlop, John Boyd 271, 302

Earhart, Amelia 356
earthquakes 158, 191, 194
East India Company 166, 170, 180, 190, 194, 223, 262, 264
East Timor 396
Ecuador 243, 245
Edinburgh 215
Edison, Thomas 288
Edward I of England 112
Egypt 96, 105, 106, 118, 364, 380
Ancient 15–19, 20, 31, 35, 38, 40, 49, 58, 59
and Britain 294, 295
and France 228–31, 230–1, 237
and Israel 395–6, 397, 405
Einstein, Albert 302, 307
electricity 248, 249, 288
Elizabeth I of England 150, 154, 155
Elphinstone, William 264
Encyclopédistes 197, 199, 203
England
Act of Union 181, 190, 215
and America 165, 166–8
and France 96, 114–15, 140–1
Medieval period 76, 79, 86, 87, 89, 96, 97–8, 104, 107–9, 112, 113, 114–15
Reformation 138, 140–1, 142–3, 150, 154, 156, 158, 162, 170
Renaissance 155–6, 158, 158–9, 162
Restoration 174
Romans 64–5
and Scotland 112, 154, 158, 181, 190, 191, 197, 215
and Spain 162
and Wales 112
see also Great Britain
ENIGMA 364, 365
Escobar, Pablo 412, 415
Ethiopia 59, 69, 298, 343, 356, 403
Etruscans 30–1, 43, 46

famine 114, 115, 116, 254, 256, 291, 373
Faraday, Michael 248, 249
Fawcett, Millicent Garrett 301
Fawkes, Guido 162
feminism 198
Ferdinand, Archduke Franz 312, 317
Ferdinand I of Austria 266–7
Field of the Cloth of Gold 140–1
financial crisis (2008) 434, 439
Finland 356
Fleming, Alexander 349
Florence 129–30, 136
Floyd, George 439
football 353, 436
France 283, 284
and Africa 294, 315
Age of Reason 174, 175, 177, 181, 187, 197–8, 198–9
and American 212–13
and England/Britain 96, 114–15, 140–1, 232, 234, 236, 245, 246–7, 313, 434
colonialism 177, 194, 197, 294, 298
Crimean War 271–2
Franco-Prussian War 273, 289, 290, 354
Indochina Wars 376
and Jewish people 305
Medieval period 81, 82, 84, 87, 96, 97, 100, 106, 114–15
Napolean Bonaparte 227–41, 245–8
Napoleon III 271–2, 273, 282, 289
post-revolution 225–35
Renaissance 135, 140–1, 154
revolution 214–17, 217–23, 264
Suez Canal 284, 380
terrorism 433
unrest 390, 394
WWI 317, 319, 320, 323, 332, 337
WWII 356, 358, 361, 366
Francesca, Piero della 132
Franco, Francisco 350, 354, 357
Franklin, Sir John 259
Freud, Sigmund 302, 304, 305
Fugger family 139

Galileo Galilei 166, 168
Gama, Vasco da 121
Garibaldi, Giuseppe 272–3
Gates, Bill 409
Genghis Khan 100, 110
George V of Britain 316
Georgia 409
germ theory 261, 300
Germany 65, 290
and Africa 294, 315, 325, 329
Berlin Wall 372, 381, 406, 409, 412
and China 299
Hitler, Adolf 343, 348–9, 355–71
Jewish people 343, 349–50, 354, 362, 367, 368
Medieval period 81, 84, 97, 100, 106
and Napoleon 237
Renaissance 123, 135, 137, 138, 150
revolution 264, 266
and Spain 354
unification 289, 313
WWI 315, 317–38
WWII 355–71
Ghana 249
global warming 439, 441
gold 144, 257, 260, 295, 308–9
Good Friday Agreement (1998) 419
Gorbachev, Mikhail 406, 409, 414–15
Gordon, Charles 295
Grant, Ulysses S. 279, 282
Great Britain 400, 442
Act of Union 181, 190, 215
and Afghanistan 262, 264, 264–5
and Africa 249, 257, 259, 291, 294–5, 298, 301, 304, 315, 376, 393, 395
Age of Reason 174, 178–83, 185–6, 187, 190, 191, 194–8
and America 206, 209, 210–13, 217, 237, 240
and China 223, 261, 262–3, 301, 435
colonialism 165–8, 180, 194, 197, 210–13, 215, 222, 223–4, 243, 298
Crimean War 271–2
exploration 205–8
and Egypt 229, 294, 295
and France 194, 232, 234, 236, 245, 246–7, 313, 434
Glorious Revolution 180
Great Fire of London 178, 180, 182–3
immigration 433, 434
and India 180, 194, 264, 291, 373–4
Industrial Revolution 223, 224, 248, 250, 255–7, 259, 270
and Iran 316
and Iraq 426
and Ireland 227–8, 254, 256, 259, 331, 337
and Japan 313
and Korea 379
Northern Ireland 391, 393, 397, 419
Roundheads and Cavaliers 170, 178
and Russia 313, 314, 316
and Scotland 154, 158, 181, 190, 191, 197, 215
slavery 187, 222, 224–5
Suez Canal 380, 385
suffragettes 301–2, 345
terrorism 428
witch hunts 158, 179
WWI 317–20, 325, 326, 328, 338
WWII 356, 358, 360, 361, 362, 364–6, 368, 369, 371
see also England
Great Depression 344, 347, 349, 355
Great Exhibition (1851) 270
Great Fire of London 178, 180, 182–3
Great Rift Valley 7, 10
Great Wall of China 53, 116–17
Great Zimbabwe 93, 94–5
Greece
Ancient 20–2, 25, 27, 30, 34–5, 43–9, 74
civil war 374, 376
and Turkey 338, 341
WWI and II 319, 360
Guantánamo Bay 428
Guatemala 35, 76, 380
Guevara, 'Che' 386–7
Gulf Wars 415–16
Gupta Empire 65
Gutenberg Bible 135, 137, 138

Hadrian's Wall 64–5
Haiti 218–19, 243, 341
Hamas 416, 445
Hannibal 48, 58
Hanseatic League 123
Hargreaves, James 223, 224
Hausa people 100, 104
Hawaii 207, 208, 223, 257, 298, 360
Henry VIII of England 138, 140, 142–3, 145, 150
hieroglyphics 15, 16
Higaldo, Miguél 244
Hindenburg 357
Hinduism 13–14, 50, 88, 374, 375, 419
Hitler, Adolf 343, 344, 348–9, 354, 355–71
Hittites 20
Holbein, Hans 136, 145
Holocaust 362, 367, 368
Homer 26–7, 30, 31
Honduras 76, 341
Hong Kong 261, 400, 435, 438
Hopkins, Matthew 178
Huang Chao Rebellion 92
Hubble Space Telescope 418–19
Huguenots 152–3, 154
Hundred Years' War 115
Hungary 110, 266, 373, 380, 382, 406
hunter-gatherers 9, 13
Hurricane Katrina 439
Hussein, Saddam 415–16, 426

Incas 112, 113, 127–8, 208, 210
India 76, 119, 190, 257, 428, 444
and Britain 180, 194, 264, 291, 373–4
early history 10, 12, 13, 39–40, 49–50, 65
independence 374–5
religious unrest 417, 419
WWI & II 319, 324, 325, 373
Indochina Wars 376
Indonesia 50, 76, 88, 89, 90–1, 170, 207, 395–6, 400, 428
Indus Valley 10, 12, 13, 43
Industrial Revolution 223, 224, 225, 254, 255, 256
internet 436
Iran 14, 39, 65, 71, 73, 74, 191, 316, 319, 341, 380, 400
and Iraq 415–16
Islamic Revolution 400, 403, 405
Iraq 10, 14, 74, 78, 82, 84, 325, 395–6, 415–16
and America 426
ISIS 425
Ireland 87, 98, 180, 227–8, 419
and Britain 331, 337
famine 254, 256, 259
revolution 267
Iron Age 18, 20–2
ISIS 425, 426
Islam
Al-Qaeda, ISIS and Taliban 416–17, 424–6, 417, 428, 433
Crusades 97, 98, 99, 100, 104, 106,
early 26, 62–3

INDEX

and Hinduism 374, 419
Iraq and Iran 400, 403, 405, 415–16
in Medieval period 72, 73–8, 80–1, 82, 84, 96–8, 99, 106, 112, 119
Palestine 341, 445
Renaissance 122, 136
Sunni and Shi'a 78, 80, 84, 96
Uighur 434
Young Turks 307
Israel 10, 29, 40, 374, 394, 395–7, 404–5
Istanbul 119, 136
Italy 112, 166, 180
and Africa 295, 298
early 6, 30–1, 46–7, 84
emigration 257
Garibaldi, Giuseppe 272–3
independence 266–7
Mussolini, Benito 342–4, 350, 355–6, 366
Renaissance 129–34, 136–8, 142, 159
Romans, ancient 46–7, 48–9, 58, 59–61, 63–7, 69–71
unification 273
WWI 319, 325, 329, 332, 342
WWII 355–6, 360, 366
Ivan the Terrible 149–50

James I of England (VI of Scotland) 154, 158
James II (VII of Scotland) 180
Japan 20, 50, 61, 63, 92, 98, 104, 110, 185
and America 261–2, 274–5
and Britain 313
and Korea 298–9, 307
Meiji Restoration 283, 284, 296–7
modern 399–400, 419, 428–9, 441
Renaissance 148–9, 162–3, 163
Sino-Japanese Wars 298, 299, 354–5, 358
Ukiyo-e 248, 254
WWI 319, 325
WWII 355–6, 360, 362, 363, 368, 370, 371
Java 88, 89, 90–1, 110, 168
Jefferson, Thomas 213, 217, 218, 232
Jenner, Edward 205, 207
Jerusalem 62–3, 74, 97, 98, 99, 100
Jesus of Nazareth 61, 63
Jobs, Steve 422
John, King of England 104, 107, 108–9
Johnson, Andrew 282
Johnson, Lyndon 384, 386
Jolson, Al 342
Jordan 36, 395–6
Judaism
and Crusades 97, 98
Dreyfus case 305
early 26, 29, 40, 62–3, 73, 74
emigration 257, 305
and Germany 343, 349–50, 354, 362, 367, 368
and Luther, Martin 148
and Palestine 338
and Russia 204, 305
and Spain 122
Zionism 305
Julius Caesar 59, 61
Justinian I 70–1

Kant, Immanuel 198, 198
Kashmir 419
Kennedy, John F. 381, 383, 386
Kenya 376, 395, 428, 433
Kepler, Johannes 166
Khmer Empire 76, 92, 98
Khrushchev, Nikita 380, 383
Kievan Rus 89, 97, 104, 106
King, Martin Luther 390, 392
King, Rodney 435
Kitchener, Herbert 295, 301, 328
knights 97, 99, 106, 115
Korea 50, 76, 77, 96, 100, 110, 299
and China and Japan 298–9, 307
Korean War 378–9
Kristallnacht 350, 354
Kublai Khan 110
Kuomintang 298–9, 305, 307, 344, 376
Kush 35
Kuwait 316, 415, 416

Lafayette, Marquis de 212–13, 218
Laos 381, 386
Lawrence, T.E. 326
Lee, Robert E. 279, 282
Lenin, Vladimir 329, 331–2, 344
Leonardo da Vinci 130, 134, 136
Leopold II of Belgum 291, 295
Lepanto 157, 162
Lincoln, Abraham 273, 278–82
Lindisfarne 86, 87
Little Ice Age 158
Live Aid 403, 406, 411
Locke, John 198
London 178, 180, 182–3, 361, 428
Louis XIV of France 174, 175, 177, 181, 187
Louis XVI of France 212, 218–21
Louisiana Purchase 232, 234
Louverture, Toussaint 218, 219
Lovelace, Ada 258
Loyola, Ignatius 145, 145
'Lucy' (Australopithecus afarensis) 11
Luddites 224, 225
Ludendorff, Erich 332
Luther, Martin 138, 145, 148, 150

MacArthur, Douglas 379
Macau 148
Machiavelli, Niccolò 132, 134
Magellan, Ferdinand 123, 125, 126
Magna Carta 104, 107, 108–9
Malaysia 376, 381, 400
Mali 112, 114
Mamluks 106, 110, 118, 203, 230–1
Mandela, Nelson 393, 417, 420–1
Mansa Musa 112, 114
Mao Zedong 344, 376, 378, 381, 385, 393, 396, 403
Marat, Jean-Marie 221–2
Marathon 43, 44–6
Marco Polo 107, 110, 112
Marie Antoinette 215, 217, 219, 221
Martel, Charles 81
Martín, José de San 244, 245
Marx, Karl 254
Mary I 150, 154
Mary Queen of Scots 154, 156
mathematics 49, 128–9, 130, 132
Matthias, Emperor 168
Mauryans 50
Maximilian I of Mexico 282–3, 288
Mayans 32–3, 35, 76, 93
Mazzini, Giuseppe 267
McCarthy, Joseph 378
Mecca 73
Medici family 129–30
medicine 180, 204–5, 207, 259, 261, 272, 276–7, 300, 349
Mehmet II, Sultan 119
Mendeleev, Dmitri 259, 261, 299
Mesopotamia 14–15, 38
Mexico 243 288
and America 341
Aztecs 112, 114, 125, 126, 127
early 10, 35, 56–7, 59, 76
and Napoleon 282–3
revolution 241, 307, 310
Mezraa-Teleilat 8
Michelangelo 133, 134, 142
Minoans 17–18, 21
mobile phones 422
Moctezuma 126
Monet, Claude 283
Mongols 100, 110
Monroe, James 249, 250
Montenegro 317, 319, 410
Montgomery, Bernard Law 364
Moors 80, 81, 84, 122
Morocco 315
Morse, Samuel 248, 251
Mount Sinai 26, 74
Mozambique 295, 396
Mozart, Wolfgang Amadeus 208
Mughal Dynasty 120, 131
Muhammad 73
music 187, 191, 194, 208, 229, 232, 342, 347, 388, 390–1, 403, 406, 404, 408, 411
Musk, Elon 423
Mussolini, Benito 342–4, 350, 355–6, 366
Myanmar (Burma) 110, 149, 298, 362, 368, 376
Mycenaeans 22, 25

Namibia 294, 325
Napoleon Bonaparte 227–41, 245–8
Napoleon III 271–2, 273, 282, 289
Nazca 52, 59
Neanderthals 6, 7, 11
Nebuchadnezzar 38–9
Nelson, Horatio 229, 232, 236
Neolithic people 9, 10, 13
Netherlands 137, 154, 170, 172–3, 176, 192–3
colonialism 166, 170, 180, 190
New Zealand 114, 205, 291, 441–2
WWI 319, 320, 325
Newton, Isaac 180, 181
Nicaragua 396
Nicholas I of Russia 249–50, 252–3
Nicholas II of Russia 305, 307, 311, 314, 316, 329
Niépce, Nicéphore 248, 249
Niger 104, 250
Nigeria 22, 23, 104
Nightingale, Florence 272
Nixon, Richard 396, 403
Nok culture 22, 23
Normans 87, 96, 97, 98
North America see America; Canada
North Korea 440
North Pole 310
Northern Ireland 180, 337, 391, 393, 397, 419
Northwest Passage 207–8, 259
Novgorod Republic 106
Nubians 35, 38
nuclear weapons 370, 371, 376, 403, 406
Nuremberg trials (1945–6) 371
nursing 272

Obama, Barack 426, 430–1, 439
O'Brien, William Smith 267
Odessa Pogrom (1821) 257
oil 316, 319, 325
Oklahoma City bombing 419
Olympic Games 288, 359, 399, 404
Opium Wars 261, 262–3
Ottomans 119, 134–6, 157, 162, 181, 184, 257, 317
Crimean War 271–2
and Greece 338, 341
and Napoleon 229, 230–1
revolution and end 307, 341
WWI 320, 325, 326
Owens, Jesse 359

Pacific islands 89, 114, 205, 207, 325
Pacioli, Luca 128, 130
Paine, Thomas 208, 210, 213
Pakistan 12, 74, 149, 374, 396, 419
Palaeolithic people 8–9
Palestine 97, 338, 341, 374, 396, 397, 416, 427, 445
Panama 181, 243, 341
Panama Canal 288, 306
Pankhurst, Emmeline 301
Paracas 31, 33, 35
Paraguay 243, 289
Paris 271, 289, 361
Park, Mungo 250
Pasteur, Louis 261, 300
Peace of Augsburg 150, 168
Peace of Munster 169–70
Peace of Westphalia 169
Pearl Harbor 360, 362, 363
Peasants' Revolt 113
penicillin 349
Pereira, António 124
Periodic Table 259, 261, 299
Perón, Juan 380
Perry, Matthew 261–2, 274–5
Persia 37, 38–9, 40, 42, 43, 44–9
Peru 10, 31, 33, 35, 52, 59, 93, 112, 113, 127–8, 208, 210, 243–4, 245
Peter I of Russia 177–8, 200–1
Philip II of Spain 150, 154, 154, 158
Philippines 284, 298, 368, 400
philosophy 48–9, 165, 166, 197–8, 398
Phoenicians 29, 30
photography 248, 249, 276–7
Picasso, Pablo 315–16
plague 71, 115, 116, 178, 180
Plato 45, 49
Pocahontas 167
Poland 319, 338, 356, 368, 373, 399, 406, 407
Polish–Lithuanian Commonwealth 150
Pollock, Paul Jackson 398
Pompeii 61, 63
Portugal 121, 123, 128, 191, 234, 319
colonialism 148–9, 180, 190, 194, 295
slavery 187, 198
Prague 168, 170, 391, 395
Presley, Elvis 388, 390
printing 92, 135, 137
Prohibition 341, 342
Prussia 106, 197, 203, 219, 232, 245, 246–7, 273, 289, 290, 334–5
Punic Wars 48, 58
Putin, Vladimir 410, 426, 435, 440
pyramids 15, 16, 35, 56–7, 59

railways 248, 255, 261, 283–4, 299, 400
Radetzky, Field Marshal 267
Raphael 133
Reagan, Ronald 403
Rhodes, Cecil 291, 295
Rhodesia 291, 319, 393, 395, 417
Richthofen, Manfred von (Red Baron) 328
Robespierre, Maximilien 220–1, 221–3
Romans, ancient 46–7, 48–9, 58, 59–61, 63–7, 69–71
Rommel, Erwin 360, 364
Roosevelt, Franklin D. 349, 355, 360, 366
Rousseau, Jean-Jacques 197, 204, 205
Russia 89, 165
and Afghanistan 262
and Britain 313, 314, 316
Catherine II 202, 203–4
and China 301
civil war 337, 340
Crimean War 271–2
Decembrists 249–50, 252–3
and France 232, 234–5, 238–9, 241
and Iran 316
Ivan the Terrible 149–50
Peter I 177–8, 200–1
and Jews 204, 305
and Poland 338
post-USSR 410
Putin, Vladimir 435, 440
revolution 329, 331–2, 333, 337
and Syria 426
and Ukraine 440, 442
unrest 305, 307, 311
WWI 317, 319, 320, 325–6, 328–9, 331, 332
see also USSR
Rwanda 416, 417

Sadat, Anwar 396, 405
Safavid Empire 149, 191
Saladin 98
same-sex marriage 436
Sartre, Jean-Paul 398
Sasanian Empire 71, 73, 74, 81
Schlieffen Plan 315, 319
Scotland 76, 78, 84, 112, 154, 158, 181, 190, 191, 197, 215
Seacole, Mary 272
Sekigahawa, Battle of 162–3, 163
Serbia 135, 317, 317, 326, 410, 417
Seven Years War (1756–63) 197, 203
sewing machine 248
Shakespeare, William 159
Shihuangdi 51, 53, 54–5
'Shining Path' guerrillas 412, 415
Sicily 58, 267, 273, 366
Sierra Leone 180, 223
Simpson, James Young 259
Singapore 362, 400
Sino-Japanese Wars 298, 299, 354–5, 358
Sistine Chapel 133, 134
skyscrapers 302
slavery 128, 165, 166, 187, 198, 213, 219, 223, 224–5
abolition 222, 224–5, 278–9, 282
American Civil War 273, 278–82
citizenship 289
smallpox 204–5, 207
Smyrna 338
Socrates 44, 45, 48–9
Solander, Daniel 205
Somalia 416
South Africa 257, 259, 260, 301, 319, 436
apartheid 376–7, 393, 417
Mandela, Nelson 393, 417, 420–1
South Korea 400, 440
South Pole 310
South Sea Company 187, 195
Soviet Union see USSR
space exploration 7, 381, 384, 396, 402, 443
astronomy 144, 148, 166, 168, 205, 418–19
Spain 80, 81, 84, 87, 428, 433
Age of Reason 186, 187, 188–9
and America 298
Civil War (1936–9) 350, 354, 357
colonialism 122–3, 125–8, 129, 170, 208, 210, 241–4, 245, 283–4, 295, 298
and France 234, 237
Renaissance 145, 150, 151, 158, 158, 162
revolution 283
War of Succession 187, 188–9
Spanish flu 337, 339
Sparta 25, 44, 47
St Bartholomew's Day Massacre 152–3, 154
St Francis of Assisi 98
St Peter's Basilica 137, 142
St Thomas Aquinas 111
Stalin, Josef 343–4, 344, 350–1, 356, 380
WWII 360, 366, 368, 369
Stanton, Elizabeth Cady 289
steam engines 224
Stephenson, George 248
stone technology 10, 11
Storming of the Bastille 216–17, 218
Sturt, Charles 250
Sudan 35, 295, 298, 433
Suez Canal 229, 284, 284–5, 360, 380, 385
suffragettes 289, 291, 301–2, 310, 313, 345
Suharto, General 395
Suleiman I 135–6, 138
Sumeria 14
Sun Tzu 40
Sweden 89, 106, 150, 174, 178
Syria 10, 14, 49, 73, 74, 80, 229, 395–6, 426

Tahiti 205, 222, 223
Taiwan 298, 299, 379, 400
Taliban 417, 425–6, 428
tanks 326, 331
telegraph 248, 251, 286–7
telephone 284, 288, 303, 422
television 355
Tenochtitlán 125, 126, 127
Teotihuacán 56–7, 59, 76
Terracotta Army 54–5
textiles 137, 223, 224, 256
Thailand 298, 428
Thirty Years War 168–9, 172–3, 174
Tiananmen Square 409, 413
Tibet 298, 379
Timur Lenk 115, 118, 119
Titian 136
Tolpuddle Martyrs 254
Trafalgar, Battle of (1805) 232, 236
transportation 215
Transvaal 294, 295, 301
Treaty of Nanking 262–3
Treaty of Tordesillas 123, 180
Treaty of Utrecht 187
Treaty of Versailles 337, 338
Troy 25, 27
Trump, Donald 433, 436, 439
tsunami 428–9
Tuareg nomads 104, 112
Tunisia 432
Túpac Amaru II 208, 210
Turing, Alan 364, 365
Turkey/Turks 8, 10, 14, 18, 24, 25, 27, 40, 75, 97, 100, 338, 341
see also Ottomans
tyres 271, 302

Uccello, Paolo 132
Uganda 395
Ukraine 89, 204, 332, 338, 440, 442
Umayyads 72, 80, 84, 87
United States see America
Uruguay 243, 257, 289, 395
USSR 373, 376
and Afghanistan 399, 406, 408
and Africa 395, 396
and China 378
collapse of 409–10
communism 329, 331–2, 338, 343–4, 350–1, 380, 383
and Cuba 383
establishment of 338
Gorbachev, Mikhail 406, 409, 414–15
Khrushchev, Nikita 380
Lenin, Vladimir 329, 331–2, 344
perestroika and glasnost 406
repression 382, 391, 395
space race 381, 384
Stalin, Josef 343–4, 350–1
and Western Europe 354, 356, 376
WWII 360, 362, 364–5, 368, 369, 371
see also Russia

vaccination 204–5, 207, 261
Vancouver, George 219, 223
Venezuela 241, 243, 245
Venice 110, 134, 159, 267
Versailles, Palace of 174, 215, 217
Victor Emmanuel II 267, 272–3
Victoria, Queen 250, 291, 314
Vienna 181, 184, 266–7
Vietnam 381, 384, 386, 388–9, 396, 400
Vikings 86, 87, 89, 97
Visigoths 65, 81
Vlad the Impaler 121
Voltaire 197
voting rights 254, 257, 289, 291, 301–2, 310, 313, 345

Wales 112
Wałęsa, Lech 399, 407
Wall Street Crash (1929) 344, 353
Wallace, Alfred Russel 259
Washington, Booker T. 291, 294
Washington, George 210–13
Waterloo, Battle of (1815) 245, 246–7
Wedgwood, Josiah 222, 225
Wellington, Duke of 234, 245, 246–7
Wilhelm II, Kaiser 313, 314, 315, 337
William and Mary 185
William of Orange 180
Wills, William John 250
Wilson, Woodrow 337, 341
witches 158, 178, 187
Wollstonecraft, Mary 198
Woodstock 400–1
World Trade Centre 416, 424–5
World War I (1914–18) 312, 317–38
World War II (1939–45) 355–71
Wright brothers 302, 311
writing 14–15, 92

Xavier, Francis 145, 148, 149
Xerxes I 42, 47–8
Xi Jinping 437

Y2K Bug 423
Yasser Arafat 427
Yeltsin, Boris 409–10, 435
Yemen 307, 341
Ying Zheng 50, 53
Young Turks 307, 317
Yugoslavia 360, 373, 410, 417

Zelensky, Volodymyr 440, 442
Zimbabwe 417
Zionism 305
Zulus 248

PICTURE CREDITS

AirSeaLand.Images: 327

Alamy: 8 (Images & Stories), 11 top right (Ryhor Bruyeu), 13 (WHPics), 14 (Heritage Image Partnership), 15 bottom (Sabena Jane Blackbird), 16 bottom (Veeravong Komalamena), 22 top (Peter Horree), 22 bottom (funkyfood London - Paul Williams), 33 bottom (Tom Till), 35 (Michael Freeman), 36 top (Tibor Bognar), 38 top (IanDagnall Computing), 44 top (Peter Horree), 48 top (Colaimages), 56/57 (David South), 58 left (Penta Springs), 58 right (robertharding), 59 (Interfoto), 61 top (Adam Eastland), 63 (John Dambik), 67 (Craig Jack Photographic), 68 (Lesley Pardoe), 69 (Heritage Image Partnership), 70 (Ivy Close Images), 71 (World History Archive), 74 (Image Professionals), 78 (Mick Sharp), 80 top (Robert Kawka), 84 (Heritage Image Partnership), 85 top (Granger Historical Picture Archive), 86 top (The Print Collector), 87 top (Pictorial Press), 93 (CPA Media), 99 (incamerastock), 106 (Penta Springs), 107 bottom (Science History Images), 111 (Heritage Image Partnership), 112 left (Granger Historical Picture Archive), 112 right (World History Archive), 113 top (Photo 12), 114 top (Zoltan Bagosi), 116 bottom (AF Fotografie), 125 bottom (Granger Historical Picture Archive), 126 (World History Archive), 128 (Dave Stamboulis), 130 (Science History Images), 134 (Painting), 135 bottom (Peter Horree), 140/141 (World History Archive), 144 (Prisma Archivo), 146/147 (History & Art Collection), 148 (CPA Media), 149 & 155 (Prisma Archivo), 159 top (Shawshots), 169 top (Classic Image), 169 bottom (Science History Images), 174 top (World History Archive), 174 bottom (Stocktrek Images), 175 (Penta Springs), 178 & 179 (Album), 180 top (Science History Images), 181 (The National Trust Photolibrary), 184 (Interfoto), 185 left (World History Archive), 186 bottom (Classic Image), 187 (North Wind Picture Archives), 188/189 (Album), 190 bottom (CPA Media), 194 & 196 (Lebrecht Music & Arts), 198 top & 202 (IanDagnall Computing), 208 top (Heritage Image Partnership), 212 (Classic Image), 213 (Heritage Image Partnership), 214 (Giorgio Morara), 215 (The Artchives), 216 (Active Museum/Active Art), 217 (IanDagnall Computing), 219 bottom (Chronicle), 222 top (AF Fotografie), 228 (Pictorial Press), 229 & 235 (GL Archive), 237 (CBW), 238/239 (Niday Picture Library), 244 top (Granger Historical Picture Archive), 244 bottom (Album), 248 (Pictorial Press), 250 (Granger Historical Picture Archive), 256 top (Pictorial Press), 256 bottom (Classic Image), 258 (IanDagnall Computing), 259 bottom (De Luan), 260 top (Sueddeutsche Zeitung Photo), 261 (incamerastock), 262 top (CPA Media), 263 top (incamerastock), 266 (Granger Collection), 268/269 (Photo 12), 272 top (incamerastock), 272 bottom (GL Archive), 273 (Peter Horree), 274/275, 289 (Pictorial Press), 295 right (Chronicle), 299 top (Heritage Image Partnership), 305 (Chronicle), 308/309 (Trinity Mirror/Mirrorpix), 312 (Pictorial Press), 313 (PA Images), 314 (World History Archive), 316 bottom (Lebrecht Music & Arts), 321 (Sueddeutsche Zeitung Photo), 323 (Glasshouse Images), 324 (Chronicle), 326 (CBW), 329 top (D & S Photography Archives), 332 (Shawshots), 333 bottom (Recall Pictures), 344 (Science History Images), 353 bottom (PA Images), 354 bottom (Heritage Image Partnership), 355 top (World History Archive), 356 (Sueddeutsche Zeitung Photo), 357 top (Granger Historical Picture Archive), 365 top (GL Archive), 368 (Interfoto), 371 top (World History Archive), 378 (The Print Collector), 385 bottom (PA Images), 395 (Keystone Press), 398 top (Granger Historical Picture Archive), 400 (Chronicle), 401 (Entertainment Pictures), 404 top (dpa picture alliance), 404 bottom (Classic Picture Library), 405 bottom (AP), 408 bottom (Trinity Mirror/Mirrorpix), 412 (imageBROKER), 415 (Archivio GBB), 422 & 425 top (Associated Press), 429 (Horizon Images/Motion), 430/431 (Kristoffer Tripplaar), 432 bottom (Keren Su/China Span), 433 (Nikolas Georgiou/ZUMA Press), 436 (PA Images), 440 (Inter-Korean Press Corp), 441 top (Newscom), 441 bottom (Kirk Hewlett), 444 (Imagespace), 445 (Geopix)

Amber Books: 322 bottom, 328, 362, 364

Anne S. K. Brown Military Collection: 262/263

Bridgeman Images: 246/247

Creative Commons Attribution-ShareAlike 3.0 Unported Licence: 123

Depositphotos: 96 top

Dorothea Lange via Library of Congress: 352

Dreamstime: 9 (Dmitryp), 10 top (Asdf_1), 11 bottom (Izanbar), 24 (Ozalpvahid), 26 (Boygointer), 30 (Perseomedusa), 32 (Ivanweb), 34 (Nikolais), 38 bottom (Electropower), 39 (Borna), 43 top (Znm), 44 bottom (Kostas1gr), 46/47 (Dmitriy Moroz), 48 bottom (Zhu_zhu), 54/55 (Dndavis), 61 bottom (Euriico), 62 (Solovki), 64 (Panglossia), 66 top (Kguzel), 75 (Krajinar), 77 top (Yunxiang987), 80 bottom (Nikolais), 86 bottom (Kalebkroetsch), 100 (Kevers), 115 (Peewam), 117 (Sepavo), 125 top (Whpics), 133 (Stelpro2), 143 (Mrallen), 154 (Karsol), 172 top (Ediliku), 172 bottom (Pytyczech), 177 (Coatchristophe), 200/201 (Zayacab), 229 bottom (Naumoid), 243 (Elovkoff), 292/293 (Annedave)

ESA/Hubble: 419

FBI: 343

From the Archive of the British Library: 108/109, 151, 190 top left

Getty Images: 6 (Werner Forman), 10 bottom (Imagno/Gerhard Trumler), 12 bottom (Sepia Times/Universal Images Group), 23 (Werner Forman), 45 (Corbis), 49 (ullstein bild), 50 (Universal Images Group), 77 bottom (Zhang Peng/LightRocket), 82 (Ismael Adnan/AFP), 85 bottom (rt Images), 121 (Universal History Archive), 150 (Heritage Images), 173 & 224 (Pictures From History/Universal Images Group), 242 (Universal Images Group), 249 bottom (Science & Society Picture Library), 271, 285 (Otto Herschan Collection), 286/287 (Sepia Times), 302 (Corbis), 311 bottom (Photo 12), 315, 318 (Bob Thomas/Popperfoto), 319, 330 (Popperfoto), 331, 333 top (Heritage Images), 334/335 (Mondadori Portfolio), 336/337, 339 top (MediaNews Group), 339 bottom (Corbis), 340 both (Universal Images Group), 341 (Roger Viollet), 342 (New York Daily News), 345, 346 (Three Lions), 347 top, 347 bottom (Bettmann Archive), 348 (ullstein bild), 350 (Oscar Manello/Central Press), 351 & 353 top (Bettmann Archive), 354 top (ullstein bild), 355 bottom (The Stanley Weston Archive), 358 (Popperfoto), 359 (ullstein bild), 360 (Fireshot/Universal Images Group), 361 top (Central Press), 361 bottom, 367 (Universal History Archive), 372, 373 (Popperfoto), 374 (Bert Hardy/Picture Post), 375 (Bettmann Archive), 377 (FPG), 381 (Three Lions), 382 & 383 (Corbis), 384 bottom (Universal Images Group), 385 top (Pictures from History), 386 top, 387, 388 & 389 (Bettmann Archive), 390 top left (Michael Ochs Archives), 390 top right (Ron Galella Collection), 390 bottom (Bettmann Archive), 391 (Express), 393 (Bettmann Archive), 394 (Alain Dejean/Sygma), 396 (Rolls Press/Popperfoto), 397 top (Charles McQuillan), 397 bottom, 398 bottom (Gisele Freund/Photo Researchers), 399 (Bettmann Archive), 403 (AFP), 405 top (Wally McNamee/Corbis), 406 (AFP), 407 (Wojtek Laski), 408 top (Pascal Manoukian/Sygma), 409 top (Bettmann Archive), 409 bottom (Doug Wilson/Corbis), 410 (Igor Kostin/Laski Diffusion), 411 (Georges De Keerle), 413 (Archive Photos), 414 (Alain Nogues/Sygma), 417 top (Dimitar Dilkoff/AFP), 417 bottom (Scott Peterson/Liaison), 420/421 (Alexander Joe/AFP), 424 (Spencer Platt), 425 bottom (Romeo Gadad/AFP), 427 (Christopher Furlong), 428 (AFP), 432 top (Martin Bureau/AFP), 434 (Justin Sullivan), 435 (Laski Diffusion), 437, 438 (Bloomberg), 439 (Spencer Platt), 442 top (Kevin Frayer), 442 bottom (Anadolu)

Getty Images/De Agostini: 11 top left (E Lessing), 17 bottom (G Dagli Orti), 18 bottom (G Sioen), 25 (G Dagli Orti), 168 top, 186 top, 226/227, 230/231, 245 (G Dagli Orti), 290/291 (Seemuller)

Getty Museum Collection: 164

GNU Free Documentation Licence: 37 (Roland Unger)

Harry Ransom Center: 249 top

ISRO: 443

John Carter Brown Library: 124

Krigsarkivet: 325, 329 bottom

Library of Congress: 105, 127, 166, 195, 198 bottom, 206, 207, 218, 260 bottom, 276/277, 278, 280/281, 282, 294, 303, 310, 317, 322 top

Metropolitan Museum of Art, New York: 12 top, 15 top, 16 top, 17 top, 18/19 top, 20 bottom, 21 both, 27, 29 both, 33 top, 43 bottom, 53, 73 both, 81, 87 bottom left & right, 98, 104, 122, 131, 135 top, 138 left, 185 right, 191 right, 210/211, 254, 255, 284

NASA: 7 (JPL-Caltech/ASU), 384 bottom, 402

National Archives & Records Administration: 209, 279, 338, 366, 369 top, 370, 371 bottom, 379, 392

Naval History & Heritage Command: 363

Official White House Photo by Pete Souza: 426

Photos.com: 304 top

Princeton University Library: 31

Public Domain: 28, 51, 76, 82 top, 83, 96 bottom, 97, 107 top, 110 both, 113 bottom, 114 bottom, 116 top, 118, 119 both, 129 top, 132, 136, 137, 138 right, 139, 142, 145, 152/153, 156, 157, 158, 160/161, 162/163, 165, 167, 170/171, 176 top, 180 bottom, 182/183, 191 left, 192/193, 197, 199, 203-205 all, 208 bottom, 219 top, 220, 221, 222 bottom, 225, 232/233, 234, 236, 240, 241, 251, 252/253, 257, 259 top, 265, 267, 270, 283, 288 top, 295 left, 296/297, 299 top, 300, 301, 304 bottom, 306, 307, 311 top, 316 top, 349, 357 top, 369 bottom, 386 bottom

Science Photo Library/A. Barrington Brown, © Gonville & Caius College: 380

Shutterstock: 5 (Bist), 19 bottom (Mountainpix), 20 top (Jess Kraft), 36 bottom (Tenkl), 40 (Hamdan Yoshida), 41 (RealityImages), 42 (Daniele Colombo), 52 (lusia83), 65 (iLongLoveKing), 66 bottom (Sergej Borzov), 72 (Zurijeta), 79 (Steve Travelguide), 88 (Reezky Pradata), 89 (Conchi Martinez), 90/91 (munduuk), 92 (Shan_shan), 94/95 (Marcus DeYoung), 101 (gumbao), 102/103 (Mark R Croucher), 129 bottom (Simona Bottone), 159 bottom (RossHelen), 168 bottom (Michael Sean OLeary), 176 bottom (lapas77), 298 (KS-Art), 416 (Everett Collection)

SpaceX: 423

UK Parliamentary Archives: 190 top right

U.S. Marine Corps History Division: 365 bottom

Walters Art Museum, Baltimore: 120

Wellcome Collection: 223, 288 bottom

Yale University Art Gallery: 60